CALL OF THE WILD DEARBORN:

Animal Tales

Edited by Henry Fischer, Linda Choo,
Kathryn Takach, and Jeff Lelek

Dearborn Public Library
Dearborn, MI

Call of the Wild Dearborn: Animal Tales

ISBN: 978-1500676964

1. Animals—Stories 2. Animals—Poetry 3. Nature—Stories 4. Nature—Poetry 5. Anthologies 6. Short Stories 7. Dearborn (Mich.)

Cover designed by Christine Fischer. Image credits for cover: cat photo by Mary Ann Zawada, dog photo by Susie Duncan Sexton, bird drawing by A.C. Fish, and mouse drawing by Mark Somers. Images throughout the book are the work of the authors themselves unless otherwise noted.

This book is set in Palatino Linotype with Verdana for headings and prepared using Microsoft Word 2010.

www.dearbornlibrary.org

Contents

Introduction

When we were planning the events for The Big Read Dearborn, a community-wide celebration and exploration of Jack London's *The Call of the Wild*, Kirt Gross, an Assistant Librarian at Dearborn Public Library, said parenthetically that it would be cool to have a writing component to the program. "People could write from the perspective of their pet." And so the initial inkling of *Animal Tales* was born.

The Big Read Committee supported the idea, and because we had witnessed the successes of the *Best Dearborn Stories* project and the rise of print-on-demand service providers as well as ebook publishing platforms (see Walt Crawford's book, *Micropublishing for Librarians*), we planned to send out a call to the public for stories, poems, or essays about animals, nature, or wildlife. We widened the criteria to include as many people as possible, but, still attempting to stay true to Kirt's original idea, we added that people could submit stories written from an animal's perspective, which was particularly fitting as *The Call of the Wild* is told from the perspective of Buck, a St. Bernard-Scotch Shepherd mix, who "might well have been mistaken for a gigantic wolf." Our plan was to compile all selected stories and produce a book of "animal tales" in various formats for our library collection.

This is our first venture into what we like to call "community publishing," which is not exactly self-publishing, as it is not one author publishing a book on his or her own and trying to sell it, but rather many authors contributing to a book that is then published by a local organization and sold as a fundraiser for that organization (in this case, it is the Dearborn Public Library; in the case of the *Best Dearborn Stories* project, spearheaded by L. Glenn O'Kray and David Good among others, it was the Dearborn Historical Museum).

The goals of *Animal Tales* were manifold: preserve community stories, put the spotlight on animals, possibly raise some funding for library programs like The Big Read, and even produce a good book. Playing on Jack London's title, the theme for our Big Read was "Do You Hear the Call?" So, we sent out "the call" far and wide for animal tales, even as far as the President of the United States (who, by the way, still has not submitted a story, but perhaps he is busy with other matters). In making the rounds, our call also went out to actor and acclaimed narrator George Guidall, who has read over 1,000 unabridged audiobooks and who performed a dramatic reading from *The Call of the Wild* as part of our Big Read programming. He said that he only had fish as a child and his only dog story was when one bit him. He did not have time to write it down but he could tell me what had happened: his neighbors had a dog that they did not take care of and was probably rabid. One day, when he was walking by, it viciously bit him. Shortly after that, the dog died. He ended the story with "my father was a pharmacist." There you have it, our first animal tale, and there are many more to come!

Our call was answered by over 100 authors. It is astonishing the range of ages, backgrounds, and styles of the contributors. We have tales about several different kinds of animals: bear, bird, bug, cat, crab, dog, fish, frog, goat, hamster, horse, moose, mouse, panther, possum, rabbit, skunk, snake, squirrel, turtle, weasel, and even a wolf. We have all sorts of tales ranging from comedy, mystery, action-adventure, local history, inspirational, coming-of-age, real-life rescue, fiction, science journalism, true crime, memoir (including a six-word memoir), all the way to poems of various shapes and sizes. Our fictional tales range from mainstream, to literary, to downright weird. We even have imaginary animals (for example, a unicorn, unless of course you believe unicorns are real—hey, you never know, right?).

We have the cutesy tales that are all part of the fun, but we also have some that delve into the wild side of nature. This is in line with *The Call of the Wild*, which looks at the soft side (the Southland) and the harsh side (the Northland) of nature. We have some tales that are really funny, such as "My Cat Called 911 on Me" by James Lawhorn. We also have our share of sad tales, so keep the Kleenex box handy. One might go so far as to say there is wisdom in this collection. For instance, Marcel Pultorak writes: "My pets helped me to learn that death is part of life."

Our assortment of characters and situations is almost dizzying. Want to see a dog find lots of buried treasure? An up-close view of hunting? A moose on the loose? A squirrel in the office? A baby deer fending off a pack of wild dogs in Vietnam? A butterfly mistaken for a jet plane? A bear helping Santa Claus? A cat flying an airship? A bee going to church? Or a whale carrying a man in a boat on its back while the ocean burns? And that's just for starters!

We have tales that explore our powerful connections with animals, such as Patty Podzikowski's "Gypsy" and L. Glenn O'Kray's "We Are Connected." One story by Hank Czerwick is about a "hairy" cricket who loses his hair—it was written to bolster the spirits of a boy with leukemia. We have so many uplifting and touching stories that it's impossible to list more than a few of them here. We have a number of nature tales as well. In a sense, this collection is an exploration of our relationship with animals and nature. It is a book of the people, and we believe there's something here for everyone.

Originally, we were thinking about separating the poems from the stories, but then we realized that all entries, whether stories, poems, or essays, tell a tale. Therefore, we decided to put the poems, stories, and essays all together and divide them up largely by animal (for example, tales about dogs have been placed in the "Dog Tales" chapter). Some tales required to be put in subject-heading chapters such as rescue or hunting tales. Still others that were particularly difficult to fit into this system of organization were placed in the "Grab-bag" chapter, which has turned out to be a highlight of *Animal Tales*.

As for editing: we tried to keep each author's unique voice intact as much as possible, while attempting to make each story consistent on its own. We did not strive for consistency throughout the collection, except in some overarching organizational and grammatical rules. We tried to stay true to the advice from Bruce Lee: "Obey the principles without being bound by them." So if consistency ever interfered with an author's unique voice, we remembered the quote from Emerson: "A foolish consistency is the hobgoblin of little minds." We mainly endeavored to fix typos or misspellings that seemed unintentional. There are things we left in that would make a grammarian scream. What we felt was most important, however, was preserving each author's individual voice for future generations.

We hope you enjoy this collection. Thank you to the authors who helped create it—without you there would be no book. Thank you to

Mayor O'Reilly, City Council Members, Mary Laundroche, and everyone else who helped spread the word. Thank you to L. Glenn O'Kray and David Good for demonstrating that there is a strong interest in community publishing. Thank you to our Library Administrators (Library Director Maryanne Bartles, Deputy Director Julie Schaefer, and Administrative Librarian Steve Smith) for giving us the O.K. to go forward with this project. Thank you to The Big Read Committee for supporting it (specifically RuthAnn Albus, Linda Choo, Eddie Fakhoury, Kirt Gross, Rebecca Hermen, Leslie Herrick, Jihan Jawad, Elaine Logan, Dina Mein, Mary Pizzimenti, Patty Podzikowski, Peggy Richard, Isabella Rowan, Kathryn Takach, and EmmaJean Woodyard). Thank you to the National Endowment for the Arts, Arts Midwest, and all local partners and sponsors of The Big Read Dearborn. Thank you to Christine Fischer for assisting with graphic design. Thank you to Linda Choo, Jeff Lelek, and Kathryn Takach, who all spent long hours editing the book. Thank you to Anne Gautreau for collecting many animal tales from her students and encouraging them to write new ones. Thank you to Walt Crawford, whose book template was used for this publication, and who gave helpful technical advice via many emails. Thank you to Lawrence Kapture for giving a presentation at the Michigan Library Association Conference regarding print-on-demand service providers and ebook publishers. Thank you to James LaRue for helping with administrative questions about the book and for writing an article about it in *American Libraries*. Thank you to the community for answering "the call" in a very big way. Thank you to God, our families, and our friends. Lastly, thank you to the animals and all the other wonders of nature that have inspired us to write these stories.

Henry Fischer
Librarian I
Dearborn Public Library

Chapter 1: A Bear Tale

Barely White by Gretchen Yates-Madick

Since his youth, Barely White had kept up with the best arctic swimmers in the *North Pole Athletic Journal*. Lately, he had lost interest. He realized a bear his age was now a has-been in the field of bear jumps, the bear paddle, underwater gymnastics and the yearly "Hold Your Breath" competition. He was also less interested in Christmas.

As a shy cub, Barely's parents, Big Bertha and Burly Bear, named him Bartholomew. They were oversized, part of why they liked each other. Bartholomew was smaller than Bertha's mom, which concerned them, so they invited his swimming coach, Crabby, over to chat.

When Bartholomew saw Coach Crabby plodding along, he hid in a snow castle. Big Bertha greeted Coach Crabby, not offering him any fish. Not impolite as polar bears hardly ever shared.

Bartholomew heard them talking. "I think Bartholomew has stopped growing," Crabby said. He takes two steps to keep up with his friends. Bartholomew knew that was true. He looked up to most of them.

"Bartholomew is good at sliding downhill," he continued. "He normally reaches the bottom first. In the class picture, though, Bartholomew is barely there." Barely knew this was true from hiding. Bartholomew was a long name for his size, so Barely became his nickname. He was a good sport about it.

Barely did not mind moving his legs faster. He won for his strong legs and small body. Fast sliding wasn't important. Swimming was. He got to the fish earlier, did not eat as much and made friends by sharing.

Now, Barely stopped hiding. He worked harder to be a good sport in competitions too. He knew you do not always win, but he won more than the average bear. He grew confident.

Getting older made Barely feel bad. He started walking every day and often ended up at the edge of the runway where Santa's reindeer practiced taking off. Toys could not be late. With magic, the reindeer pulled it off every year. Practice kept their confidence high.

North Pole fishing was plentiful. Global warming was melting ice. The southern bears complained about distances between patches. Barely felt that migration would have to be towards the North Pole. He worried about differences of opinion over food and islands of ice. Might be a problem.

Santa saw Barely and knew his reputation. Barely was peace-loving and tender-hearted. Santa waved at Barely who waved back. Santa noticed the slower walk, more frequent growls of complaint and mood changes.

When Santa returned from listening to what children around the world wanted for Christmas, he got a little tired. Barely and Santa were getting older. Santa sometimes figured a wrong number of trucks and dolls he would need. Each year new toys came into the hearts of children and out their mouths. If Santa hadn't predicted correctly, the elves had to work faster.

When Santa saw Barely he wondered if getting older could be part of Barely's problem. That night Santa slept soundly and snored loudly. He dreamed of having Barely on his lap, telling him what he wanted for Christmas.

The next day, at the runway's end, Santa invited Barely aboard for a little ride.

Barely was frightened, excited and happy. Santa liked having Barely in front of the sleigh. Barely protected Santa from the wind, kept his feet warm and liked the cold from living outside.

Santa told Barely what a wise bear he was. Santa didn't put Barely on his lap, because his lap was sore from so many children. What would Barely want for Christmas? Barely decided quickly. He wanted more rides on the sleigh. For other bears, he wanted to drop fish off the sides of the sleigh, so bears everywhere could have a day off from fishing with lots of Christmas food.

Barely's heart was so big, generous and kind-hearted. Of course, he could come along. A little magic would rid the sleigh of the fish smell.

When the snow melts, if you find a dead fish or bones washed up on the beach, you can know for sure, Barely's been working. He fills the dreams of so many bears around the world.

Barely is feeling better. He's happy about his size. He fits in the sleigh and doesn't block Santa's view. Doing good deeds for others is great medicine. And a touch of magic around you is remarkable.

Bears don't have long tails, but whenever Barely thinks about Christmas, he wags in that direction and looks like he is dancing.

If Christmas Eve is cold and clear and the Milky Way crosses the night sky, watch carefully. You may see a low streak of red. It's Santa's sleigh and in front, you might see Barely there.

An Edsel Ford High School graduate, Gretchen Yates-Madick holds a B.A. degree from Western Michigan University with an English Literature major and an Elementary Education minor. Having worked as a teacher, a supervisor for a word processing department and as a reporter for several newspapers, Gretchen's greatest joy is her four sons: Mark, Todd, Christopher and Brian. frederickfrog@charter.net

Chapter 2: Bird Tales

The Superior Animal by Joseph Bongero

Birds don't punch a clock;
Neither do squirrels.
They don't have mortgages
or monthly car notes.
They don't wear clothes
or cook their meals.
Transportation is free
and unemployment unknown.
They dance and sing
and soar above the trees
in effortless flight
seeing everything that's important.
They never visit a doctor, dentist,
optometrist, barber or masseuse.

Are we better off than they?
Are we so special as to decide
the fate of these creatures
who breathe the same air
and share the same space?
Or, are they better off than we?
They can fly, swim and roam
without the presence of man.
Could we exist without them?

Joseph Bongero (1938-2011) was a United States Postal Service Letter Carrier and an English major in college. He loved being out-of-doors, observing nature and its constantly changing phenomena. He endured Parkinson's Disease the last 15 years of his life but even as the last five years meant limited mobility, he loved nothing more than being able to sit on the porches of his vacation home in Greenbush, Alcona County, Michigan, watching the ever-changing Lake Huron and landscape and searching for whatever birds, waterfowl, and wildlife he could see, making records of them in his journals, and often writing short stories or poems. His wife, Agnes Bongero, sent in this poem.

The Cardinal by Dan Colovas

It wakes the world with its sparkling song,
This cardinal in the red sarong.
Perched alert on wire high
Its melody saturating the morning sky.

Bright notes through open window slip
Stirring me from slumber's grip.
Cajoling in most joyous way
Must you tarry in the bed all day?

I've been awake from sun's first glow
The erudite troubadour lets me know.
Stealing from your garden green
The twisting worms you've never seen.

Oh how I treasure these serenades
As I throw open wide the window shades.
And fill my heart with the brilliant song
Of the cardinal in the red sarong.

Dan Colovas is a retired mechanical engineer living in Dearborn with his wife JoAnne. He has resided in Dearborn for 72 years. He graduated from Fordson High School in 1956, Henry Ford Community College in 1958, and University of Michigan in 1962. He has been writing poetry for 20 years.

Chickadees by Beaufort Cranford

If you pride yourself on being of sound mind, the chickadee can be a dangerous bird. Few other creatures have similar power to evoke in otherwise sober people the use of the word "cute" to describe its habits.

They're certainly familiar to anyone who owns a bird feeder. *The Atlas of Breeding Birds of Michigan* even proposes that "the *chickadee-dee-dee* call of this small, mild-mannered bird is familiar to everyone except those totally alienated from the natural world."

I think I know some of those people, but never mind.

Among common backyard birds, chickadees seem to have no peers for popularity with the possible exception of the cardinal, but they have more going for them in the cuteness sweepstakes: They're infinitely more acrobatic, talkative and tameable – something lively and quick out there in the yard when even the wind seems frozen solid.

Michigan has two chickadees: the black-capped, a permanent resident throughout the state, and the boreal, which is confined to the Upper Peninsula. Our local black-capped (*Parus atricapillus*) is similar to the more southern Carolina chickadee, whose range it slightly overlaps. Black-caps live in a variety of habitats from forests to subdivisions, though their numbers tend to thin out in cities and heavily cultivated areas.

In cooler parts of their range, suburban populations of chickadees increase in winter – proving among other things that even though their brains may be smaller than raisins, chickadees are no dummies.

Atricapillus runs 4¾ to 5¾ inches long, reaching what sharp-shinned hawks, a major predator of chickadees, would consider eatin' size on a diet of pine, hemlock and other seeds as well as insects and their eggs. At feeders they seem partial to sunflower seeds, particularly the black-oil type, and suet concoctions.

At nesting time, they use holes – usually inherited, though they'll make their own if they can find wood soft enough for them to work. *Atricapillus* won't turn up its beak at man-made boxes, either. Females build the nests themselves, lining them with the softest materials available – moss, hair, fur, strips of bark. I've taken apart several old chickadee nests made almost entirely of moss, and others made largely of feathers and string.

Chickadees are among the first birds to greet springtime, adding a whistled *fee-bee* to their repertoire, a sound easily mistakable for the *fee-bee* of the uh, phoebe. In summer, chickadee life is like that of other 4-F nesting birds – mostly just feed 'em, fledge 'em, fly 'em and forget 'em.

Chickadees gather in flocks in winter, however, and often forage with other small birds such as nuthatches, titmice and downy woodpeckers. You can be in a dead, snowblown and empty woods one minute and in the next be surrounded by chipping, peeping and pecking tiny birds busily examining every bit of loose bark. Then, just as swiftly, they're gone and the woods is still again.

The usual chickadee winter flock contains an even number of birds, because it's made up of male-female pairs. But there are also what zoologist Susan M. Smith calls "floaters," unpaired birds who live in loose congregations or pass among flocks. According to Smith, when interacting with organized groups, floaters always rank below all "regulars" of their sex.

So what good are they? Simple, yet marvelous. When a higher-ranking flock member dies or is killed, you'd expect the bird ranked immediately below to move up. But among chickadees that's not what happens at all. Instead, a floater of similar rank among its own kind – in other words, an outsider – moves into the vacant position. When the No. 1 female dies, for instance, the No. 2 female stays with her mate and the neighborhood's No. 1 female floater slips quietly into the late No. 1's empty boudoir.

What this neat arrangement accomplishes is to keep all the flock's existing pair bonds in place. Which is pretty neat, if you think about it.

Usually only the top two or three pairs in a flock will find territory in which to mate when spring comes and the gathered pairs disperse. So somehow I wasn't surprised to learn that floaters don't bother moving into a flock at all unless they can inherit a fairly high-ranking spot.

This is purely instinctive behavior, of course, which is all the more reason that it's perfectly reasonable. It converts into a good moral, too: Why go through all the hassle of changing your life, even if you're a little bird, when the game may not be worth the candle?

Which just goes to show that cute can run pretty deep.

Beaufort Cranford retired from Wayne State University in 2013.
beaufortc@gmail.com

Patchy by Elle Vee

"Come on," Patchy hollered to his friend as he flitted toward the odd visitors.

"I don't *think* so," Tuffy mumbled.

"It's easy. Just watch," he said to the Tufted Titmouse who was cowering in the bushes. Patchy zoomed down the woodland path and landed on a branch above the humans. There were four of them: two tall ones and two shorter, fast moving ones. The man put his finger to his lips and the little ones stopped running around. All four held their hands out, offering sunflower seeds.

Patchy swooped down and landed on the hand of closest person—the little girl. She jerked away and the seeds plunged to the ground but not before Patchy nabbed a tasty treat. He flew back to Tuffy's bush and devoured the seed.

"See? Nothin' to it," Patchy said.

"That kid nearly killed you!" Tuffy protested.

Dawn flew over. "What's all the fuss about?" she asked.

"Patchy is trying to get me killed," Tuffy peeped. "Do you think you're the boss of the forest because you're the only Black-capped Chickadee around here with a patch of white on your cap?"

"Fine, just starve then," Patchy scoffed, and he flew off to grab another seed. This time he aimed for the woman's hand. She held perfectly still, so Patchy picked leisurely through the pile for the plumpest seed before returning to his friends.

"You make it look so simple," Dawn commented as Patchy gobbled the sunflower.

"Well, there isn't much of a choice is there?" He looked pointedly at Tuffy. It had been the harshest winter that Patchy had ever seen. What wasn't buried under feet of snow had been mostly picked clean long ago.

"It's worth a try," Dawn said. "We Downy Woodpeckers aren't known for being fond of humans but considering the circumstances..." Patchy watched as his friend made several wide passes without landing. He moved in nearer to coach Dawn. Tuffy followed close behind.

"Aim for the tallest ones. They are usually the stillest. Dawn tried again. She landed for a split second on the man's hand but rocketed off before she could swipe a morsel.

"That was so close!" Patchy encouraged. "Next time you land, just close your eyes and dig in." Dawn kept trying unsuccessfully for what felt like forever. She looked like she was about to give up when the adults started to pack up to leave. The man poured the edible treasures into a little plastic bag and passed it to the woman. Just in time, Dawn dove for the food. Success! She came away with a seed to munch.

"Yes!" Patchy shouted. "I knew you could do it if you kept trying."

The woman handed the bag to the children. The girl started to dump her seeds, but the littlest one, a boy, didn't stir. That's when Tuffy made his move. Like a bolt of lightning, he shot from the overhanging branches to the outstretched hand and then soared off to his favorite bush with a seed securely in his beak.

"You did it!" Patchy cheered. All three friends celebrated, confident that they would make it through the long winter months ahead.

Author's note: Many common birds have a genetic mutation that causes white markings on some of their feathers (those with the pigment melanin). These partial albinos have normal coloration otherwise. From: http://birds.audubon.org/faq/birds

Elle Vee is a graduate of the University of Michigan-Dearborn. She was a student tour guide in the U of M Environmental Study Area, and, though the birds were not tame enough to approach people at that location, she has fed them at Kensington Metropark.

Five Little Birds on a Wire by A.C. Fish

Five little birds on a wire
Five birds as I drive by
Each bird is a prayer
I send to you up there

For the grace, mercy and blessings to my family, a prayer
For the grace, mercy and blessings to my family in God, a prayer
For always answering our prayers and giving us what we need, a prayer
For always being with us through good times and bad, a prayer
For personal salvation through your love and sacrifice, a prayer

No man is ever isolated; through our life we touch the lives of so many others. We never realize how many people have been affected, until one of the lives that have touched ours has returned to you. Like the number of grains of sand on a beach, that is the number of other souls that we touch as we go through this life. You bless us with delivering your love, support, understanding, teachings and messages, by words and actions, which we convey both consciously and unconsciously. Sometimes, only when a soul has gone home, do we finally realize how much that soul has touched ours.

A.C. Fish:
"I live in a shoebox borne on a deer,
A little left field, a little bit weird,
Jack of all trades, master of none,
Just writin' this doodle 'cause it's fun!"

The Bird Who Couldn't Fly South by Maleka Sharay

Full Title: The Bird Who Couldn't Fly South for the Winter

I was walking home from hockey practice when I spotted a dark grey pigeon slowly spinning in circles on the sidewalk ahead of me. The snow was slowly falling down from the sky in big beautiful snowflakes.

(Insert an animated picture of the pigeon on the sidewalk and large snowflakes falling from the sky.)

By the time I reached the pigeon, she was just about to topple over and into a pile of snow that old man Reuben had shoveled off to the edge of his sidewalk. I reached into my backpack and retrieved some crackers and sprinkled them on the ground for the pigeon to eat, but the pigeon was just too cold and too weak from struggling in the cold to get her balance so she could eat. I couldn't just leave her like that on the ground so I scooped her up in my arms and I carried her home.

(Insert an animated picture of a teenage boy carrying a pigeon home.)

"Poor little one," my mother said when she saw me carrying the pigeon in the house. I told Mom how I found the pigeon and she said it was kind of me to bring the pigeon home so we could help her. Dad said we could try for a little while to help the pigeon and if the pigeon did not get better, we could take the pigeon to a veterinarian which is an animal doctor who can help the pigeon get better.

Dad made a little joke about calling a limousine service for the pigeon. "Maybe we can hire a homing pigeon to put the pigeon Freddy found on her back and fly it down south for the winter."

(Insert an animated picture of Dad's imagination over his head.)

Dad was always making jokes about everything which is why Mom said she loved him so much. Mom suggested we could make a cozy and warm place for the pigeon in our basement. Dad carried a space heater down to the basement while Mom retrieved a bowl of wild bird seed with black sunflower seeds from the pantry and placed them in a little bowl and filled another little bowl with water for the pigeon. I went outside to our backyard in search of a sturdy branch for the pigeon to perch on.

About a month later, the pigeon who I affectionately named Lucy was flying around in our basement, eating and drinking plenty of water.

(Insert an animated picture of a pigeon flying in a basement with her makeshift habitat.)

Mom, Dad and I take turns mopping the basement floor with hot water and flower-scented bleach to keep Lucy's environment clean so we will all remain healthy. We also open the window a crack to give Lucy fresh air while we mop and to see the outside world so she never forgets that it is still there.

My name is Freddy Knight. I'll let you know how the pigeon makes out in the spring when we release her back outside. For now, it is too cold to let Lucy back outside because we are having one of the coldest winters ever in Michigan.

(Insert an animated picture of Freddy smiling.)

Maleka Sharay: "I am an animal lover and I support spaying and neutering pets. I live with a menagerie of animals and I go out every night and feed stray cats and dogs in East Dearborn and Southwest Detroit. Pet food donations welcome! You can call me at (313) 768-4251 or email me at mommasharay@gmail.com *with pet food donations."*

Pete the Parakeet by Shirley Foisy

How many of you reading this story went to Edsel Ford High School? If you attended in the late 1990s you will probably remember the parakeet named Pete. He was such a popular member of the Thornley Court animal menagerie that numerous pictures of him were featured in the yearbook that year. Now you will learn his background.

My aunt gave me money to buy a birthday present and I decided to get a parakeet. The store had quite a large number of birds to choose from and it was a hard choice. Pete really caught my eye. He was a lively little fellow and seemed to promise a lot of activity. There was a problem, though. He was attached to another little girl in the group. Even though he moved about, he was paying a lot of attention to a little girl. How can anyone break up a romance? As you can imagine, I bought both birds.

Pete was a real charmer. He had me wrapped around his little wing (well, he didn't have fingers) in no time. Even though he was devoted to his partner, he loved contact with my daughter and myself. When out of the cage, he flew to us and would sit on our fingers and it almost seemed as if he was trying to communicate with us.

Since we had both a male and a female bird, my husband decided to get a nest box and try to get this little couple to breed. We also bought a few more birds shortly after this to expand our bird breeding which was successful. Pete and his mate were able to give us two different clutches of eggs but both were infertile. My husband at that point told me to get rid of "that bird." I was heartbroken. I loved that little guy. At least I felt better knowing that he was able to go to a good home by giving him to the Thornley Court program at Edsel Ford High School where my daughter was a student. The plus for me was that when going to pick my daughter up at school, I was able to go and visit Pete.

Pete was given free flight in "his room" during class time and loved to visit students and throw pens and pencils off the desk onto the floor. I don't think anyone in school during that year did not know who Pete was.

One day my daughter was called out of class on an emergency. Something was wrong with Pete. Sadly to say, Pete died. Both students and faculty mourned the passing of this little member of the school.

Drawing by Christine Fischer

Shirley Foisy was born and raised in Dearborn and has spent the majority of her life there. Animals have been a large part of her life. The longest she has ever been without an animal companion is a couple of months. She has been blessed with many parakeets, rabbits, dogs, and ferrets to share life with. Currently, she has two ferrets.

The Amazing Baby Blue Jay by Laurine Griffin

Full Title: The Amazing Baby Blue Jay...A True Dearborn Happening

One day, a mother Blue Jay was distressed that her baby had fallen out of the neighbor's pine tree. I was concerned because it was on the ground and the neighborhood cats might get it, so I put the baby bird on a fence rail among the evergreen limbs. It sat there a while and then jumped up on to one of the overhanging evergreen branches. I waited to see if it would chirp to call to its mother and to see if she would feed it. But the baby bird did not chirp and did not sit still on the branch; it hopped from branch to branch until it had circumnavigated that section of branches and was back where it started. Next time around the tree it hopped up on to a higher branch and again went around the tree. The amazing baby Blue Jay continued to hop up on to higher branches, go around the tree, find another higher branch it could reach, hop up and continued up and around until it reached the nest and hopped in. I had stood, hardly breathing, watching the whole time.

Born in Marshall, Michigan, B.A. Western Michigan University, M.A. University of Michigan-Ann Arbor, Dearborn resident for almost 50 years, retired elementary teacher, interested in the environment and in genealogy, newsletter editor for Friends of the Detroit River, past treasurer for Dearborn Genealogical Society and for Michigan Genealogical Council, Laurine Griffin walked the Mackinac Bridge on Labor Day for her 80th birthday. She is the widow of Don A. Griffin and has three children who graduated from Dearborn High School. griffinretired@yahoo.com

Spring Ritual by Michael Louis

It was a beautiful day for flying. Bright blue skies and calm winds made for a great flight. You could see every field and sparkling pond for miles. It was time for this flock, having flown from Goose Creek to Central Michigan, to pick a pond and field. So the gaggle put down, settled in and gabbled until the sun dipped into night.

Sentinel, the designated sentry, would have to keep watch for suspicious movement throughout the long night. Guard duty was taken seriously so that every goose could get enough rest for their next leg on the trip to Canada. They were proud "Canada geese" intent on making it to the country named after them.

With the rising sun awakening the day, every goose was rested and ready. Every goose was ready except for Sentinel. The long night did him in. He fell fast asleep in his sentry position, standing up.

Sentinel stayed behind as the departing flock took flight. In addition to Sentinel, another goose named Hachi stayed behind. Being born in the Florida Panhandle, her name is derived from the Seminole Native Americans and means "stream."

Sentinel and Hachi settled in and became familiar and welcomed guests in the community. They were observed to take on family nesting on a church carport as Hachi decided this would be a great place to nest.

The great thing about a carport is that Hachi could see all around her from the height. Sentinel would have a good view from the field across the road. It was at a nice, quiet little church. Perfect! What more could a mother goose want?

Except for the lazy traffic on the road slowing to stop, the little church and the carport provided a sleepy little spot for Hachi to care for the eggs with four expected little hatchlings. Tree branches that covered her nest would provide a soothing lullaby and shade for peaceful rest. So, lazy and sleepy it was.

But on the first weekend, Hachi's sleepy little spot lit up! You might say that it really lit up, literally. The normally quiet parishioners came to life with barbeques and picnics on the weekend. Grills were lit right under the roof of the carport.

As Hachi peeked over the side of the carport roof, she was struck with horror! What kind of birds were the normally nice people flipping on the grills? Tiptoeing back to her nest on the center of the roof, she decided it would be a good thing at the time to be very quiet.

Tiptoeing quietly was hard to do with huge webbed feet! Rising heat made it uncomfortable and Hachi's tiptoeing turned into a hot-footin' stompin' dance across the roof! It was impossible to be surreptitious!

Sentinel could only gawk from his position across the street. How could Hachi seemingly have such a good time with birds grilling and people laughing, dancing and singing right under her feet? She even appeared to be dancing to the beat of the music!

With the weekend party over, Hachi could again settle down to her original purpose: caring for and protecting the eggs. It was time again to settle back to nurturing and to enjoy the fruit of her labor.

Except for an occasional flyby of some hawks running reconnaissance on the eggs, the remainder of the four weeks seemed uneventful. There were no more grilling parties, but there was a weekend when people gathered to sell clothing and gifts. Hachi was beginning to bond with these friendly people, while Sentinel stood his ground across the street "protecting" her and the nest at a safe distance.

The big event finally arrived with a mix of excitement and sadness in the community. Sentinel and Hachi became proud parents of four little goslings. Carefully instructing the goslings on how to glide from the top of the carport to the ground took patience and coaxing.

The little procession of proud parents and goslings occurred properly at the crosswalk at the intersection. It would not be long for Sentinel and Hachi, and the four new Canada geese to resume their flight as planned.

As has happened for the past three springs, Sentinel and Hachi will return again to the same place. The nest will be remodeled slightly but it will be as good as new, ready for another generation of geese.

Michael Louis: "My grandchildren and I spend a lot of time observing geese. We do observe individual personalities in the geese and enliven our stories with their character. If you would like to add the first names of my four granddaughters as co-writers you are welcome to do so. They have been an important part of our team as 'field researchers,' having spent many hours 'in fields' and near ponds. Their names are Sydney, Cassie, Savanna and Ansley." mdlouis@bellsouth.net

Chapter 3: Bug Tales

The Steel Butterfly by Abeer Alhassan

The steel butterfly
Feels real but seems locked in place
Because of its fear.

Abeer Alhassan is a student at Lowrey Elementary School in Dearborn, Michigan.

If I Were A Butterfly by Ali Aljahmi

If I were a butterfly, I could have been in the sky long ago.

Ali Aljahmi is a student at Lowrey Elementary School in Dearborn, Michigan.

A Fire in the Belly by Beaufort Cranford

If everything on Earth can be said to have a purpose, then fireflies are probably here to entertain little children. But maybe I speak too soon; I haven't seen little children chasing fireflies in years.

What's the matter with these kids? My cousins and I used to have great fun with what we knew only as lightning bugs — catching them and letting them go, or putting them in jars. We'd watch them flash, turn off and flash again, winking with a cold, ghostly light. Wow. Of course we were easier to please back then, but it was amazing.

Somewhere along the way I stopped interacting with fireflies, but they still seem to be a necessary part of summer. Even as long as I've lived in Michigan, when I see them every June I think of miserably muggy Georgia twilights, of sitting outdoors listening to the wood thrushes and watching lightning bugs come up out of the grass and bushes.

Odd, isn't it, that there are more insects alive than anything else, yet we routinely pay close attention to so few. Cockroaches, yes, and mosquitoes; on the other extreme, butterflies. But not much in between. Fireflies are special, though; it's hard to miss them when they're around.

The first thing to remember about fireflies is that they aren't flies, they're beetles. The second is that they aren't on fire, either. Well, not really, except that most of them sailing around out there — wouldn't you know — are gloriously hot to trot. That, of course, is because flashing on and off is part of the real purpose of fireflies, which is simply to make more fireflies.

Fireflies have special light-producing cells, called photocytes, on their abdomens. These cells contain a chemical called luciferin, which, when it comes in contact with oxygen and the enzyme luciferase, produces that familiar blink.

The sun sets and the light by which to locate a mate goes away, but insects have risen to the occasion. Katydids make music, moths perfume the wind with pheromones, and — perhaps most spectacular of all — fireflies strike tiny candles of love against the darkness. What a concept.

Firefly bioluminescence can be true yellow or have a blue, red or green tint. Of our common fireflies, for instance, the pyralis firefly (*Photinus pyralis*) glows yellow, while the Pennsylvania firefly (*P. pennsylvanicus*) has a greenish light.

Different species blink their bulbs to different rhythms, and more than 20 patterns have been identified. Standard procedure is pretty much the same, though: Males generate most of the lightning, frantically flying around looking for love while females wait till the right guy comes by. 'Twas ever thus, even among higher creatures. Some female lightning bugs are wingless, in fact.

When the female sees an inviting signal, she flashes back in her species' code; then male and female wink at each other until they're beetle to beetle.

The need to locate a mate is one reason fireflies flash; another is that signaling in short bursts doesn't give predators an easy target. Even so, fireflies are routinely snapped up by frogs, bats and nighthawks. And in one of the crummiest jokes in all the animal world, species of predatory fireflies exist in which the females lure males of other species to their boudoirs only to turn the unrequited suitors into snacks.

On the other hand, while all firefly larvae I've ever heard of are carnivorous (and glow, too), many adults don't eat anything, and none lives long.

As a rule, to have lightning bugs you need woodland, bushes or tall or otherwise unmowed grass nearby. One night last summer I was at a house whose yard, backed by weeds and heavy cover, was lit high and low by the lightning of bugs; the next night I was at a condo with a large, well-tended green over which not one firefly flew. It's true that many "well-tended" lawns are as sterile as scalpels because of pesticides that annihilate everything, lightning bugs included; on the other hand, any well-mowed grass isn't particularly good firefly habitat, though males may check it out.

You probably chased fireflies when you were little, so don't feel silly introducing your kids to them. Run down a few and keep them a while in a jar; at times even this can be challenging, since some fireflies are programmed for evasive maneuvers.

Or try this: Arm yourself with a small flashlight, and hunker down near the ground. When you see a firefly flash, count two seconds, then flash your light at it for 1/2 to 1 second, depending on how fast you are. Sometimes male fireflies will actually turn and head your way. The odds of man meeting insect close-up improve if you can keep the attention of one in particular. Other people say this really wows their wee bairns, but my record at it is pretty spotty.

Fireflies have courtship down pat. With millions of years of modifications and refinements, they get right to work—no pain and sorrow, but no fun, either. Even so, it would be wrong to underestimate their wooing just because it's mechanical; fireflies have tapped into something not only physical but philosophical, too. I mean, all of us have tried to shine for somebody at some point.

Beaufort Cranford retired from Wayne State University in 2013. *beaufortc@gmail.com*

Buzerbie's Great Adventure by Hank Czerwick

Buzerbie was a worker bee who lived in a city of bees called a colony. Colonies were usually located in a box called a hive. Humans called beekeepers provided hives for bees. Buzerbie's colony was situated on a small farm, near the small town of Dryden, in the state of New York. The colony's keeper was a kindly man whose name was Farmer Hank.

Buzerbie's mom was the queen. But then, she was the mom of every other bee in the whole colony! That was the queen's job, having lots of baby bees to keep the colony going. Buzerbie's dad Droner was a lazy lay-about who Buzerbie hadn't seen since the first winter after Buzerbie was born. He wasn't sure just what ever happened to Droner.

All the worker bees had various jobs to do. It was the main job of the colony to gather nectar from flowers, and to convert it into honey. The honey would provide food and energy for the queen, and for the workers, and for all of the baby bees that were being cared for in the nursery. Some worker bees would fly great distances from the hive to collect the nectar. Other worker bees would make beeswax, which was used to construct ever-larger nurseries where more baby bees could be brought up. It was the job of some workers to ventilate the hive by flapping their wings and thus regulating the temperature. There were workers charged with housekeeping and they kept things tidy by carrying all unnecessary refuse out. Some worker bees were charged with making storage space for the extra honey, which would be used to feed the colony during the cold months when there were no flowers.

A busy hive always made way more honey than it could use and it was this honey that Farmer Hank would remove from the hive. He was always careful to leave an abundant supply for the bees.

The colony that Buzerbie lived in was in a safe place, next to a shed, and alongside a great pasture that was frequented by many grazing cows. The cows were great neighbors; they seemed to ignore the bees that went about doing their jobs. The pasture had many different wild flowers and provided an ample supply of nectar for the colony. On occasion, Buzerbie's hive and its neighboring hives, of which there were several, would be disrupted by woodchucks who seemed to have less regard for the bees than did the cows. Farmer Hank would come to the rescue by chasing away the woodchucks and straighten out the hives that would get tilted by the tunnels that the woodchucks had dug.

All of the bees in all of the hives were very loyal to their queens. They would do everything and anything to protect her. But it was a rule that there could be only one queen at a time in charge of a colony. If a second queen were born, she would have to take her followers to another place to start another colony. This group of bees is called a swarm. When the bees are about to swarm, Farmer Hank, and all the other beekeepers as well, would prepare another hive for the new queen and her colony. Sometimes however, a new swarm occurs before a beekeeper can provide a new man-made hive. If that would happen, the new queen and her followers would fly off to find a new home.

Such was the case when the nursery where Buzerbie was working produced a new queen! Although Buzerbie loved his mother the queen, he had to follow the new queen for whom he had cared in the nursery. He and many of the nursery workers became part of a swarm. The problem was that Farmer Hank did not have another hive ready and the swarm had to go somewhere. Unfortunately, since many bees in the swarm were nursery workers and not nectar gatherers, they had never been outside of the hive. The new queen had only her instincts to rely upon, as she also had never been outside before. But true to their nature, they gathered outside the hive and formed a large living ball of bees, surrounding the new queen to protect her and to await the direction in which she would take them. Luckily this all happened on a day when the sky was blue and the sun shone brightly. The new queen, quickly learning how to direct her loyal followers, aimed for a large branch on a nearby stately oak tree. Here she would assess how well the swarm could stay together as she planned her next move.

As many years as the old oak had stood, it had never before hosted a swarm. The cows in the nearby pasture, who in the past largely ignored the hives, all took turns slowly walking up to the oak and looking up to see what was making all of the noise.

Of course Buzerbie was in the middle of it all! Having been one of the workers who had been closest to the cell in which the queen was hatched, he now had the honor of flying closest to her and relaying her commands to the other bees.

In addition to this being a lovely day, it was also a Sunday. The queen, who had a great skill of communicating as bees do, with vibrations of wings and special bee dances, was feeling some strange, but pleasant, new vibrations in the air. These, as it turned out, were coming from a church organ. The lovely old church had stood at the top of Simms Hill Road for almost a hundred years. Here the farmers would worship, singing hymns accompanied by an equally old organ. Organs make sounds by vibrating reeds inside large and small pipes with air. The pipes make sounds of different musical notes depending upon the size of each pipe. It was these vibrations that the queen was detecting. Everything was perfect for the move in the direction of the pleasant vibrations. It was a nice day and the church was gleaming with its coat of bright white paint. Bees like bright objects; it is why their hives are usually white and why beekeepers' protective clothing is also white.

The queen left the branch of the old oak tree and led her swarm toward the great white target, the church. It was lucky that the congregation was singing when the swarm arrived, as no one inside could hear the great buzzing outside. It was also lucky that the swarm landed on the backside of the church roof where no one would see it! Just under the place where the queen and her colony landed there was an opening, just like the entrance to the hive that the bees had come from. In they all went...and immediately began to set up bee house-keeping. The queen's caregivers attended to her needs while other bees flew off to gather nectar with which to make honey for food and beeswax with which to build a new hive.

The church members were unaware that there was a great hive being built in the wall of their church, until some time later, when the ladies working in the church kitchen, which was at the back, reported strange noises coming from the wall. Then George, the church's handyman and groundskeeper, saw all of the bee activity up near the roof as he was cutting the grass. News of the bees' presence alarmed the congregation. Something had to be done! Buzerbie the worker bee was unaware of the commotion that his presence, that of his queen, and the rest of the colony, was having on the humans with which the bees were sharing the church. By this time, Buzerbie was in charge of a large nursery and many new worker bees had been born. These new bees were producing great quantities of honey, some of which was starting to seep down the wall and into the basement of the church.

Now anyone would be happy to have a free supply of fresh honey, but not when it was coming out of a wall! Something had to be done! Fortunately, Andrew and Alysandra, two of the younger members of the church, had an uncle who could help. That's right, their uncle was none other than Farmer Hank!

Farmer Hank was the man in the neighborhood that everyone went to when they needed help with bees. And so it was that the children told their uncle about the honey in the wall at the church! Little did Farmer Hank know that the bees at the church were from his very own hives!

The very first thing that Farmer Hank had to do was to visit the church to determine how the bees could be safely removed. Since these were honeybees they were valuable and care had to be taken in removing them from the wall. Fortunately, Farmer Hank had removed bees from similar places before and he knew just what had to be done. Farmer Hank prepared a new hive. The new hive had special wax furnishings, which were already inside. There would be a nursery and everything else that the bees needed to get started once they moved in. The big question was how would Farmer Hank get the bees to move into the new hive? The answer was...a vacuum cleaner! Farmer Hank put on his protective bee suit and placed a ladder against the church so that he would be near the place where the bees went in and out. The worker bees that were guarding the hive entrance were in for a surprise. Farmer Hank proceeded to puff smoke at them from a special device that makes bees very sleepy. He then removed a few boards to have a better look. The vacuum was attached to the new hive with a short hose. Then a longer hose from the hive was placed at the entrance in the church wall. The vacuum would be turned on. Inside the church wall the alarm that something was wrong was given. Buzerbie and many other bees rushed to the queen to protect her, but before they knew it, they became very sleepy and stopped in their own tracks. Using the long hose, Farmer Hank proceeded to vacuum all of the bees out of the wall and into the new hive. He was very happy to have another hive to take home. As for the honey in the wall, it was scooped out and given to the ladies of the church. They would surely use it the next time the church put on a pancake breakfast!

As for Buzerbie, when he awoke, he was in the new hive. So were the queen and all of his friends. Before Buzerbie went back to a new job in the hive, he thought that he would take a peek outside. What he saw was very strange. There were the same cows, still basically ignoring the bees. There was the same pasture, with all the wild flowers. There was the old oak tree...and there were the pesky groundhogs, still burrowing under Buzerbie's hive. Everything was still the same except for one thing...that summer, Buzerbie and all of his friends had gone to church!

Author's note: Farmer Hank is my son, who is a beekeeper. In addition to tending his own hives, he provides a service of removing swarms from trees and buildings. Once he had removed a swarm from a church and the story above is based on a real occurrence.

Hank Czerwick is a 66-year resident of the city of Dearborn and product of its schools. He retired from Ford Motor Company as an engineer and from Henry Ford Community College as an educator. His writing has been published in many magazines.

"Hairy" the Cricket by Hank Czerwick

This is the story of Hairy the cricket. Yes, his name really was Hairy and not Harry! Crickets as a rule usually do not have names, but Hairy was called Hairy because he did have hair! There certainly are no barber shops for crickets, so when Hairy's hair got real long, his mother cut it for him. Once she cut his hair so that it looked like someone had put a bowl on his head and just cut straight around it. Hairy looked just like Ringo Starr, the famous drummer. All of the other crickets teased Hairy and told him to go play with the other beetles. That was the last time his mom cut his hair that way because the real beetles knew that he wasn't one of them and wouldn't play with Hairy.

Most of the time Hairy wore his hair in a ponytail. That way, it stayed out of his eyes as he hopped around in the sun, looking for crumbs of bread and other little goodies to eat. Hairy was pretty curious as crickets go. He would hop over and under things that other crickets would usually avoid. He and his family, and his friends too, lived in a great big yard. There were many interesting things in this yard. There was a bird bath and some bird feeders. When Hairy was thirsty, he would climb up the bird bath, sit on the rim of the bowl and take little sips of water. He had to be careful and avoid being seen by any birds. It was O.K. if he shared the bowl with sparrows, who only eat seeds, but you didn't want to be there when robins were around. Robins eat insects and Hairy was an insect. He was an especially interesting insect because of all that shiny black hair on his head! When Hairy was hungry, he would hop over to the bird feeder and look for seeds that the birds had overlooked. Here too, he had to be real careful.

Another hazard in this yard were the Humans. They seemed to come in two sizes: big and real big! They were easy to see, but you had to be real quick in getting out of their way or they would squash you. Sometimes the smaller variety of humans would chase Hairy and his friends and catch them. Usually, the crickets were able to escape by crawling through the little spaces in the things that the humans would hold them with. Hairy was caught only once, and luckily, he escaped. That made him very wary of the humans.

When Hairy wasn't on the lookout for birds that would eat him, or humans that would squash him, he would hop all around the yard being his usual inquisitive self. One day, Hairy hopped into a shoe. Of course, Hairy didn't know that it was called a shoe, but to him it was a nice place to be. It was out of the sun and it was out of the sight of birds. In fact, it was pretty cozy in there. "How much nicer this is than the little tunnel by the rose bush, in which I live," thought Hairy. "I think that this will be my new home."

Just about that time, Hairy got sleepy and nodded off for a little rest. It seemed like he had slept for a very long time, and it certainly was, for when he awoke and hopped out of the shoe, he was no longer in his yard! He was in a very strange place. There was no bright sun. There was no grass. There were no birds. There was just Hairy and more humans than he had ever seen before. Hairy would hop from one hiding spot to another to avoid being squashed. The humans seemed to make noises that were much louder than Hairy remembered when they were in his back yard. Instead of the big sun, there were several smaller ones and they were not as bright. They would come on and go off in much shorter periods than the sun that Hairy was used to. When they would go off it was really dark and very quiet. Hairy would chirp in the hopes that other crickets would answer him, but the only thing that would happen was the little suns would come on and the big humans would appear to be looking for Hairy.

There were many large things in this new land. They certainly were not shaped like the things that Hairy had seen all his life. Some of these things were white and they made whirring noises, especially when the humans were around. They were easy to hide under, and sometimes there would be a drop of water near them to sip on. Another large thing would also make a funny noise, and when it did, cool air seemed to come from above and made this place very chilly. Hairy certainly couldn't complain that there weren't enough things to explore. One of his favorite places was this large, soft mountain. Hairy didn't know what a mountain was, nor did he know that the mountain was actually a pile of clothing that the humans wore. It was a nice warm place to hide, especially when the very cool air came from above. Hairy had to be careful, because every now and then, a human would pick up Hairy's mountain and put it in the big white thing that whirred and made water drops.

Food was abundant in this new place as the smaller humans seemed to be dropping tasty crumbs all of the time. You would think that Hairy would be happy in this new place what with all the places to explore and the never-ending supply of crumbs. But strange things were happening in addition to Hairy being very lonely. Of course, he would chirp every time it got dark, but he would never hear an answer. Only the small sun coming on and another human looking for him. Hairy missed his family and he missed his friends. He even missed the birds, the bird bath, the bird seeds and especially the warm sun. He missed the long days and the long nights that were much more regular than the little suns. One day, as he hopped around looking to find his way back to his own back yard, he noticed a strange feeling on his head. First, his head felt much cooler than usual, and second, he couldn't feel his ponytail bobbing up and down on his back as he hopped around. He wasn't sure why, but when he was drinking water from one of the little drops, he could tell from his reflection that something was quite different. By this time, his hair would have grown quite a bit and it would be time to cut it, but such was not the case. When he felt his head with his front feet, it was definite. His hair was gone! Hairy wasn't hairy any more! Being in this new place had made Hairy not hairy!

Well, not having hair didn't make Hairy less of a cricket. He was indeed still a cricket and he was still himself! He was still curious and he could still hop! This he continued to do, checking out all of the different places, looking for crumbs, and finding water when he was thirsty. But his activities didn't make up for his loneliness.

One day after a particularly filling meal (he had discovered a bit of peanut butter), he felt particularly energetic. He decided to hop up the stairs that the humans would come down whenever they came looking for Hairy. Of course, Hairy didn't know that these were called stairs, but nonetheless, with great effort, he hopped up each one till he got to the top. It was here that he suddenly realized that he was close to his yard and the brightness was that of the real sun. Hairy figured it was a shoe that transported him away from his every day world, so he figured a shoe would take him back. This time he went under the shoe, and doing what crickets can do, he attached himself to the bot-tom and patiently waited. Before too long, he could feel the shoe moving and in a few large steps, Hairy could tell that he was once again in his own wonderful world. Once the shoe stopped in the tall grass, Hairy let go and quickly hopped in the direction of the rose bush and his mom.

"Hairy, where have you been?" said his mom as she hugged him. "We were so worried that you might not come back."

Hairy was so happy to once again be back home with his family and his friends. "Perhaps I shouldn't be so curious in the future," he thought. "It certainly got me into places where I didn't want to be." Then the thought occurred to him: neither his mom, nor his brothers and sisters, nor his friends, paid any attention to the fact that Hairy had lost his hair! They were just happy to have Hairy back.

In time, with the bright sunlight and the blue sky and the fresh air, Hairy's hair grew back and he had his ponytail again. He decided not to be so curious anymore and he was cautious as to where he hopped. But what this taught Hairy was that he was still a cricket, he was still Hairy, and that his family and friends loved him as they always did!

For Vinnie and Erin,

Mr. C., March 10, 2008

Author's note: The story of "Hairy the Cricket" was written for then six-year-old Vinnie, our neighbor's grandson. Vinnie was undergoing chemotherapy at the time and had lost his hair. His dad shaved his head so the both of them would look alike and I wrote the story to further bolster Vinnie's spirits. I am glad to report that Vinnie's leukemia is in remission and that he is about to enter middle school.

Hank Czerwick is a 66-year resident of the city of Dearborn and product of its schools. He retired from Ford Motor Company as an engineer and from Henry Ford Community College as an educator. His writing has been published in many magazines.

Beautiful Butterflies by Gloria Edmonds

The Monarch butterfly was created to amaze and mystify humanity. Those feathery wings were created to take them on a long flight from their North American home all the way to a warmer destination. It was our creator's gift to mankind. How these fragile wonders of nature could travel to a predetermined home so far away certainly amazes and poses many questions for the human brain. We drove our car with our two young children that fall day so long ago, in eager anticipation of the wonder we would show them. We exited the car and our enthusiasm to see this wonder of nature took hold of us as we hurried along the path to the warm sandy beach.

Our vision spread wide into the deep blue background of the sky that adorned, as if in a picture frame, and enclosed the wonder of thousands of Monarch butterflies dressing the limbs of the almost bare small trees of Point Pelee National Park. The sun that came through the sparse clouds brought us a vision of the magical transformation of fluttering leaves into beautiful wings that were prepared to take them to their predetermined destination. Their adornment in the trees that lay in front of us was nature in all its glory. The black and brown wings with white tips were a design masterpiece that no artist could outdo. The black veins in the wings form a strong framework for gliding, like the crossbars of a kite. This allows them to follow the same migration pattern every year covering thousands of miles.

While my children observed in wonder, I stopped to take pictures of this day. The memory of this day still awakens those glorious times when life was still innocent and enjoying nature was so affordable. It was just a drive to a beautiful place to sit and gaze at the things that were a really important part of life and were there for all to see. For as long as the day kept its light we could quietly gaze in wonder without the blaring of horns or outrageous sounds disturbing our relaxed, sensuous rendezvous with nature.

Too soon it was time to pick up our shoes and say goodbye to the troubles that we left half-buried in the warm sand. As we awaited our turn in line at the immigration booth we found the papers that would have to be displayed to cross back to Michigan. The man in the booth executed the transaction, stamped "Approved" and waved us on into the night. We headed home towards the sadness of crowded streets where winds whipped harsh coldness the Monarch butterfly could not stand. We, however, held the memory of that day on Point Pelee as hope in our hearts for the coming of spring.

Gloria Edmonds: "Writing has been an interest of mine from my younger years in grade school until now. Even though I have become blind in my later years, I still have a love of writing. I am currently studying with the Creative Writing classes at the Senior Center in the Ford Community and Performing Arts Center in Dearborn."

Tiny Lives, Big Hearts by Malak Fawaz

Noli looked around her: Which way should she go? She needs to find food, or she will be reprimanded when she gets back to the colony. She was supposed to be helping the other working ants gather corn seeds, but she forgot one of the important rules and stepped on a fallen leaf. A gust of wind carried the leaf and dragged it away from the colony, with Noli holding tight onto one of its veins so that she would not fall off.

When the wind calmed down and the leaf settled on the ground, Noli looked around to see how far the wind had carried her. One quick look around and Noli's heartbeat quickened. She was lost, and had no food to bring into the colony whatsoever. Finding her way back will take some time, but returning without food, for the third time in a row, will prove to her colleagues their view of her as useless...a failure.

A tear trickled down her cheek, and a small prayer escaped her lips. "Please, please, show me where to find food."

She crawled and crawled aimlessly, trying to catch a smell that would save her pride. But the only smell that her nose caught was the smell of the trash towers that humans periodically stuff with food and pretty, colorful shapes—for an extremely huge mountainous monster to eat. The trash towers always fascinated Noli, but she saw so many of her peers get eaten alive by the monster for her to think of violating their Book B, part 7 rule, ever.

However, at that moment, she was desperate. She needed to get something—anything—to save her from humiliation; and if this was what it took, then she was willing to take the risk. Not the "Ultimate Risk"... She did not have the courage to actually climb the towers to get the really good stuff inside... But she was willing to get close enough to the towers in hope of finding food crumbs around them.

Luckily, a huge sack that was resting at the top of one of the towers had been torn open by some animal, and Noli was able to see grains of rice scattered all over around the tower. She only needed one grain.

***

"Ants!"

A roar came from behind. Noli's heart sank. She recognized the language. It is Human. Forget about the trash-towers eater. Humans are heartless monsters themselves. Countless working ants are murdered on a daily basis by humans crushing them under their feet or killing them with poisons sprayed on plants to kill as many innocent lives as possible. Once, when she was still a child, Noli herself got poisoned so that her colony almost lost hope of her recovery, and they all agree that her being alive and walking the earth is a miracle. These thoughts slammed into Noli's mind all at once, freezing her in her tracks.

The expected blow was so painful. Noli bent her body as low as she could, pushing as much as possible of herself into the creek in the ground. Another blow came, and Noli lost consciousness.

***

"Poor child. She had it rough," said a gentle voice.

"Those heartless humans! They deserve their being tortured by the trash monster indeed! I wish he would eat them all."

Noli stirred. "Nobody deserves to be eaten alive," she wanted to say; but her voice did not come out.

The old ant with the gentle voice, however, noticed her moving in the bed, and she put her hand on Noli's forehead to check whether her fever had gone.

Noli's eyelids fluttered open, but the light hurt her eyes; when she tried to pull her right hand to shield them from the light, pain shot through her arm like knives. Her countenance twisted with pain while she took quick inventory of the damage: "I cannot move my left-back foot, my lower back is wounded, and my right arm will probably take days to heal. I am totally ruined!"

Then her mind froze mid-thought: This is not my colony! Where am I?

Auntie Chloe, the ant with the gentle grandmother's voice, was watching, and hurriedly reassured Noli: "Don't you worry about a thing, dear child. You just forget everything and let us take care of you." The gentle voice was soothing, so Noli closed her eyelids and sank back into sleep, letting her thoughts and pain be carried away with the gentle breeze.

***

"Aw, Noli, that's so sweet of you. I've been craving chocolate for weeks!"

Noli grinned: "I know, Auntie Chloe; this was exactly the same thing you said about the cheesecake last time, and about the pecan pie the time before."

"All right, all right, out with it. What are you bribing me for?"

Noli's smile faltered. She thought she practiced enough, but when the moment came, she stood there, twisting her hands and trying to remember how to say the words without hurting Auntie Chloe's fragile heart.

Auntie Chloe, seeing the struggle and pain through Noli's eyes, let the tears she was holding back slide down her cheeks.

"Time is up, huh? I knew it for days now. I was noticing how your eyes darted over the horizon with that determined look of yours, and I knew what that meant. You're leaving us, huh?"

A repressed sob escaped Auntie Chloe's lips, and she tried to hide it with a cough, raising a hand to her heart. Noli came closer and held it with her own hands:

"You know I will never forget you. You saved my life, taught me how to gather food, and made me see my strengths and respect my weaknesses. You healed my wounds and my heart with your love. From under your wings I am reborn! The best way I can think to repay you is to stand for all you taught me and go back to my home colony to spread the love and light that you planted in my heart."

"But...you can spread love and light here instead. You know we love you and want you to stay!"

Noli's eyes softened: "More love and more light are always appreciated here. But there, on the other side, it is so dark I almost choked with darkness with every sun and with each breeze. And light always spreads outward, or it dies."

***

She did not take anything back with her. The journey was long, and she no longer thought she needed to prove herself anymore. Off she started, towards the horizon on the other side. A long distance stretched in front of her; but step by step, she will make it shorter. Food and water were now at the bottom of her priority list. She only wanted to get home to touch the hearts the way her heart was touched. But the days were long and hot, and when she saw a field of walnut crumbs at the end of the wooden path, she could not but slow her steps and reach for a small crumb to quiet her rumbling stomach.

Just as her trembling hand touched the crumb, a large shadow, like night, stretched over the area where she stood.

She looked up...way up...and she saw a human beast looking directly down at her. Her heart froze. It is the end. She took her chance...and lost.

Noli braced herself, waiting for the painful blow to tear her small body to shreds. But then, she saw the human bend down towards her. "Poor little one. You should not be here, or someone might step on you."

Two giant hands spread a white sheet in front of her, and Noli noticed that she needed to get away...fast. She started running away from the huge white sheet, but the human moved it faster and put it right in her track; and Noli found herself stepping on the sheet that she had just left behind. For five long seconds, the sheet floated in the air, between the human hands, and then was set down, right next to Noli's home colony.

Noli could not believe what was happening. And while she tried to make sense of what that human was doing, a shower of walnut crumbs sprinkled down around her and around the colony's entrance.

"Now you don't need to travel back to that dangerous porch. Stay safe, little one."

And the human turned his back and left, stepping so softly on the ground that the ants who gathered around Noli and the walnut crumbs did not take notice.

Although a good painter, Malak Fawaz is not very fond of painting. She loves to relax while reading a good book and drinking a cup of cappuccino. She also enjoys writing when she has time and is in the right mood.
malak_fawaz@yahoo.com

Spencer, the Spider by Phyllis Tippett

Oh, little spider, in corners you hide
your eight little eyes watching on every side

With four pairs of legs you're swift as the breeze
to hide from critters meant to seize

Your body makes silk spun from spinners
in myriad ways each a winner

Your web in the corner stitched like fine quilt
snares bugs so nature's balance won't tilt

You spin a fine web over garden and plant
one thread a highway for you to prance

You wrap your eggs and line your retreat
in silk so fine it's your grandest feat

But little spider, no matter your size
don't appear before my eyes!

Phyllis Tippett's favorite pursuit in writing is haiku, the diminutive Japanese form that celebrates the natural world. Recently, she published a book entitled Alphabet Critters *which is available on Amazon.com.*

Chapter 4: Cat Tales

My Cat Tom by Bonnie Bilbrey

I looked out of my door this morning
    Snow was everywhere
Footprints on my porch running down the stairs
Little prints of birds the bigger ones were Tom's
    There was a little blood
      More than I like to see
        At the bottom of the stairs
Tom my cat was eating Chicken Fricassee
It could have been a pigeon, robin or perhaps a wren
Only feathers were left from where the bird had been
Tom has been doing this ever since I don't know when
    When Tom was just a kitten
I caught him with a little mouse that he gave to me
He brought it into the house and laid it at my feet
He looked up at me as if to say, I brought lunch
    I love you Mom, today's your day
Tom is not a bad boy when he cuddles up to me
    But the birds had better worry
    And stay up in the trees
I love the birds and watch carefully
    And try to shoo them high into the tree
For Tom is old and not so bold and will never do as he is told
    I love my Tom and he loves me
    What happens next we'll have to see

Bonnie Bilbrey is 63 years old and retired. She goes to school and volunteers for the Volunteer Reading Corps (VRC) in Detroit.

When Shadow Met Faith by Amy Bruhn

Hi, I'm Shadow. I was taken to the Dearborn Animal Shelter when I was five weeks old and was there for over three months before my Mommy-person brought me home. She was sad because her buddy Tigger had passed away at Christmas. Tigger was 20 years old and after that many years together he couldn't be replaced, but my Mommy-person couldn't stand having an empty house any longer. She saw me on her first visit to the shelter but didn't even think of taking me home because she didn't want a black cat (how silly is that?). On her second visit I won her over with my antics when I poked my paws through the cage bars and tried to get at the cat in the cage above mine. When she finally gave in and held me for the first time, I instantly started to purr and lick her chin and then nuzzled against her neck. It was love at first sight. She commented that my mischievous ways would be a handful, but she didn't realize how right those words would prove to be.

The day I came home was Groundhog Day, so she named me Shadow – partly because I was black, but also because the groundhog saw his shadow that day. I've also lived up to my name in that I am literally her Shadow. I love to follow her around all the time and have to be involved in whatever she's doing. They don't call us cats curious for no reason! I also love to check out anything that isn't nailed down or locked away. My Mommy-person calls me a kleptomaniac. I'm not

sure what that is, but I think it has something to do with me taking her glasses and hiding them while she's in the shower.

I'm Faith. I came to the shelter when I was only three weeks old. I was born wild and didn't like people very much at all, but the nice ladies at the shelter worked really hard with me. I was only in the adoption room for one day when my Mommy-person came in, saw me, and decided to bring me home. She had another cat, Shadow, who was always getting into mischief, so she thought he could use a friend. My Mommy-person named me Faith because despite my tiny size (I was only 1.5 lbs.) I didn't have any hesitation when she brought me home and I went exploring as if I had always lived there. And then when I met Shadow, I just knew he wouldn't hurt me, not even when I'd walk under him, bite his belly, and then run. Since he outweighed me by nine pounds, my Mommy-person said that took a lot of faith.

Shadow and I were kept separated when I first came home because our Mommy-person wanted us to get to know each other gradually, and she was really worried about our size difference. She slowly let us play together, which was really Shadow chasing me and me hiding under and behind furniture where he couldn't get at me. But when I was in my separate room, Shadow would always come and lay outside my door.

Our Mommy-person feared that we would never get along and that Shadow would never stop chasing me. The turning point came

one day when Shadow chased me right through his food dish. I stopped to eat and he stopped dead in his tracks and lay down to watch me eat. The look on his face was priceless. None of his toys had ever eaten his food before!

Shadow inched a little closer to see if I was really eating his food. He couldn't believe his eyes!

He finally decided that he may as well join me before I ate everything up. From that day on we were inseparable and we like to eat out of the same food dish together.

Shadow started to teach me how to play with all of his toys. We love it when the Mommy-person tosses toys down the hall for us to run after, and then we run back to see what she'll throw next. We call this game "Kitty Olympics" and by the time we're done we usually have about thirty toys that need to be picked up. One of our Mommy-person's friends said we have too many toys, but we don't really think that's possible, is it?

We love to chase each other through the house and up and down our six-foot cat tree, and sit in the windows and watch the birds at all the feeders that our Mommy-person keeps full. We get to see cardinals, finches, woodpeckers, and of course – lots of squirrels and chipmunks!

All of this activity wears us out, so when we get tired we curl up and take our cat naps together. Our Mommy-person often wonders how sane she was to go from one well-behaved 20-year-old kitty to two rambunctious, mischievous kittens, but she says that our antics make her laugh, and that's what it's all about.

Amy Bruhn is an animal lover.

What Did I Do? Am I Guilty? by Susan J. Cleereman

This is the sad story of how I killed a cat. I did, he is dead. And if I hadn't taken him to the veterinarian, he might still be alive. I have been crying ever since I told her to put him to sleep. I even cried while I said it, but I did say it.

He adopted us one winter during a horrific snowstorm. I don't know where he came from, but he appeared on our deck surrounded by the deepest snow we had seen in years. Poor thing, he was skinny and shivering and very unhappy. We, my husband and I, don't normally feed strays. "Feed them once and they never go away." You've heard that, maybe even said it, but where else could he go? We put out a dish of food and it was gone in minutes.

The snow didn't clear for a couple of weeks. Every day we would look outside, hoping that he had given up on us and moved on. Every day he was outside, still skinny and still hungry. Every day we would relent and give him another dish of food.

One day was colder than normal. I don't remember just how cold it was. My coat was all buttoned to the top. I was even wearing my hood. I came home after dark, very happy to walk into a warm house. "Hi Hon," I said shivering and rubbing my hands together. "Any chance of a warm cup of cocoa?" I love cocoa, especially when I'm cold. Just then he appeared with a steaming cup of cocoa in his hands, already for me to drink. "How is the cat?"

"Well, he's not too cold."

"It's awfully frigid outside tonight."

My husband looked embarrassed for a minute and pointed toward the computer room. It was shut. We always keep it open. I looked at him in amazement; it had been his rule never to let the cat inside. Of course, it had been his rule never to feed the cat either. The cat was in the computer room, staying a lot warmer than he would be outside. I put down the mug of cocoa and hugged him, "You softy."

From that day on, whenever the temperature seemed cold, the cat would appear in the computer room. Just so he didn't freeze, yeah, sure. So now we were feeding him and keeping him warm.

I suggested naming the cat. My husband vetoed that. If you name a cat you are claiming it as yours. I had to admit that he was right. It did seem strange to refer to him as "that cat." Oh well.

With the end of winter the weather became much more comfortable. One day the temperature was in the 70s. The cat was looking worse than ever. He was still skinny and filthy. I was afraid that he would scratch me, but I wanted to give him some kind of a bath. I got a brush and a bucket of warm soapy water outside on the deck. I started by brushing him with the warm soapy water. He loved it. I started to rub his fur with my fingers and the soapy water. He still loved it and started to purr. I washed him all over, he was purring the whole time. What you do with a soapy cat? I called my husband out to see. He took the bucket and filled it with warm, clean water. He poured it over the cat. The cat was not offended in the least! He hugged me, only poking my wrist lightly with one claw! He was still a bit soapy, so my husband got another bucket and doused him again. No scratches, just a very wet, loving hug.

He looked a lot better after that. We were still feeding him. He was never gone from our deck for more than a couple of hours at a time. Whenever it rained the food would get wet and be ruined. So we put boxes out to keep the food under and dry. The cat would curl up in the boxes and take naps. He had decided that we were his people and we were going to acknowledge it, someday.

One rainy day in April, my son came by. He was tempted to take the cat. He called him "Twerp." I thought it would be nice for Jeff to take the cat. We had two cats already, but Jeff didn't have any. I started calling the cat "Twerp." I figured that if he named him, he might take him. Turned out Jeff didn't really want the cat, but the cat was now named "Twerp."

Twerp got along with our older cat, "Shadow," just fine. Whenever Shadow wanted to go outside and Twerp was in the way, Shadow would pretend to claw at him and he would cower with his ears back. This was funny because Shadow couldn't really fight at all. He had been fixed and declawed as a kitten, 13 years earlier. Twerp would take on any other cat that came into our yard. We frequently heard cat fights.

Our younger cat, "Scooter" was a totally different story. Twerp was always jumping on poor Scooter and clawing at him. Scooter was not happy with Twerp around. He would not go out any door that Twerp was guarding. Shadow could go in and out, but Scooter couldn't. He would make me let him out a different door.

Now the story changes. In May, I discovered that I was very ill. After a month or so of misdiagnoses, it was determined that I had a children's bone Cancer. I had to have treatment. Ugh, I can tell you that chemotherapy is <u>not</u> fun. I went bald and I was miserable. This is not my story, so just take my word, Cancer is not a nice problem to have. After several weeks of treatment, I decided that I wanted a "Make-A-Wish." I was not a child, but I had a children's Cancer. I figured I deserved it. My "Make-A-Wish" would be to adopt Twerp. He was a nice cat, he liked me, and I liked him.

Before we could adopt him, we would have to get him neutered, declawed, and vaccinated. Hopefully the neutering and declawing would mellow him out so that he wouldn't attack Scooter anymore. Scooter had to be safe, at least in the house. We weren't sure just how it would work out. Twerp was such a nice cat. He liked everyone except for Scooter. He deserved to come inside.

I called the veterinarian and she suggested that before the surgeries we have him tested for feline leukemia and feline AIDS. That sounded really smart. I was nervous that he would test positive, since he had never been protected and he was always getting into fights. I took him to the vet's office. He didn't like the car ride, but when we got inside, he started to purr! I have never had a cat purr in a vet's office before! He sat in my lap and snuggled really close. When the vet came into the room he purred for her too! "What a wonderful cat," she said. "Most cats don't cuddle like this." I left him with her. She would test him and call me with the results.

About a half an hour later she was on the phone: "He has feline AIDS." Now what? He was so nice, but I couldn't have a sick cat in the house that didn't know how to use the litter box. He would attack Scooter. I still had Cancer myself. If he had been healthy it would've been hard enough. I told her that I had to talk to some other people. I called my husband and I called a friend who is a vet in another state. I could hardly talk. I was crying so hard. If we just left him outside he would continue to pass the virus on to other cats in the neighborhood. By taking him to the vet, he was now my responsibility. Whoever got rid of him as a kitten had been responsible before, but where were they? I had to face it, I couldn't take care of him and nobody else would. I called the vet back and gave her verbal permission to put Twerp to sleep. I was in tears and I still am. Did I murder him? I don't know.

Susan J. Cleereman is a Cancer survivor. This is a true story from 1999. She has been Cancer free since 2000. majsjc@aol.com

Feline Beeline by Snuffy Cook, as meowed to Rose M. Cook

The day was July 7, 2013, 10:15 p.m. I had to do it. Take a chance. Catch my own food and feel the grass under my paws. Follow my instincts just like my father and forefathers before me. See, I've lived in a house all of my 54 cat (9 human) years. I was tired of being a prisoner in their home. I needed to escape!

However, I want to make something perfectly clear. My humans are good people. They treat me right. Three squares a day. Fresh water with ice cubes. Treats, high-grade catnip, my own bed, scratches and pets anytime I'm in the mood. So let's get one thing straight. It wasn't them. It was me. I had to see if I could make it on my own. Sometimes, a cat's gotta do what a cat's gotta do!

Now that we got that out of the way, I'll let you in on my story. Some names and places have been changed to protect my co-conspirators. I take full responsibility for what I did and the pain I caused. I'm that kind of a cat.

The air on the July night in question was warm and humid. My humans were busy unloading the car, coming in and out of the side door and not paying attention at all to my whereabouts. I realized that this was my chance. It was now or never. I bolted out of the door, unnoticed. Free at last. Free at last.

It was about an hour or so when it happened. I was just starting to get my bearings outside, when I heard their frantic calls. "Snuffy! Snuffy boy! Where are you?" From behind an evergreen in the neighbor's yard, I saw them, my humans. They were traipsing around in their pajamas, flashlights in hand, looking under cars and bushes, clanging on my metal food bowls, calling my name. I must admit, the pitiful sight of them, to say nothing of what the neighbors must have thought, almost caused me to cave and come out into the open. With a great deal of trepidation, I held fast, turned around and ran.

After a night of roaming the neighborhood, I woke from a short nap. That's when it hit me...HEAT. Under my thick fur coat it felt like 100 degrees. Found out later that it was the first day of the hottest week of the summer. In retrospect, should have paid more attention to Rich Luterman's weekly weather forecast. After what seemed like an eternity, I found a leaking garden hose in a yard on Hubbard Street. That faulty faucet turned out to be my main water source during my time in the wild. Thank goodness for human frailties and the fact that no one took the time to repair that faucet.

The smell of fresh air and the warm grass under my paws was exhilarating. It was midday when I suddenly realized that I hadn't eaten since I left home. My predatory instincts took over and I began to scout the area for food. Put the kibosh on a few grasshoppers and crickets. That barely touched my hunger. Knew I was gonna have to speed up the hunting process if I was going to maintain my svelte 13 lb. frame.

The next few days were teeming with adventure. I surveyed the neighborhood, hunted, survived a few scuffles with some young feline ruffians, dodged cars and runaway dogs and had a tryst with a long haired calico beauty. I also discovered a number of amazing human cat lovers in the neighborhood. Some of them even left food and water outside for vagabonds like me.

Eight days into my adventure, I decided to take a trip back to the "old neighborhood." Passed 50 or so signs with my mug shot on them. They were on light posts, storefronts and just about anything else my people could put a nail into. There was even a $200 reward being offered for my safe return home.

By the time I got to my human's house, it was completely dark. To my surprise, my water bowl and food dish were on the back steps. Both filled to the brim. That really touched my heart. As I ate the dish of food and drank most of the water, a feeling of nostalgia swept over me. I was starting to miss my humans and the good life they provided for me. I thought about sticking around till daylight, but decided to leave and find a bed for the night. I had a lot of thinking to do.

For the next two days, no matter where my travels took me, it wasn't long before I saw them, hitting my food dishes together, calling my name, handing out flyers with my picture on them, asking dog walkers and joggers if they had seen me. Always the same query: "Our Snuffy boy is lost and we really miss him. Have you seen him?"

I was starting to feel some remorse for all of the pain and grief I was putting them through. Guess it never occurred to me that I was such an important part of their lives.

My escapade ended on July 17th, 6:45 a.m. My female human was in the backyard watering the flowers. Her eyes were red and puffy and honestly, she looked downright pathetic. I decided right then and there that I needed to stop their pain. They needed me. It was my feline duty to return to them.

I walked out from under the firethorn bush in the corner of the yard and meowed. She looked over at me, dropped the hose and let out a big yell. When her mate heard the commotion he came running outside and scooped me up in his arms. The three of us stood there for the longest time, enjoying a glorious group hug.

It's been a couple of months since I returned home. We've settled into our routine. As for me, I have no immediate plans to leave. I'm content daydreaming about my ten days in the wild.

My humans, however, are extra cautious coming in and out of the door when I'm around. I do believe they have a new found respect for me and realize that "You can take the cat out of the wild, but you can't take the wild out of the cat."

Rose M. Cook is a daughter, sister, friend, registered nurse, wife and mother of Jai and Heather. She finds pleasure in gardening, yoga, meditation, writing, outdoor activities, animals (especially her cat, Snuffy) and laughing. nmbr1roze@aol.com

The Ghosts of Dandy and Bowie by Dannielle DiMeglio

I have always been fascinated by ghost stories and disappointed that none of my loved ones who died came back to say goodbye.

However, two of my cats did. The first, Dandy, when he was outside and wanted to come in, would jump on my kitchen window sill with a distinct sound that I called the "Dandy Thump." Several weeks after he died I was at the kitchen table when there was the distinct sound of the Dandy Thump. My heart froze and my other cat leapt to the inside sill and meowed excitedly. I am convinced that Dandy came to say goodbye to us.

The second cat, Bowie, died and was buried in my back yard. This was around the time of Stephen King's *Pet Sematary* in 1983. I was outside on the patio one night when I saw Bowie struggling out of his grave and come running toward me. I immediately thought, "This cannot be happening" and he disappeared. Had I not thought that, would he have kept coming?

Dannielle DiMeglio is a retired pediatric nurse and has four companion cats. None of her pediatric patients ever returned to say goodbye, but memories of some of them still haunt her. danitraveller@aol.com

The Wild Tail of Walter Kitty by A.C. Fish

Part 1: One Sunny Day

Walter sat in a spot of warm, congenial, shimmering sunshine that pierced the grey dullness of the apartment. All the other windows had the drapes pulled, since Mother did not like the light fading the plethora of photos, dollies, and strange things that populated every good landing surface in the apartment. Walter looked down upon the kaleidoscopic display of chaotic color in the Great World below. Walter Kitty was bored. Very bored. Bored to the point of ceasing existence.

Well, Walter thought, I am rather boring. My whole being is just random shades of grey, and I do tend to blend into the shadows and get sat upon a lot. I am neither large nor small. I do not talk a lot. My eyes are even grey that blend into the greyness that is my existence. I eat the same thing each day at the same times, get the same snacks, and every day is the same. I am so boring that I am named after Mother's husband Walter, the former insurance agent, and her son Walter, a government employee, and her grandson Walter, the accountant, and her great grandson Walter, the baby. Walter, Walter, Walter! I never know who she is talking to or about! Walter's tail twitched, and flailed nervously.

Dust motes float through the air, even though Mother would deny the existence of the motes. Mother is always taking a cloth and pushing the dust around, making the motes dance up from the landing surfaces into the air to continue the pattern of the ballet. This is somewhat interesting, because the motes always change their dance. Walter Kitty took a swipe at the motes, and the dance changed again.

Walter jumped onto the grey carpet. If I lay here, Mother will not see me and step on me. The same if I lay over there, or even over there! Walter Kitty slinked into the kitchen, where Mother was making hot water for tea. Mother always makes tea at this time of day. The same kind of tea every day. Boring. Walter weaved through Mother's legs, but as usual, Mother pushed Walter away, and kept watching the pot of water, waiting for it to boil.

The whole environment of this apartment is one of waiting. Walter could feel the oppression of waiting. Waiting for food, waiting for attention, waiting for sunshine, waiting for some undetermined life-changing event, waiting for visitors to relieve the boredom. Rejected, as usual, Walter Kitty slunk from the kitchen and back to the table under the window sill.

Finally, a knocking noise comes from the door. Walter, the great grandson is visiting today. He is pulling a lot of the things from the landing surfaces onto the floor, pulled my tail, pulled Mother's hair, and even pulled his own feet to his mouth! Walter, the baby, is in a great pulling mood.

Mother does not scold Walter Baby when he pulls the things off the table. Mother makes funny noises at Walter Baby, and then picks him up and holds him. I wish Mother would give me as much attention as Walter Baby gets. Walter Baby does not even seem to want the attention, and wiggles to get away so he can go and pull at something else.

Walter Kitty jumped to the floor and quickly darted to the door. Walter of the pulling mood just pulled open the door...

Adventure lurks just beyond!

Part 2: Walter Kitty's Jungle Adventure

Walter Kitty rocketed out of the cracked door courtesy of Walter Baby. The floor was different here; it did not have fur! Walter slid across the slick light brown shiny surface. This is kind of fun, to be able to slide all I want! I slid once with Mother, but I got yelled at when all the things fell off the landing surface. Sliding is good, but there is a cracked door across from Mother's door, and it must be investigated!

Walter Kitty crept cautiously across the hall and nudged the door open with his nose and paw. The room was a green jungle! A hard green floor amplified the soft grey thuds of Walter's padded velvet feet as he reconnoitered his surroundings. Plants in the corners, plants hang from the ceiling, plants in the window, plants on the floor, plants on jumping surfaces, and even a plant by the door. Vines stretched from ceiling to floor and from floor to ceiling. Unlike the plants in Mother's apartment, these would break, and ooze goo, and some could even be eaten! Flowers peeked out of a number of randomly shaped glass things. This is not boring. Maybe this is adventure...

Also hanging from the ceiling is a bunch of wire enclosures with noisy multicolored birds. Blue, yellow, white, brown, red. All colors of birds. The biggest bird sat on a chewed branch in a giant enclosure that hung low from a large vine-enclosed stand on the floor. The giant bird was blue, red, white, green, and black with shiny yellow eyes.

It talked too. It said "BORED! BORED! BORED! BORED!" when it was not chewing on the branch. The other birds were also busy making noise at each other, and being rather silly. Walter Kitty now understood what Mother meant when she called him a birdbrain. Mother was not being nice when she called Walter that!

Walter Kitty sauntered over to the big enclosure to get a better look at the really big bored bird. Rattle, rattle, clickety-clickety-click. Arfff-arfff-arfff-arff! Walter's tail got bit by the ferocious, funny-looking, curly-haired, short-tailed cat. Walter leaped up on the giant enclosure to get away from the stupid cat. The rude cat leaped up and bit Walter's tail again. Walter climbed even further up the cage.

Walter Kitty turned his head towards the cage to continue the climb, and encountered a yellow eye very close to his.

"OPEN! OPEN! BORED!" The large sharp beak pointed at a hook on the cage.

Walter could knock that a couple of times with his paw and open it if he could get up there. Just need to climb the cage and not fall off. Walter's tail throbbed with pain as he advanced up the cage.

Walter Kitty slowly inched his way around the cage, and up to the latch. Whack, whack, whack. I almost fell! That would not be good. Try again. Whack, whack, whack.

Yellow Eye now looked into Walter's, and then squawked, "DOG!"

Don't know what a dog is, but the hook is almost loose. Whack, whack,

"SQUAWK!"

Walter fell off the cage as Yellow Eye launched himself from cage to ceiling and back down onto the funny-looking cat.

Yellow Eye, who is much larger than the funny-looking cat, flattened the cat so his four legs stuck out in four different directions, and proceeded to bite that cat's tail. Yellow Eye paused momentarily to look at Walter Kitty and squawk, "DOG!"

Ah, this is what a dog is. Pestilent little beastie. Should have known it was not a cat, because cats would have better manners than to greet each other by biting tails.

The dog wiggled out from under Yellow Eye and scuttled for the shelter of the big cage. Yellow Eye jumped up on the cage, slammed the gate behind Dog, and flipped the hook back into place.

Serves him right, after all, Dog bit my tail not once, but twice. One time could have been a mistake made because of the excitement of a new visitor, but two times is just plain malice. "DUMB DOG!" Walter agreed. "BORED!" screeched the colorful bird.

Walter Kitty introduced himself, while Yellow Eye looked longingly at the door.

Yellow Eye illuminated with a shriek, "POLLY!"

"Polly is a girl's name," queried Walter Kitty, "and aren't you a boy?"

Polly screeched in offended tone, "MAN!!!"

Walter suggested, "Paul!???"

Then a unanimous decision was made that Polly would be re-christened as Paul, almost like Saul from the big black book that Mother reads out loud on occasion, but without the piercing beam of light and the chorus of approving angels.

Dog complained from the cage. Dog did not like seeds, berries, cuttlefish bones, millet, or tree branches. On this Walter agreed with Dog, with the exception of the tree branch and maybe the cuttlefish bone. The branch had possibilities and the cuttlefish bone just smelled interesting. Dog is boring, and there is nothing worse than boring!

Walter noticed this apartment was colorful, and might be a nice change.

Paul screamed, because he did not know how to whisper or talk normally, "BORING! GREEN! NITWITS! DOG! SAME! SAME! SAME!"

Walter understood, even though Paul usually did not exclaim in more than two words at a time. Walter Kitty described the grey world of existence to Paul.

"BORING!" quipped Paul.

Walter exclaimed, "ADVENTURE AWAITS!" Paul's way of talking is kind of fun!

Paul turned one yellow eye on Walter, and then on the slightly opened door. "OPEN!"

Walter turned one grey eye on Paul. "WALK! NO FLY!" This new way of talking left no misunderstandings. Paul walked on two legs, just like Mother, but not as smoothly, to the door. Walter Kitty followed Paul.

Paul stopped at the door. "OUT!?! SAFE?!?!"

Walter Kitty was perplexed. Safe is boring. I have been safe all my life. I went out on an adventure and got a couple of bites on my tail, but I got to meet Paul and slide around in the hall. Walter considered Paul with one grey eye. "RISK GOOD! SAFE BORING! GO!!!"

Walter Kitty gave Paul a mighty shove through the crack made by the open door. A couple of small grey feathers floated to the floor. So Paul is grey too! I am in good company, thought Walter as he squeezed through the door just in time to see Paul sliding across the floor. "FUN!!! WHEEEEEEEEEEEEE!!!!!" Thud! Paul slammed into a wall, knocking off a few more feathers, "NO RISK!! NO FUN!!!" as he ran into a prolonged slide down the hallway instead of across it. Wow, Walter observed, Paul is quite intelligent in spite of his limited speech capacity.

Adventure is risky.

Part 3: The Furry, Feathery, and Scaly

Walter Kitty and Paul Parrot explored the hallway between sliding sessions. Neither of them feared the discovery of their respective escapes. Walter's mother barely noticed him except to feed him and open the one shade a peep so the light would come in the window and push Walter out of the way of the daily routine. Paul's mother was gone. She always departed when the light came up, and then would return when the light went away. Paul's mother only talked to the plants and made funny noises like the small silly birds, but Paul was lucky if his newspaper got changed once a week. Granted, Paul's feedings are regular, but what does that matter if the newspaper on the bottom gets so encrusted that the once-a-week changing is a monumentally mammoth maintenance mission interlaced with a surfeit of incomprehensible infuriated expressions?

The hallway contained a multitude of identically boring doors. All the doors looked the same, except for the doors to the mothers' apartments. Those two doors were opened a crack. Various objects, like umbrella stands, boxes, and bags with interesting smells, were placed by the hallway doors. These were excellent obstacles for the sliding festival!

The wall at the end of the hallway looked funny, and it needed investigation. There are three big cracks running from the floor to the top of the wall. A warm purring noise comes from the wall sometimes, and sometimes it is quiet. The wall seemed like it should open, but it did not do anything, even when Walter swatted at it with his paw, or Paul pried at it with his beak. Walter and Paul soon lost interest in the wall, and proceeded to slide into each other, walls, doors, and anything that got in their way.

The wall at the end of the hallway suddenly purred, groaned, clinked, and clanked. A sliding noise, like Mother's broom on the kitchen floor, emanated from the wall as it whisked open in a sideways manner. Walter, the accountant, the father of Walter Baby, revealed himself to be inside the wall. Walter Kitty and Paul hid behind a conveniently located box in the hallway. Walter and Paul peered around the edges of their hiding place to observe Walter Accountant.

Walter Accountant wearily worked his way up the hallway, neither looking left nor right, but at the floor, mumbling to himself about boring, errands, dead-end job, jerk boss, nagging wife, broke, supermarket errands, crooked clients, budget, stupid job, stock market, and boring again. Walter Kitty felt that Walter Accountant may be a kindred soul, but after an abbreviated discussion with Paul, they both agreed that having two Walters in the group would be too confusing, plus Walter Accountant is a wet blanket, and would never ever even dream of having an adventure.

Walter Accountant knocked on Mother's door, entered, and exited with Walter Baby under his arm. Walter Baby screamed, wiggled, bit Walter Account, and was a general pain. Walter Accountant muttered something about spoiled, brat, monster, and some other unrecognizable words as he pressed a white spot on the wall next to the funny-looking wall at the end of the hallway. A light appeared behind the white spot. Again, the noises emanated from the funny wall, and it opened. Walter Accountant, showing no fear, only resignation, with Walter Baby securely tucked under one arm, reached into an unseen part of the sliding wall. The wall closed again, with the prerequisite noises.

"AMAZING! INCREDIBLE! GONE!" Yes, that was incredible. Even weird, but not boring. Walter Kitty looked up at the white spot on the wall. Walter leaped up to bat it with his paw, but missed. Walter tried many times, but since Walter is a cat, and even cats can be vertically challenged, he could not get up high enough to hit the white spot. "PAUL! FLY! HIT SPOT!" Hopefully this is not too many words at once. Paul spread out his wings, and pushed off the floor. He flew towards the spot, could not stop fast enough, and slammed into the wall, resulting in a shower of various feathers.

The white spot on the wall lit up like a beam of sunshine was coming out of it. Paul smoothed his ruffled feathers while standing next to Walter Kitty and listening to the purring of the wall. Something is going to happen. Something different. Something that is not boring. "ADVENTURE!"

Again, the same noises, and the wall opened. This is not so scary. Walter and Paul walked into the box. It was like sunshine came down from the ceiling, and there were a lot of little round white spots on the left side of the inside of the box. Maybe like the white spot on the outside, one or all of these spots must be hit. Paul tilted his head and focused his brown eye on the little white spots as the wall slid shut again. "NO FLY!" Walter thought this was a good idea, because he did not want to see his adventuring companion losing all his feathers.

Suddenly the box lurched, purred, clicked, clacked, and started moving. Well they were still in one piece, even though it seemed the world is moving up, or they were in some kind of box falling. Strange, but it still did not hurt. Some small lights on the wall wiggled and undulated. The box lurched again, and the world stopped moving. The wall opened up, and a woman with a stroller started pushing her way into the box. Both adventurers made their escape from the amazing moving falling box as the wall closed again.

Walter and Paul gazed down another long hallway. It looked just like Mother's hallway, but different. No umbrella stands in this one, but there were some plants in containers, boxes, and even interesting bags. This hall even has the slippery-slidey floor too. There is an open door about halfway down the hall, and another mother is putting out some bags, and now carrying a big box this way towards the funny wall!

Walter and Paul practiced their stealth skills again by hiding behind a plant. Mother pressed the white spot on the wall next to the funny wall and waited with the box in her arms. Grey eye looked at brown eye, a nod was exchanged, and the both of them made a mad dash for the open door.

The apartment is the same size, same shape, same sameness as both the other mothers' apartments. Talk about boring. Epitome of boring, except for the really big green dog draped across the entire back of the brown sofa. The dog looked at Walter and Paul, scratched behind her ear with one scaly claw, and then put her head down on the sofa again.

Walter and Paul exchanged looks. "NO DOG! NO BITE TAIL!" Walter came to that conclusion, since the green dog has manners, that this dog must not be a dog. Paul's brown eye locked on the snack bowl at the end of the sofa. "FRUIT!!!" He tottered over to the bowl, uninvited. So much for manners when it came to food...

Green took a deep breath and lifted her head again, looked at Paul eating her fruit and then Walter patiently sitting on the floor. She scratched again, dislodging a few more bits of dead skin, and languidly expressed, "Visssitorsss, I never get visssitorsss. How esssiteing!" She pushed her body off the couch and gracefully glided to the floor and looked into Walter's grey eyes. "I have sssseen katsss in the petsssshop. You are a katsss. I too have ssseen parrotsss in the petsssshop. I am not a dogsss, I am a lisssard, an iguana. I am called Isssey."

Walter Kitty introduced himself and his gluttonous companion Paul. Isssey exclaimed, "Katsss and parrotsss are not friendsss. Parrotsss are birdsss. Katsss eatsss birdsss." Walter replied, "I have more manners than to eat a companion, a kindred spirit, who longs for a little adventure and relief from boredom!" Walter considered Paul. "It is more likely that really big bird will get hungry and eat me!"

Isssey looked sad, even depressed. "Mother getsss visitorsss. Mother getsss to leave the apartment. All I do is eat, sssleep, move with the patch of sssunlight, and ssstare out the window at the world. It looksss marvelousss. Do not get me wrong, I love Mother, but I am ssso bored, I do not feel that I am living. Would it be posssible to join you in your adventuresss? I can sssee that you do not think too far ahead, sssince you have no food with you. I could be a help, becausssse I am good at thinking. That is all I do all day, think."

Walter looked over at the occupied Paul. "It would be a good thing to have you on this adventure, because it seems as though Paul is always hungry." Isssey retorted, "Either he hasss tape wormsss or isss more like the sssmall birdsss than he admitsss!" Paul raised his head from the metal bowl and glared at Isssey. "NOT BIRDBRAIN!! HUNGRY! EXERCISE!!! STUPID IZARD!"

Issey rolled her eyes. "Ssssee, driven by hisssstomach." Issey sashayed towards the kitchen, as Walter watched Paul take the last bit of apple and toss it in the air and catch it in his beak. Issey returned with some fruit, nuts, and wiggly white worms in a small grey plastic bag. Issey slipped the bag over Walter's head saying, "You are taller than usss, and the bag will not drag. Pleassse carry the bag for usss?" Isssey could be a cat too, because she has excellent manners! Walter batted the bag around his neck, and Paul examined the bag with a shiny eye.

Down from the end of the hallway, the now familiar funny wall noises were getting louder. Isssey declared, "Mother isss returning from taking out the trasssh. We mussst leave!" The trio escaped into the hallway, with Walter looking a little silly wearing a very small bag of fruit and worms.

Walter directed Isssey behind a large box and Paul into a potted plant. Walter blended into the shadow behind Isssey's box. Mother, whistling, half skipped down the hall, oblivious to the adventurers, entered the apartment and snapped the door shut.

Paul knew what to do, and launched himself at the white spot on the wall, and lost a few more loose feathers in the process. Walter and Isssey dashed to the funny wall. "Elevator, not a funny wall. I have ssseen many thingsss, and know many thingsss. Mother doesss take me out sssometimesss. I will help you ussse the elevator." The elevator door parted and the co-conspirators ducked into the elevator. Isssey stretched herself up the wall, and indicated that Walter should leap up on her shoulders and swat the second button from the left on the bottom. Walter performed the acrobatics, swatted the button, and the doors closed, as the elevator lurched to life again.

Adventure is moving down in the world.

A.C. Fish:
"I live in a shoebox borne on a deer,
A little left field, a little bit weird,
Jack of all trades, master of none,
Just writin' this doodle 'cause it's fun!"

The Mystery of Blackie by Annie Franco

In 1963 the six of us lived in Lynchburg, Virginia, along with our cat, Blackie. In those days there were no laws about pets running about, so Blackie was an outdoor cat. She had many lovers and therefore lots of progeny which she chose to birth in a weird variety of places, such as the washing machine or in the bushes.

The time came when my husband decided it was time for a new job in a new state, so we made plans to move and called the moving van. While the movers were packing up our furniture, we were busy loading the car and making a special little bed for Blackie who was pregnant – again.

Since we had no furniture on the last night in Lynchburg, we stayed at a motel and left Blackie at the house. The following morning when we went to retrieve her, she was nowhere to be found. We called and called, then checked with the neighbors to no avail. Finally, we had to make the decision to leave without her, asking the neighbors to take care of her when found. We left Lynchburg with four crying kids, ages 2, 4, 6, and 8 and two heartbroken adults.

We spent two nights in a motel in Asheville, North Carolina, our new city of residence, waiting for the movers to arrive at our home. On Monday morning the movers, with all doors of the house open, were putting things in place when I decided to wander into the open, attached garage. There, high up on a window sill was a black cat. I assumed a neighbor's cat had wandered in, but it looked vaguely familiar, though not too friendly. Finally, I dared to call out "Blackie" and she responded.

Apparently Blackie had sought refuge in the moving van while it was parked at our house in Lynchburg, either out of fright or to have her babies and had spent the whole weekend therein. She had no water, no food, and no obvious "mess." It was really a mystery how she survived.

Two days later Blackie gave birth; this time accepting the bed we made for her. I thought it was such a unique story that I submitted it to the local paper and it was published. Good thinking, because when the kittens were ready for a new home, I advertised "Blackie's kittens – free" and had more requests than I could fill.

Blackie survived another move two years later to Huntsville, Alabama, where she protected her young by riding a nosy dog out of her yard with claws bared and hairs raised. She lived to a ripe old age but lost a final fight with a dog.

Annie Franco is twice a widow and has 5 children and 12 grandchildren. She lived in Michigan for 27 years before moving to California in 2001 and has returned to Michigan permanently. george0299@sbcglobal.net

The Airship *Piscea* by Jacob Hildebrandt

Full Title: The Airship Piscea: *A Feline Adventure in the Steam-era Skies*

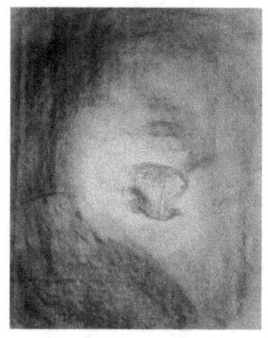

This was Moppet's very favorite. This place, this weather, this warm glow in her tiny kitten heart. Everything about this clifftop picnic was exactly what made the uncoordinated calico happy. Her father, a sturdily built tabby with deep black stripes, lay nearby mirroring her contentment. A storm had been brewing in the distance for some time, though the sky above their noontime feast remained clear enough to furnish the duo with cozy sunbeams in which to lay. Fond memories of the dried trout they had just finished filled their bellies as they both stared across the sea below them.

With a crinkle and a pounce, Moppet skittered away in pursuit of a blowing early autumn leaf. Tom was aware of this, but knew his daughter was safe and continued to watch the dark, rolling clouds in the distance. As his eyes focused again after a particularly slow blink, he noticed a thinning towards the center of the nearest cloud formation. Like one of his own sleepy eyes, the space slowly rolled open wider. A tired ray of sunlight began to filter through, contrasting the dark plumes around it. Suddenly, the tomcat's ears swiveled forward as something caught his attention. It was not much more than a speck at this distance, but something was definitely coming through the hole in the clouds.

"Moppet!" he called out with sharp joy. "Come here! There's a ship on the horizon!

"Ship?" mewed the kitten as she flopped up alongside her father on the sandy cliff's edge.

"Yes, little kit, an airship! See it there? Among the clouds? It seems as though it is headed right towards us!"

The two cats strained their eyes forward, tails swishing with excitement behind them. Airships were one of Tom's very favorite things, and tiny Moppet couldn't help but share in the excitement. The small yard behind their house contained evidence of more than a few abandoned attempts to construct such a vessel, but neither member of the family had attained any altitude beyond what their claws could provide against a tree. Enthusiasm was a thing Tom had in spades, but follow-through and general carpentry skills were sadly lacking. This didn't stop his friends from routinely calling him "Captain," however, and he was often seen wearing a modest pair of flying goggles on his forehead.

A few moments later, the ship was plainly visible. Looking something like an oversized rowboat suspended beneath an enormous lemon-shaped helium envelope, it blew swiftly towards the shore. Smoke and steam billowed out from a pipe on the stern of the ship, mingling and blending with the still darkening clouds from which it had just emerged.

"An engine! Moppie, it has an engine!" Until this point, Tom had assumed that the craft was a sailing ship. It had appeared to be approaching at a greater speed than the breeze that had been ruffling their fur, but Tom knew that a skilled sailor could accomplish this with some clever rigging. Now that it was only a few hundred yards away, however, he began to see that this was an airship like nothing he had ever seen. He had read of a few pilots on the East Coast who were brave or mad enough to affix small steam motors to their craft, but he had never thought he'd encounter one in person. Leaning as far forward as he could and cursing the fact that he had left his spyglass at home, Tom put every ounce of his being into seeing as much detail on the vessel as felinely possible. A few glints of brass were all he could make out of the mechanical portions, but it looked amazingly complicated. Lost in his tight focus, Tom failed to notice that the ship was maneuvering about and lowering an anchor down to the beach below.

"Are they fishing, Pa?" Moppet asked with poorly concealed excitement.

"Fish...what now?" Tom replied, shaking off his daydreamy concentration.

"Fishing, Father. Is that what the cats on the ship are doing?"

"OH!" cried Tom, suddenly noticing the line that had been lowered from the craft. "No, little one, I do believe they are attempting to land—or at least come aground! I think we ought to welcome them..."

Moppet couldn't take her wide eyes off the ship, but she didn't need to see her father's face to know there was a giddy twinkle in his eyes when he said this last sentence. Wordlessly, the two scrambled down the sandy bluff as fast as their paws could carry them. They ran across the beech, dodging driftwood as they went. Under any other circumstances they would have relished the fishy smell in the air and the warm sand beneath their paws, but at this moment there were such grander things to be excited about. With only a few dozen yards to go, a second line of rope descended from the bow of the airship. Instead of an iron anchor, however, the weight at the end of this line bore a very different silhouette: that of a female cat.

The pilot and the two picnickers arrived at the anchor point at precisely the same moment.

"Uh, err, terribly sorry Miss ahh Madame ahh..." Tom stammered, trying to apologize for the sand his daughter had inadvertently kicked at the woman when attempting to stop short of running directly into her.

"Fitz. *huff* Agamemnon Fitz," the newcomer said cheerfully between heavy breaths. "Aggie, if you like." Though her brown trousers and white vest appeared dry, what visible fur she had was soaked with rain. In one motion she doffed her elaborate goggles and wiped the water from her face with the drier of her two forepaws. Before Tom or Moppet could greet her properly, however, she dashed away out of sight behind a small dune. A cat in a hurry to get to sand... Moppet put two and two together and suppressed a giggle. A moment later, the molly returned looking drier and more at ease.

"Oh, I'm so terribly sorry! You must think me a might odd. You see the storm ruined my litter box and there was this nice beach in the distance and..."

"Ah, no need for blush-inducing explanations Miss Fitz! We understand an adventurer such as yourself..."

"'Adventurer!'" interrupted Agamemnon with a laugh, "'Inventor' is what I am. Any adventuring was purely accidental I assure you."

At once Tom became much more aware of Agamemnon's bright blue eyes and gleaming gray fur than his own vocabulary.

"I'm called Tom!" he blurted out. "Er, Tom Kittinger. 'Captain,' my friends call me. 'Professor' to my students. And this here is my daughter, Moppet." Moppet gave a small curtsey.

"We live just outside of town here. Just the two of us," he added with a small amount of awkwardness.

"Students? Of what subject, might I ask?"

"Oh!" Tom was somewhat surprised at her interest. "I teach Latin at Beatrix University."

"Ah, then you might appreciate the name of my ship here. I thought it appropriate what with the fins and whatnot."

Tom followed her gesture and began to study the port side of the craft. There, above a webbed stabilizing fin and below an incomprehensible mass machinery, the wooden hull bore a plaque. With flourish and elegance, the name *Piscea* was engraved onto it. Tom immediately recognized the Latin root, and smiled. He had barely finished saying the word when Moppet bounded over, overflowing with excitement. It took some convincing, but Tom soon made it clear to her that "fish" was only a rough translation of the airship's name, and not an announcement of snacks.

"Captain" Kittinger poured over the exterior of the machine. His mind whirled as he tried to identify and understand the various mechanisms and controls he could see. This was clearly much more than a balloon with a propeller. This was a masterpiece; an orchestra of linkages and gears, suspended by a wonder of chemistry. Following one particularly interesting armature from bow to stern, he finally managed to work out one mystery that had been bothering him since the craft arrived. Though the wind had died down a bit since their picnic began, it was still very present. Yet the *Piscea* seemed wholly unaffected. The anchor and line mooring it to the beach was of a good size, but certainly not enough to hold a ship of her proportions as steady as it was. What Tom now deduced Aggie had done, was to somehow connect the wind measuring devices on the front of the craft and the anchor line in the center to the throttle and rudder at the rear. When pointed into a wind, the ship would adjust its speed and heading accordingly to precisely counteract the wind. So long as the gusts weren't greater than the top speed the ship was capable of, the *Piscea* would stay just where she was.

"I would invite you two up to take a closer look, but I'm afraid there's something of a catch," Agamemnon said, watching the handsome tomcat study her work.

"A catch, Miss Fitz?"

"Well, you see I have a tendency to overdo it when it comes to automatization. The very second I pull this rope to be hoisted back up, she's rigged to pull up anchor and resume course. Coal is running low, so I won't be able to go against the wind for more than a few yards and I definitely won't be able to land without a proper dock. If you wish to come aboard, I'm afraid you had better be prepared for a journey!"

Tom wasn't sure if Aggie was only inviting them to be polite or not, but one look at Moppet's smile and swishing tail told him that now was not the time to be reserved. The fall semester was still nearly a month away, and there wasn't much he needed to do. They had yet to visit the grocer this week, so there was nothing left in the cupboards to spoil...

"If you'll have us, Miss Agamemnon, I believe a little adventure is just what the kitten and I need."

"Well then, let's not waste any more coal fighting the winds!" the feline aviatrix replied with welcoming excitement. She picked her now sun-dried goggles up from the sand and strapped them to her head. "If you'll both hold tightly onto this rope, we'll get going immediately."

The three cats dug their claws tightly into the hemp line that Agamemnon had descended on earlier. Aggie tugged on it sharply, eliciting a hearty clank from the ship above. Instantly, a sand-filled counterweight dropped from the starboard bow hoisting the trio swiftly into the air. Following their pilot's hollered instructions, they all three let go of the rope a moment before it ran through a complicated looking pulley. This sent them flying up over the gunwale, landing safely on the deck. No sooner had their soft paws hit the planking, the ship sprung to life. A downward jerk and a rumble of cogwheels meant the anchor was being reeled in, as the various wings and fins adjusted themselves to put the wind and the sun at their back.

Responding wordlessly to a hospitable invitation from Aggie, Moppet dashed to the front of the vessel and sat herself in the pilot's seat. A delicate whirring of cams and clockwork told the real pilot that the ship was running as automatically as she planned, leaving the kitten to harmlessly pretend. The *Piscea* began to pick up speed as Agamemnon Fitz and "Captain" Tom Kittinger stood beside each other with their forepaws resting on the port wale. Neither knew precisely where the ship was headed, but both had an unfamiliar comfort about the coming days. Never had the promise of adventure seemed so welcome, nor had the feelings of friendship ever formed so quickly. They gazed off towards the horizon, tails tentatively entwined.

Jacob Hildebrandt is a lover of cats, science, and making things. He is a lifelong resident of Dearborn.

Why I Love My Adopted Cat by Carol Kalat

I would like to introduce you to Winky, our adopted five-year-old tabby cat. Four years ago I attended the Dearborn Women's Expo at our Performing Arts Center. While browsing the aisles, I spotted a lady walking a very tiny, very cute cat. He was wearing a halter and leash and walking very properly as if he were a dog out on a stroll. I went over to her, and asked if I could pet her cat and as she picked him up, I realized he only had one eye. She then explained he was not her cat, but that he was up for adoption through our local Dearborn Animal Shelter. I held him and petted him for several minutes, went on viewing the show, but kept getting drawn back to see him at the shelter's display.

He was now in a cage, but was still very playful and alert. He kept reaching his paw out to me through the bars of the cage. After several more visits to the display, my friend dragged me away from him saying: "Oh no you don't, you already have a dog and you know your husband is just going to say no to another animal."

After two days of non-stop talking about the cat, I pulled his picture up on the shelter website and showed him to Roy, my husband. He agreed to go visit him and off we went. When we got to his cage, he crawled right out of it, into my arms, and into our hearts.

The shelter explained he had come to them with a seriously injured eyeball and the veterinarian decided the best treatment was to remove the eyeball completely. After his surgery he went to a foster home for several weeks. He had been around dogs in the foster home, so we knew he would be fine with our dachshund, Lucy. We filled out adoption papers and waited two days to be approved. When we picked him up, we decided the name the shelter had been using was just fine, so Winky he was.

The missing eye does not hinder him at all. He climbs, jumps, chases imaginary mice, begs for treats and generally teases the dog daily. They share two beds in our kitchen, the same water bowl and sometimes the same couch. His favorite pastime is lying on the back of the couch and watching the world go by out on the street. He will often chatter at the birds and squirrels outside the window. He is loving, friendly and a major part of our everyday life. He loves to visit with the neighborhood dogs when they come over and will even share his toys with his doggie friends, Brody and Annabelle. He loves watching the cursor on the computer, lining up with the dogs for a treat, sitting outside the shower waiting for us to get out or curling up on the bed.

We do have a small problem with jigsaw puzzles. Pieces are often a little damp and sometimes even missing. He just can't quite fit them in the right place yet, but they don't go far; we always find the missing piece somewhere nearby.

Winky has brought a lot of love and joy into our home. He is hilarious when he tries to get a piece of candy out of the dish by fishing with his paws for a piece at a time. We do find it in our shoes and under the couches, but he never tries to eat it, just bats it around and has fun with the shiny foil wrapped pieces.

His gentle personality shines through with everyone; he loves to be petted and scratched under his chin. He will roll over for anyone to pet him and loves to sit on everyone's lap. Winky doesn't know the word aloof. To be the center of attention is his daily goal and he quite easily achieves this by being his silly, playful self. If allowed, he would probably spend his day in the middle of the dining room table, where all the action takes place. Instead, he joins us by sitting on one of the chairs and trying to sneak up on the table at every possible chance.

There were many beautiful, healthy cats for adoption at the shelter, but I am so glad we took Winky. His handicap doesn't bother him at all. He is happy, healthy and curious. He loves to share a piece of fruit, or a little yogurt or even a bite of cookie. Dog food is not on his list of favorites, but treat time ranks up there with the best part of his day.

Adopting Winky was a wise decision, both for him and his forever family.

Carol and her husband Roy have lived in Dearborn for over 40 years. They love their neighborhood, the Ford Homes District, and their city. They are proud to be residents of such a vital community and enjoy participating in the city activities. cakrek@aol.com

My Cat Called 911 on Me by James Lawhorn

This is a true story. It really happened. I'm guessing it was back in 2008. I had just moved back to Dearborn from Wyandotte.

If you have a cat I assume it goes by many names. Right now I have two and they go by Mr. D (aka LD, Little Dude, Dude, Dman, etc.) and Mr. Lo (aka Pablo, Pablo Dude, Pablo Lo Mein, etc.). Mr. D needed to go see the vet. He hates riding in cars, just hates it. Mr. Lo doesn't mind at all—just position the carrier so he can see out the window and he's fine.

When I first got Mr. D and took him to see the vet he clawed my hands up pretty good. We were running late because I couldn't get a hold of him to put him in the carrier. Once he was in the carrier I just wrapped some paper towels around my bloody hands and off we went. For a while after this I called him Slash.

So now he needed to see the vet again. As before, it wasn't easy to get him and put him in the carrier. When we got in the car I decided to turn the ringer off on my phone. It was an old, dumb cell phone. It wasn't lauded as being smart. It was constantly locking or unlocking itself—you only needed to hit one button to do it. There was no camera. It didn't even flip. I hated that phone.

Anyway, we're in the car, the phone is in my coat pocket, and the cat is just howling bloody murder. At first I tried sweet talking him but it didn't work. It wasn't long before he was getting on my nerves. He was impossible to ignore.

By the time we were on the Southfield Freeway I just couldn't take it anymore. I don't know how many times I told him to shut up. I told him he was going to hurt his throat if he kept it up. This went on and on and I'm sure there were some expletives thrown in now and then.

I just kept thinking we couldn't get there soon enough. At one point I told him, "If you don't shut up I'm gonna pull over and put you in the trunk!" Thank God it's not too far to Lincoln Park.

I was so glad when we got there. I signed in and sat down and he still didn't stop crying. Soon enough someone came in with a dog. That did the trick. The cat shut up.

While we were waiting to be called to the examination room I checked my phone. I had received a message during the ride. I didn't bother to listen to it. There wasn't anything I could do about it at the vet's office so I just put the phone away telling myself I'd check it when I got home.

The message was from the Southgate Police Department. It said someone from my phone had called 911 and all they could hear was a cat crying. It went on to say that if there really was an emergency and I needed help I should call back.

I was so embarrassed. I wanted to call them and explain but I just couldn't. How was I going to tell them that while driving my cat to the vet my phone had unlocked itself and called 911? All I could think of was them hearing me say, "If you don't shut up I'm gonna pull over and put you in the trunk!"

I like to tell people that's the story of my cat calling 911 on me.

James Lawhorn, librarian, retired from the City of Dearborn in 2010 after 25 years of service.

Oreo's Story by Anita Polzin

Leah was seven. It was spring and the walk home from school to her family's small farm was refreshing. Oh how she could not wait to see the bunnies! A while back she had discovered little white fluffy bunnies in one of the two back rooms of their

gar-

age.i999999999999999999999hhhhhhhhhhhhhhhhhhhhhhhhhhhhhhhhh
hhhhhhhhhhhhhhhhhhhhhhhhhhhhhhhhhhhhhhhhhhhhhhhhhhhhhhhhhh
hhhhhhhhhhhhhhhhhhhhhhhhhhhhhhhhh8888888888888888888888888
88888888888888888888888888888888888888888888888888888888888888
88888888888888888888888888888888888888888888888888888888888888
88888888888888888888888888888888888888888888888888888888888888
88888888888888888888888888888888888888888888888888888888888888
8888888888888ttttttttttttttttttttttttttttttttttttttttttttttttttttttttttttttttttttttttt
ttttttttttttttttttttttttttttttttttttttttttt8888888888888888888888888888888888888
88888888888888888888888888888888888888888888888888888888888888
88888888888888888888888888888888888888888888888888888888888888
88888888888888888888888888888888 8888888888888888888888888888888
88888888888888888888888888888888888888888888888888888888888888
8888888888888888888888888888888888888888t5689999999999999999999999
99999999999999999999999999999999999999999999999999999999999999
99999999999999999999999999999999999999999999999999999999999999
99999999999999999999999999999999999999999999999999999999999999
99999999999999999999999999999999999999999999999999999999999999
99999999999999999999999999999999999999999999999999999999999999
99999999999999999999999999999999999999999999999999999999

As I began to type my story "The Straw Filled Room," I decided I wanted a soft drink. As I was out of the room, Oreo, my cat, typed this paper. I found him sitting on my desk between the laptop and the edge hitting at the keyboard with his paws. He was greatly annoyed when I removed him from the computer. This is an authentic animal story.

Anita Polzin is retired as a court clerk at the 36th District Ct. in Detroit. She has been a Dearborn resident since 1997. The story "The Straw Filled Room" was based on a childhood experience growing up on a small farm in what is now Southgate, Michigan.

Missing Fiona by Drew Prosch-Jensen

Why do I still see you,
though I know that you are gone?
You aren't perched on the back porch rail any more,
yet there's your shadow stretched 'cross the lawn.

I come down from upstairs now and
at the bottom I still say "Scoot over babe."
You were always curled up and taking my seat.
How long before that habit fades?

It's not that you would ever move.
Can a cat even be trained?
You'd just look at me with those big dark eyes.
Your expression would be total disdain.

But after I had moved you,
You would crawl back on my lap.
And after obligatory petting and purring
you would go back to your nap.

I'm still cleaning up your cat hair,
like you had never left.
Free-form weaving under a chair.
Our time's warp and our time's weft.

Occasionally I will find a grey hair on my robe

Too long, so I know it isn't mine.
But it's like you've sent a message to me
Through some weird portal in time.

Sleep well my dear old friend
Underneath the old apple tree
Next to old friends of yours
And new ones you will now meet.

All too soon I will join you, I suppose.
To all life's beginnings, there must be an end.
I look forward to seeing you
And you may nap on my lap once again.

Drew believes that everything is art, and art is everything.

Cats in Six Words by MaryAnn Rowe

Hair balls. Fur balls. Love balls.

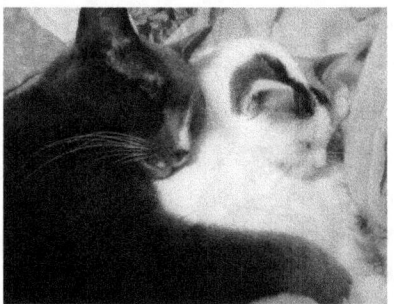

MaryAnn Rowe: "I'm a retired physician assistant and Army Veteran and a lifelong cat lover. Anne Gautreau who is conducting a writers' workshop for Veterans at UM-Dearborn, suggested I submit this six-word memoir. I'm also attaching a picture of my cats Dude and Snuffles who inspired this memoir."

The Cat Who Went to the Bowling Alley by Julie Schaefer

Growing up, my family always had at least one cat as a family pet. Normally, we had two or three at a time. The one consistent cat in the family is one that we obtained when I was in kindergarten and who lived her entire existence with us as her family until she was about 17 years old. She was a kitten when we obtained her and an old lady cat when we finally had to let her go because of increasingly poor health. We named her Nicole because my mother said she always loved that name and in fact had wanted to name my sister or me that when we were born. My father vetoed that name on the grounds that it sounded too fancy for him, but accepted it when we begged to name our kitten that name when we found her in the pet store.

During our youth, Nicole was our constant companion. She acted more like a dog than a cat but since we were young and thought all cats were like that, we accepted her behavior as normal. In fact, as we have grown into adults and acquired our own family cats, Nicole is the barometer against which we measure all other cats and find they always fall short. The other animals are never smart enough, friendly enough, adventurous enough, or they might not purr like Nicole did or act as nurturing as Nicole did or as intuitive.

All you have to say now to my sister or my brother when we gather together is "remember Nicole?" and that will start us off on a round of Nicole stories.

Why was Nicole so special? Maybe it was her all-seeing, all-knowing green eyes. She watched all we did and reacted to our behaviors. If we cried, she nuzzled us or sat by us. When we played outside, she played outside. When we walked to school, she would run behind on the sidewalk, or walk stealthily in the bushes across the lawns and at some point, when we crossed into the school yard, she would disappear. But when 3:30 rolled around, and we walked back home, she would be waiting at the end of the street to walk the last block home with us.

She slept nearby and kept us company all the time. She delivered a steady hum of purring, nearly constantly. It was a very comforting sound to hear at night in the dark. Once Nicole got very sick with some kind of feline infection and turned her nose up at her usual cat food. She continued to not eat and the vet said she would not live unless we could get food into her body. My mother cooked her favorites to coax her to eat, such as chicken livers, and let her drink melted vanilla ice cream and we nursed her back to health. After that, she expected, and received, cooked chicken livers on a regular basis!

On Saturdays we would head to the neighborhood bowling alley which was about four blocks away across a busy street. One particular Saturday, my sister and I walked to the bowling alley as usual for the afternoon. As we were walking there, we noticed Nicole trotting after us. We let her follow for a bit, but when we came to the busy street to cross, we stopped and yelled at Nicole to go home. We were worried she would cross the street and get lost or hit by a car in the parking lot. Nicole ran into the nearby shrubbery, and we crossed the street and entered the alley. A little while later, we heard someone talking in the bowling alley about some cat who was hanging around the front door and seemed to want to come in and bowl a few games! As soon as we heard that, we ran to the door of the alley and looked around and sure enough, there was our Nicole, waiting for us to walk back home.

After that day, we made sure Nicole was inside the house when we set out to walk to the bowling alley.

Nicole was part of our family for my entire school career, including college. It seemed impossible to have a home without Nicole as part of it. Other cats have come and gone in our lives since Nicole, and we continue to seek out an animal with Nicole-like qualities. We cherish and love all of our pets but the one with the special place in the hearts of my brother, sister and me is Nicole. Her glowing, all-knowing, all-seeing emerald eyes are embedded in our memories and we still sigh from time to time and state "I miss Nicole."

Julie Schaefer has worked for the City of Dearborn for over 25 years. She has been a cat lover and owner for all of those years, with the exception of the past 3 years. Due to allergies in the family, she is cat-less currently and must get her cat-fix by looking at photos on websites and reading stories of cats in Animal Tales. *jschaefe@ci.dearborn.mi.us*

Focus Full of Wild Cats by Gary Setter

On the morning of November 1, 2011, one of my co-workers catches me walking into work and says, "Hey Gary, Pete said there's a car full of cats in the blue Focus in the back lot." Why me? Everyone here knows I volunteer at the Animal Shelter in Dearborn. Anytime there's an animal emergency, I'm the go-to guy. So it's no surprise. Sometimes it's a bird in peril, a snake or a stowaway gecko caught in a glue trap. Many of my co-workers donate their empty returnable bottles for supporting animal rescue.

A few decades ago, this was all farmland and the barn cats that once lived here eventually lost their homes and became wild. The nearest homes now are several miles away on the opposite side of the Interstate. But there are homes further down the railroad tracks that young intact males looking for love could follow. Then there are the dumped cats. Long before I started working at this plant, people were dumping cats on the property next to us. Used to be you make a grim discovery while working in the sheds. There was a time when I trapped a cat here; it would go to the animal shelter to be evaluated. If it was possible for the cat to be placed in a home, it would go up for adoption. But feral cats can be dangerous and so were put down. However, a new way of controlling feral cat populations is emerging. Trap, Neuter and Return or TNR has been gaining popularity because it works. This new sighting was the opportunity I was waiting for to try TNR.

Steve showed me to the vehicle that Pete said "was full of cats." The car was missing the rear door window and Pete was assigned to close up the opening. Well, the car full of cats turned out to be one four or five day old baby on the front floorboard. Its eyes were barely open. This was a complex problem. If I remove the kitten, it would have to be hand raised. Ever done that? Find out what it takes. It's a 24 hour a day job. You'd be lucky to find anyone available to foster orphaned newborn kittens. But how many kittens were there? Did the mother move any others by the time I got there? I do know it's most important for kittens to have their mother's milk in the first weeks of their life. It was a hard decision to leave them alone. To let the baby grow up in the cold. And, as it turned out, without other siblings. But any other path would have ended badly. We left some canned cat food near the kitten for the mother, hoping she would return for the baby. About an hour later we went back to check the car and saw the mama cat standing on the back of the front seat. As soon as we saw her, we turned around and left. Later, I went back to find the kitten and food was gone.

So where did she go? Were there others? That same day, I set up a makeshift feeding station made of a sheet of plywood held up by, and attached to, a wooden box. An old cracked windshield leaned against the plywood as a wind break. I keep cat food on hand for these situations. Before I'd left for the day I checked the food dish and found it empty. So I knew Mama was probably still around. Every morning I'd fill up her bowl before my shift. Other than Christmas day, we were operating seven days a week at the time and I could leave food out daily. More than a week went by without anyone actually spotting Mama and baby, but the food was eaten by the time I checked her bowl at lunch time. Then one day our customer, who rents the lot, was patrolling it. He spotted Mama and called me to report the sighting. She was possibly holding up in the blue SUV that had been used in a rollover test. The car had a crushed roof, no glass and was exposed to the elements for a few years.

I went to investigate and there was the baby sitting in the front seat looking up at me. I spoke to him and put my hand out slowly to scratch his chin. His head wobbled around and I was able to touch his nose. Then he hissed and dove under the driver's seat. I went back to the wood shop for a scrap piece of plywood to replace the missing windshield. An old car cover went over the whole vehicle. The next day I filled up the whole front floor of the car with fresh straw. Some time had passed and no other kittens appeared. I was starting to believe Mama had only one baby.

It now was mid-November and there were many colder days ahead. Thank God it turned out to be a very mild winter that season, compared to how it could have been. I gave Mama and baby a small pink covered cat bed and left it on the driver's seat, hoping it would give them more protection from the cold nights.

Early one cold and sunny morning, as I was bringing food I could see into the car. The fuzzy pink bed was lit up by a sunbeam and steam was coming out of the front. I called out "Ma-ma....bay-bee" and out rolled a steaming, yawning, little chubby kitten. He calmly looked at me as if he was greeting me with "good morning." He wasn't a bit spooked. It was all just routine to him. Mama just stayed in bed. I showed him the food and left it center console. At lunch time I'd return to clean up, remove the dish, refill it and move it to the feeding station. I never leave food inside their home for fear of attracting raccoons at night.

For a feral cat, Mama didn't show much fear of me especially around her kitten. After a while, we would see each other more often

but it wasn't every day. A few more weeks went by when I noticed pieces of dead mice inside the car. Looks like Mama was starting to feed him solid food. One day I found a whole dead mouse on the driver's seat. It could mean that the baby was old enough to learn how to kill bite its prey or was in training to do so. There wasn't any snow on the ground and sometimes I'd find the baby playing in the leaf litter around his home. Well, I'd hear him more than see him.

Before I could catch him, I had to wait until I was sure the baby was eating solid food and didn't need mother's milk. He should be at least eight weeks old to be trapped. The weather wasn't cooperating at the time he was old enough to catch, so trapping had to wait. By the time the weather improved, he was over ten weeks old. In the first attempt, the trap was positioned in a spot where I knew he played. No luck. The adults were interested in wet food and he probably was timid of the trap. For a couple weeks, to get him use to the trap, I wired it open and left treats inside. It was exciting when I did catch him but I also felt sorry for Ma. What will she think about this? I took her baby before she was ready to shed him. It could make her go into heat, considering the weather was getting warmer, signaling mating time. However, that's not going to happen. After the baby was settled into his new home, it was Mama's turn to be trapped.

Around the time the baby was roaming around on his own, a huge Main Coon cat appeared at the feeding station. He was beautiful! The sunshine made his fur glow yellow. He didn't notice me immediately so I was able to watch him. Mama was there first but moved aside to let him eat. Could this be the papa cat, I wondered. Mama wasn't afraid of me until Papa saw me and darted off. Mama looked puzzled, what was the danger? Then she split. Ever since then Mama became a little leery of me.

At the beginning of March, Mama cat was caught and taken home to wait for her spaying appointment. I kept her in isolation until she returned home from the vet. Normally a feral cat is released back a day or two after surgery. But the weather turned bad again and Mama needed de-worming. After Mama had her surgery, it was Papa's turn to be trapped and held in isolation until his neutering day. When I brought Papa home from his altering, I set him up in another cage next to Mama. I didn't know much about how deeply they felt about each other at the time. Mama would sing a sad song to Papa every night. I thought about putting them together but I wouldn't know what to do if they fought. So I kept them apart but near each other.

The baby, who I've named Cookie, didn't recognize his own mother. He hissed and growled at both his parents. Talk about having a short-term memory. Cookie was now adopted by Seven, who herself was rescued, and Scooter, her best friend. Seven is a little chubby girl with a squeaky voice and a strong maternal sense. She took to grooming Cookie and looked after him as if he was the kitten she never had.

Scooter, a black cat with a white spot, was never homeless. He was dumped on me by a friend of a friend of a friend.

You know how it is. You rescue a few cats and everyone thinks you collect them. Scooter was tiny and may have been taken away from his mother too soon. I didn't have the heart to take him to an already overcrowded shelter. Cookie didn't have other siblings to play with when he was wild, so Scooter became his big brother. They play all the time and are great pals.

Cookie grew up to be a wonderful cat. He has a constant look of alertness. Well, whenever he isn't sleeping, he loves to cuddle in my lap and has a very unique purr. Sounds like a tree frog. Especially when I sing to him "Ma-ma...bay-bee," it really gets him cooing.

Twelve weeks is about the borderline age for taming feral kittens. Any older than that, the kitten my not ever socialize well with humans. Even though I caught Cookie at about that age, it only took a few days for him to trust me enough to hold him. After all, I was the food guy and Mama's monkey friend.

Ma & Pa were returned to the back lot just after Easter that spring of 2012. Since then, I've built a few shelters and an elevated feeding station for them and their friends if they should drop by. I can keep an eye on all the critters through a wild life camera.

On November 1, 2012, one year to the date I found Mama and baby cat, Mama blew me away when she came out from under a car, spoke to me for the first and only time I've known her, then rolled over on her back and blissed out right in front of me. That said a lot about trust. When a cat slowly blinks at you, it means they're comfortable and pleased with you. Sometimes on a nice day, Ma & Pa will come out of hiding when they see me and we visit. I blab away and they just sit and blink slowly at me and it's as if I was a part of their pride.

Ma & Pa help save other cats that may have not been noticed by leading them to the feeding station. I've learned a lot about feral cats from them, especially in their relationships with each other. There are many photos of Ma & Pa together. In some, you can see them looking at each other lovingly.

Wild cats. Just give them some help and they'll be happy.

Gary Setter has lived in Dearborn for more than 30 years. From 1994 to 2006, he volunteered with the Friends for the Dearborn Animal Shelter. During that time, he cleaned the kennels on weekends, started an annual fundraising event, orientated new volunteers, photographed animals for the shelter's website, picked up and delivered food donations to the shelter, ran satellite adoption events, was photographer for Santa and Easter photo shoots and even spent some time on the board of directors. Presently he is experimenting with the Trap, Neuter and Return (TNR) method of feral cat population management at his work place. Read his cat rescue blog at
www.sosanimalslounge.com/evolution-of-my-feeding-station-121.html;
protodog69@hotmail.com

How Donnie Got His Name by Donald G. Smock

Full Title: How Donnie Got His Name...and His Home!

A few months ago a pretty large orange-colored cat began to hang out near my house, and at first—being protective of my tiny dog Lena (a Brussels Griffon who weighs about 7 lbs.)—I would basically chase him away. (The cat reminded me of the one that I used to see a few years ago in my backyard when I had my little terrier Mary and I used to chase her/him then too.) This one was very persistent however and I would see her/him just about every day at my house, and after a while I saw that the cat seemed friendly enough (and not mean as was my impression with the one at the time that I had Mary).

So I made the fatal mistake of being nice to her/him (I actually thought for several months—up to the crisis in fact—that the cat was a female; even after a while started calling her "Lucy"). I gave her water then started giving her some food. After a while, she seemed to sometimes want to come in my house but I never let her do that for a variety of reasons (fearful for my dog, for messes and odors, for damage by scratching furniture or knocking things over, etc.). She was not a mangy animal and seemed real clean and looked cared for so initially and for a very long time I kind of assumed that she was someone's pet that lived nearby, although I couldn't figure out why she was ALWAYS at my house. And always hungry!

So I started seeing her virtually every day—when I opened the door to let my dog out at 6 a.m. she was right there at the door; when I came home from work whether at 4 p.m. or 6 p.m. she was likewise right there. By now I was actually feeding her a regular amount of food twice a day. I had also by this time figured out that there was actually another cat that looked just about the same (color, size, etc.) but seemed to be mean that sometimes would be there at the same time as Lucy and so there were two of them that looked alike, but the second one was distinctly unfriendly and had a mean look about him. Lucy would actually start hanging out with Lena and me in the backyard after work and I saw that she was nice and very friendly to both me and my dog, always rubbing up against both of us, playing a little sometimes with Lena. So this went on and by the time the crisis came up she had actually been hanging at my house for a few months, three, maybe four.

By now it was October and I began to think about the possibility of either letting her in the house or making some kind of warm shelter for her with the cold weather just around the corner. I also began to think that maybe she really was just a stray and did not in fact belong to anyone (or else why would she be CONSTANTLY at my house no matter what time I opened the door?) I was just starting to mull over these possibilities when on Friday a couple of weeks ago the crisis came up.

I came home from work a couple of months ago (mid-October) on a Friday and like normal this cat was right there to greet me the very minute I arrived (and of course to be fed!). I noticed when she ran by my car in the driveway that it looked like she had something in her mouth. What a surprise I got when, on the porch where I had a food bowl and a water bowl I got a closer look! The poor cat's tongue was so swollen it was sticking out of her poor mouth looking like a piece of liver, she was drooling and meowing plaintively; it was so swelled up that it was quite impossible for the animal to eat or to drink water, and it looked like it had been bleeding on her fur. Very distressing for me and most certainly for the poor cat!

I was somewhat at a loss as to what to do, however. Without belaboring the point too much, I had no money and very little left in credit cards either. If I could have done so I would have taken the animal immediately to an animal hospital, but that was quite impossible for me to do. I racked my brain trying to come up with an idea of what to do to help this poor animal, and the only thing that I could think of was the Dearborn Animal Shelter. It was somewhat of a calculated risk because she might be euthanized or given to someone else but I just had to do something for this poor animal and it seemed like my only option.

The Animal Shelter was closed—it was a Friday evening after 5:30. There was a sign in the window which stated that for after-hours emergencies a phone number for the police department should be called and so I did that and explained to the officer my situation with the cat. They were very busy so she told me that it would be a while until someone could respond; she could not answer my question as to what they would do to help the cat. She put the call "on the board" and asked me to call back if I left so that she could take the call off the board. So I sat there for a good while waiting and as I sat there I tried to figure out a way that I could help this cat myself. "I think I still have a little bit left on this credit card and a little left on that one," etc. After waiting for about an hour I had determined to go home for a phone book to locate a local pet hospital and see if I could help this cat by pooling what little financial resources I had available to me (besides it didn't seem like the police would actually be able to help the cat anyway and I began to wonder what would they do with her?) so I called the PD back to inform her that I was leaving and she could take the call "off the board."

As I was still talking on the phone with the PD, a woman came out of the Animal Shelter who is as it turns out (fortuitously for both the cat and me) the shelter's director. When I explained the predicament, she took charge of the injured cat and at the same time took down my info from my driver's license. I was much relieved for the cat but also a little sad because I wasn't sure if I would ever see him again. All that weekend I worried about him, prayed for his recovery and realized that I had actually gotten quite attached to him being around. My prayers continued the following week when I was able to talk with the shelter director who told me that the medical intervention had been quite expensive (somehow his tongue had become impaled on one if his teeth; they thought that maybe he got hit by a car) and if it turned out that he had a tumor or something she would probably have to have him euthanized simply because the shelter had so many other cats to take care of. It was at that time that I found out too that the cat was a "him" not a "her" — shows you how much I know about cats.

So he recovered in a week or so, and I had decided to try to adopt him by then, although I still had some reservations. I had not had cats since almost 40 years ago. I discovered that this type of cat is called a "Mackerel tabby," which I had never heard of. Now that I knew that he was a boy I thought of different names to replace "Lucy," maybe "Leo" or something. Perhaps "Lucky" would be appropriate. When I went to the shelter to visit him and to look into the adoption process, I found out that they were calling him "Donnie." As I found out later in talking to the director, when she had seen to it that night of the crisis that he received prompt medical attention, at the veterinary hospital when she was asked for his name, not knowing what it was, she used my name from the info that I had given her off my driver license.

The adoption request was favorable and I adopted "Donnie" and he is now living with Lena (my beloved little Brussels Griffon) and me, inside a warm house with plenty of food, and getting fat. Although I can't claim that there hasn't been a certain amount of getting accustomed to "cat ways" (and I remain basically a dog lover more than a cat lover), he's a real nice cat. I am very grateful that he recovered and that the Dearborn Animal Shelter took such good care of him in his hour of need. And I still call him Donnie.

Don Smock is a lifelong dog-lover who currently has a little Brussels Griffon (Lena) living with him as well as a recently adopted cat named Donnie; he has at one time or another had about seven dogs and several cats, and a miniature lop-eared rabbit. His activities/jobs have included mechanic, tour bus driver, water wells driller, author & poet, folksinger, press operator, men's clothing salesman, agricultural extension worker, agricultural machinery researcher, and Peace Corps volunteer in Africa.

The Purrfect Christmas Gift by Mary Weber

It was Christmas Eve, 2000. My sister Samantha and I were on our way to adopt a new member into the family. Her co-worker, Marjon, had found a small black kitten in her backyard. The kitten nearly froze in the snow and was brought in out of the cold. The hope was that she would be placed into a good home.

Soon we arrived at Marjon's house and met her cat Simon. Simon was an older orange cat and he didn't seem interested in a playful kitten. Just as I was about to ask Marjon where the kitten was, a tiny black paw came out from under the television stand and touched Simon's tail.

We brought the kitten home in a carrier. It didn't take long for her to explore the new place. There were many chairs to pounce on and cabinets to hide under. The kitten was very small so Samantha and I blocked any holes where she could get stuck or hurt.

We named the little black kitten Molasses. Molasses enjoys roaming around her nice warm home. We are all so happy that she is part of the family now and is in out of the cold.

Mary Weber has sponsored and fostered special needs animals in both Michigan and New York. She also volunteers her time to help hunger and poverty non-profit organizations in the Metro-Detroit Downriver area.

The Day Mama Lost Her Spots by Arleen Wood

Let me introduce myself: My name is Mama. I am a calico cat – a *Felis catus*, and this is the story of the day I lost my spots. It was a Tuesday. I have been told my nine spots are exquisite. I am inclined to agree. They are irregularly shaped rounds and oblongs marbled with a kaleidoscope of stripes colored brown, orange and tan.

My adoptive family owns a pet treat bakery and we all live above it. Although I am a feline, I am expected to participate in the family business in capacities suited to my feline sensibilities. This means as the treat taster, customer greeter and, best of all, the new apprentice baker. The Tuesday in question started as any other without a hint of the catastrophe I would face later in the day. My routine was simple: I rose before dawn, woke up the family and had breakfast. Afterwards, I washed my face, paws and legs, counted my nine spots, slipped my baker's hat over my ears and, with a flick of my tail, pushed through the cat door and ran down to the bakery.

Each morning before the sun came up local farmers and fisherman delivered flour, sugar, eggs, goat milk, special greens and fresh fish for the day's baking. With loud, rolling purrs I greeted all and conversed a bit. But, between you and me, their quizzical expressions made me think they did not quite understand what I was saying. Given my position as the apprentice baker my spots were scratched and counted as each took their leave. After putting away the deliveries, the baking began. To create perfect treats in an organized manner, I created a rhyme:

Get out the list and start to gather
The things you will need to make all the batter.

Take down the bowls, waxed paper and pans,
Then mix together butter, flour and spiced fish jam.
Jump in the bowl and use your four paws as paddles
To knead bread dough for bagels and edible babbles.
Next, put the treats on a sheet or pour batter in pans
Sprinkle lightly with cheese and bake at four hundred degrees.
When crispy and brown, ease onto a plate
Set aside to cool, then cover and date.

After baking all morning, I usually took a mid-morning nap before greeting customers. But that Tuesday there would be no nap for me. As I looked in the mirror to remove my chef's cap a white cat stared back. I mean white. Like an unpainted canvas or freshly fallen snow. I howled in surprise. Where did my spots go? Where were my exquisite stripes? I can't be white. I am a calico cat with nine unique spots. So,
I looked under the table.
I looked in the bowls.
I looked in the drawers – no spots – Oh no!
I looked in the fridge.
I looked in the oven.
I unrolled wax paper and found – the salt shaker.
I looked in the spices and sniffed all the greens.
I looked on the counter.
But, no spots could be seen.

As it happened, Monsieur Renee, a favorite customer, saw me searching here and there. "Mama, your spots are gone. Where did they go? Quelle Catastrophe!" In response, I meowed loudly, but s-l-o-w-l-y, so he would understand my panic.

"Perhaps, I can help," he said. He scratched my back, tail and head. He suddenly stopped and studied his fingertips. "I have an idea, but I will need your brush," and off he went to find it.

"Seriously," I meowed after him. "My spots are missing. This is not the time for a brushing. What if they were kidnapped for ransom? What if someone is pasting them onto their body right now? What if that dog that always barks at me took them and buried them under a tree?"

With brush in hand, my owners appeared with Monsieur in tow. "Mama, Monsieur Renee told us your spots had fled. He thinks he knows why. Monsieur, please proceed with brushing her coat."

I meowed in despair; they did not understand. I heard murmurs of concern, then, suddenly a voice exclaimed, "Voila, it is flour, as I suspected. Mama, you must have dusted yourself with it when you were paddling the bread dough." Monsieur held a mirror in front of me. A catastrophe averted! My spots in all their exquisiteness had reappeared. There was still time for a nap, after all.

The next day an insurance salesman stopped in to purchase pet treats. I can't be sure he understood, but I asked if there was a policy that covered lost cat spots. For fifteen minutes one Tuesday I was a white cat. I wouldn't recommend it. I AM A CALICO.

Author's note: This story is based on a true event. Mama did lose her spots one day; luckily, they were quickly found. If she ever misplaces them again, I will know where to look and it won't be under a tree in a dog's backyard.

Arleen Woods is a native of Detroit, who moved five years ago with her cats in tow to a rural northeast Michigan town for a job. She has been telling them stories about themselves for years, so she thought she'd try writing one down.

I Am a Princess by Mary Ann Zawada

Let me introduce myself. My name is "Princess of Oakwood." I am three years old and am quite a beautiful Ragdoll cat. I reside in a very comfortable apartment overlooking the river at Oakwood Common Retirement Center.

MEOW!

I know that my owner, my mom, had me in mind when she settled on this lovely apartment with a balcony especially for me. If I cry loudly enough, she allows me to sit on my beloved balcony for hours at a time. I have a special spot to watch the birdies fly by and a nasty squirrel who crawls around. My coat is very silky and shiny and I spend hours keeping myself beautiful. I am truly to be admired.

My mom has a friend who is very friendly to me. But as I do not want my fur to be soiled with too many fingerprints, I only allow her to scratch under my chin. She does a very good job but she wants to rub my furry tummy. If Mom is not around to do it, I may allow her friend to fill in.

I am very special. When I am thirsty, I put my paw under the faucet. My mom kindly allows it to drip so I can take a sip from my paw anytime I get thirsty. Sometimes I like to hide on counters, and maybe in a drawer. I do need my quiet time.

Recently, my mom bought a wonderful machine for me, I am sure. It has nice cool, clean air coming from the top. I sit on top of it to cool off and to fluff up my fur.

Well, that is the end of my interview as I must get my beauty sleep. More later if I feel up to it. MEOW!

(as dictated to my human Secretary, Mary Ann Zawada)

Mary Ann Zawada: "Princess is owned by a dear friend at Oakwood Common Retirement Home. When her owner/mom is out of town, Princess allows me to pet and feed her. When 'Mom' returns, I again become a stranger."

Chapter 5: A Crab Tale

How I Got Crabs by Michael Dorantes

My family has had a few pets, from invertebrates and crustaceans to avians and pisces. When I was nine, I captured my first pet in Florida, an anole named Godzilla. In fact, a majority of our pets came from Florida, including three hermit crabs (ordered in descending size): a huge one named Bubba (named after Bubba Trammel, an amazing baseball player), the average guy Hermie, and Scooter (he scooted, a lot). The story of the hermit crabs, our first actual foray into becoming a respectable, pet-owning family, actually involves me getting hurt not once, but twice.

We had been visiting my granddad's friend in Florida and like many youngsters my little sister Olivia and I were drawn to three things: ice cream, mini golf, and pet stores. At the time we lived in an apartment so we were limited in pet choices. Olivia and I never particularly wanted a dog, or a cat, but we were attempting to persuade our father for a pet every chance we had and on this trip there was a pet store that we passed by a few times. My mom, despite loud protests from my dad, let us go inside and we immediately went for the hermit crabs. They were strange, alien, and most importantly they fit in a small terrarium and were low-maintenance. Olivia and I asked to get a crab. Dad was stubborn, and needless to say we left the store with as many crabs as we had when we entered.

Later on, our family was playing putt-putt golf after a long day at the beach. Olivia and I are horribly competitive, and she was swinging for the fences on every putt; Tiger or Nicklaus had nothing on her that day. I was standing behind her minding my own business when all of the sudden I felt the hammer of Thor come down on my brow. I was dazed and confused. I didn't say anything at first. But then Olivia started screaming, seeing the blood come from a substantial gash on my eyebrow. I was fine; I played it cool as a piña colada, but then my mom said I needed stitches and because I have a fear of needles I flipped out.

Fast-forward to a few hours and a hospital trip later and we returned to the store where we saw the hermit crabs. My mom persuaded my dad to get me one, a consolation prize of sorts. I picked one and back we went to the hotel room. By the way, Godzilla had escaped and was loose in our hotel room by now, so technically Hermie was pet #2. When we got back Olivia and I, being the budding marine biologists that we were, decided to play with the scared-out-of-his-shell Hermie, who promptly decided "not fun" and withdrew deep into his shell.

We poked and prodded but he didn't come out. As my finger neared to poke him yet once more, out came a claw and Hermie hung on for the ride. He was anchored pretty firmly and I was waving like a pre-teen girl at a Bieber concert. I screamed and hollered. Suddenly, Hermie went flying across the room and landed on the wall with a thud. My finger was swelling and it hurt pretty badly. Hermie was O.K. and in time the pain was forgotten.

My mom and dad loved it so much we doubled down and got Bubba and Scooter before we went back to Michigan.

Michael Dorantes is a recent Michigan State University graduate with a major in Comparative Cultures and Politics and a minor in Spanish. He is pursuing a career in the legal field. He enjoys cooking and writing poetry or prose when he isn't working as a Crowd Manager at Comerica Park.
dorante2@msu.edu

Chapter 6: Dog Tales

Of Sophie and Murps by Ayat AlTamimi

When I met Sophie for the first time, she was a chubby blob with stubby arms and legs sticking out. She had a head that was small and pink like my favorite ball, a mop of thin, dark hair, and this crooked split in her face that always seemed to lift upwards. Her parents called it a smile, and they said that I had one too.

When we met for the first time, I padded over to her and when I thrust my nose out to sniff at her, she grabbed me by my ears, squealed and started pumping her legs. She started giggling and her parents started clicking away at this little box that they called a camera. Sophie kept on giggling and stuck her face right in front of mine, and when I licked her face, she laughed even harder and her parents laughed right along with her and I figured that this little blob was going to be all right, because she seemed to lift her lips up a lot and looked like my favorite ball and smelled like baby powder, instead of cigarettes, like the old family I lived with.

When Sophie was two, the family referred to me as "Doggie," because her parents insisted that they wanted her to name me. They would pat me on the head and reassure me that it wouldn't be much longer now, that Sophie was going to give me a name that was perfect and I was going to love it. I had to wonder, who exactly was going to love the name, me or them?

When Sophie gave me this so-called name I was going to love, it was an uneventful winter day, not exactly Christmas, but almost there by the looks of the tree and the decorations that her parents had put up. I was curled up by the fire and Sophie walked over—which was apparently still really exciting even though she had learned how to do so a couple of months ago—and plopped herself on top of me. She didn't weigh much, but a warning still would have been nice before she decided to unceremoniously crush my rib cage. There wasn't much I could really do except give out a little, helpless whimper, which her parents—and here I'm going to ask, what exactly is wrong with these people?—found adorable, and they whipped out their camera faster than you could say "cheese"—which humans for some reason said when they were taking pictures—and started clicking away.

After about half an hour, once her parents had settled down instead of swarming around us like those really annoying bugs in the summer, and Sophie had settled into me like I was a couch or something, she suddenly sat up and turned to face me. Her parents, somehow sensing that something pivotal was going to happen, also sat up and whipped out their camera again, and honestly, where do those people even keep that thing? Like, is it always on them or something? It seems like even when Sophie is getting her bath on, they're hovering over her with it. Anyways, Sophie grabbed me by the ears, looked me in the eyes—and I'm not going to lie, I held my breath in because, oh my God, I have never seen something so tiny look so serious—and squealed out, "Murpy!" and gave my ears a good tugging. Then she broke out into a fit of giggles, which erupted into full-blown laughter. Her parents started cheering and from then on, I was referred to as Murpy, even though it sounded downright ridiculous.

When Sophie was six, she started going to this thing called school. The night before her very first day, she had just gotten out of the shower, her long, now lighter brown hair dripping wet and soaking her Spider Man pajamas, because she refused to wear princess ones, much to her father's dismay and her mother's glee, oddly enough. Her mother claimed she was going to grow up unique and independent, but her father was heartbroken that he wouldn't have a little girl to take to father-daughter dances, though I was absolutely positive he would, because that girl played with her mother's makeup like nobody else's business.

Once Sophie's mother got her hair dried and braided, and Sophie brushed her teeth, her mother tucked her into bed, and I hopped up onto the end of it. That was my rightful place, you know? I was a dog and no one was going to rob me of this right, even though I was robbed of a cool name, like Rex. When her mother kissed us both on the forehead and left the room, Sophie sat up and looked at me. She grabbed me by the ears, which seemed to have turned into a habit at this point, looked me in the eye and sighed. My head perked up at this, because Sophie wasn't down very often.

"Murpy," she started softly, "I'm scared of going to school..." She started crying then and I cocked my head to the side and started whimpering. Why was Sophie so sad? Was school really that scary? All the kids on T.V. seemed to like it, except for this dreaded thing called homework, and yet, here Sophie was, crying because of it.

"Murpy, what if all the kids are mean to me? What if no one wants to play with me or be my friend? What if the girls think I'm weird because I like playing soccer instead of playing house, what if the boys don't want to play with a *girl*..." and here the tears really started coming. She buried her face in my fur and cried. I let her cry for a bit, because people, I've learned, need a little time to let it out before you comfort them, and then I pulled away from her.

Unfortunately, I couldn't give her a lecture about what a great girl she was, how nice and fun she was and how everyone would love to be friends with her and if they didn't, they were crazy, but I could lick the tears off her face and that seemed to do the trick because she started giggling and wiping away the slobber and snot and tears that were running down her face.

When she lay down in bed again and all that was left of her tears was the occasional sniffle, she whispered, "Thanks, Murpy, I love you."

When she came home from school the next day, she ran to me and showed me a picture she colored in school of what was apparently me, but looked more like a blob with sticks coming out of the sides and gave the unabridged account of what happened at school complete with all the snacks they ate and a story about this girl named Laney who spilled her grape juice and almost started crying until Sophie shared her juice with her and this boy named Russell who started crying for his mom until Sophie asked him to come play blocks with her and Laney.

"I loved it, Murpy!" She squealed and started giggling again.

When Sophie was eleven, she started middle school. She would get on the bus every morning and sit next to Russell and Laney, who stopped crying and spilling grape juice respectively, but not before she would give me a kiss on the head and a scratch behind the ears.

One particular evening, after Sophie came home from Laney's house, she didn't eat as much at dinner. When her parents asked her what was wrong, she said that she wasn't as hungry, because she had a snack at Laney's house, and that she was going to go do her homework now.

"Come on, Murpy," she called and I trotted up the stairs after her. Instead of sitting down at her desk to do her homework, she stood in front of her mirror.

"Hey, Murpy," she began, pinching at her sides, and then she lifted her shirt up and sucked her stomach in, her ribs protruding from underneath her skin. "When I was at Laney's house today, she said she and I needed to go on a diet."

I gave a confused bark in reply and she sat down on her bed next to me.

"A diet is when you don't eat as much food so that you can lose weight."

At this, I was even more confused, because who wouldn't want more food? Anyways, it's not like Sophie was big, by human or dog standards; she still played soccer every single day and was skinny, so skinny she looked like a walking stick, even though she inhaled everything in the kitchen, including the kitchen sink.

"Laney says boys aren't going to like us if we're fat, so we need to stop eating so much. She said I eat a lot especially, and I told her it was because I played soccer and I needed to keep my energy up and she said that wasn't an excuse. The thing is, I don't even want boys to like me, but Laney says she won't be friends with me anymore if I don't stop eating so much."

I started whimpering when Sophie started crying, because what could I do about it? Laney wasn't even here so I could bite her, and then the worst thing ever happened, even worse than her ribs, because at least with her ribs, she didn't look near tears; Sophie started pinching at her thighs and looked up at me desolately, tears rolling down her cheeks.

"Maybe she's right, Murp, maybe I really am fat." I started wailing at this, because there was no way that Sophie was fat and I swore to myself that I would bite Laney the next time I saw her.

The next time I saw Laney was two weeks later, when she was over for dinner. Every time Sophie would pick up her fork to take a bite of her pasta, Laney would shoot her a glare and kick her leg. After about ten minutes of that, I was done. How dare this little brat make Sophie feel so worthless? I ran under the table and bit down on her hand and she started screaming but I wouldn't let go until I tasted blood and she was crying.

Sophie's parents were screaming and everyone was in a commotion, but when I looked over at Sophie, she wasn't smiling; instead, she was looking down at her plate, tears silently dripping down her cheeks and onto the tablecloth.

When Laney's parents came to take her home and Sophie's parents went outside to talk to them, Sophie came and sat back down at the dinner table. Every time she tried to pick up her fork to eat, I would feel this little burst of hope, because maybe what I did was worth it. Maybe all those "bad dogs" and threats of sleeping outside had paid off, but then, every time, she would shake her head and put her fork back down, like Laney was still there, whispering in her ear not to eat, until she finally pushed her plate away.

I growled and her head snapped up to look at me, her green eyes opened wide in shock. I had never growled at her before, but when I nudged her plate towards her, she started to tear up again, and it was my turn to be surprised.

"Is that why you did this?" she whispered. "So that I'd stop listening to Laney and eat?" I started whimpering and turned my face towards the floor. The hard wood was looking especially lovely this evening.

"Oh, Murpy, you didn't have to bite her for me." Sophie gave me a big hug and turned to her plate. She took a deep breath and picked up her fork. "Well, here goes, Murp." She took a bite and a grin spread across her face. Grabbing me by ears, she broke out into the biggest grin I'd seen from her in the past two weeks. "Oh my gosh, Murpy, this tastes so good."

When Sophie's parents came back in after Laney left, they were both surprised to see Sophie eating, like nothing had ever happened, and her best friend didn't just go home with her hand wrapped in bandages.

"Mommy, Daddy," Sophie began when her parents sat down at the table again, "The reason Murpy bit Laney is because she told me that I have to stop eating so much. She was kicking me under the table every time I wanted to take a bite, and I guess Murpy saw her doing that, so he bit her."

Her mother frowned, and it was her father who started talking. "Listen, Sophie, you do *not* need to stop eating or lose weight or whatever the case may be. You're healthy and active and you need to keep up your energy. Tell Laney that she can diet if she wants, but to leave you out of it. As for you, Murpy," her father turned to look at me and I started whimpering again, because I was in for it—Laney's mother had been hysterical and I knew I was going to get chewed out—but Sophie's dad just stood up, walked over to where they kept my food and pulled out some dog treats, "You're such a good dog." He bent down to feed me the snacks and scratch me behind the ears. I barked in response and Sophie came over to pet me too, and her mother, Lord help that woman and her scary obsession, pulled out her camera and took another picture.

Ayat AlTamimi's biggest dream is to become a published author. This is his first published story. altamimiayat@hotmail.com

Rikki: The Amazing Treasure Hunting Dog by Mary Althaver

Dogs, like people, vary greatly in intelligence. Some are brilliant; others a little slow on the uptake. I wasn't sure about Rikki, my sister's young Sheltie. I tried to teach him to sit and shake, which isn't difficult for most dogs, but Rikki was not inclined to participate. Oh, sure, he liked the treats, but for some reason, he was not about to shake with me. After a few attempts to teach him this simple trick, I decided Rikki was not real bright and abandoned the project.

Then one day my sister Sara told me of an article in her treasure hunters' magazine, which was about training dogs to find money. Based on my previous experience, I wasn't sure Rikki had the brains for this, but we decided to give it a try.

First we showed the dog a dollar bill. He sniffed it thoroughly and we told him it was money. After we placed the bill across the room in plain sight, we asked Rikki to find the money. He quickly went to it and brought it back to us. After his reward, we made it more challenging, by placing the bill partially out of sight. Again, on command, he fetched the bill and claimed his treat.

We then hid the bill in the house, out of sight, and that was no problem for him either. Later we went outside and concealed the money in a shrub. Rikki raced to it, apparently led by a very keen sniffer. He was really into it by then, gobbling up his rewards and looking for more challenges, so we kept making it more difficult and were amazed at how good he was at finding money. In about an hour, my sister and her husband had a treasure hunting dog, though the magazine had indicated it took a lot of training for dogs to learn this skill.

Always avid treasure hunters, Sara and her husband Bill started taking Rikki out to public places and asking him to find the money. They did this nearly every day, enjoying the exercise and time out-doors. This dog was amazing! They would come back from an outing with reports of him finding ones, fives, twenties, even fifty-dollar bills. I revised my opinion of Rikki's intelligence.

For years Rikki entertained us all with his skill and, according to my sister, added $30,000 to their bank account. This dog paid for himself many times over, yet his reward was the same tiny treat for a dollar or a fifty-dollar bill, so I knew his intelligence had some limits! I joked that he needed an agent to represent him to make the reward more proportionate to the denomination of his finds.

Rikki would dive into shrubs, under decks and bleachers, wherever his nose told him money waited. The sight of him emerging from such locations with a mouth full of bills was a thrill. He could even smell buried money and easily dug up a number of impressive stashes.

Sara and Bill also used a metal detector on their outings. After a while, Rikki learned that coins were money too. When the detector would ring, he would race over to retrieve the coin in his sharp little teeth and carefully present it for his reward.

Rikki had penetrating black eyes and could focus with an intensity that was almost frightening. He held your gaze like a hypnotist, demanding compliance. If it was time for his dinner, there was no delaying it. When he decided it was time for an outing, his knife-like gaze was fierce. He lived to hunt, a true working dog.

I wonder still why a dog as clever as Rikki refused to participate in my first training session, but perhaps he was so smart he didn't see the point of sit and shake. Rikki was saving his skills for the more interesting challenge of hunting treasure.

It was a sad day when Rikki moved on to dog heaven. After a period of mourning him, a new Sheltie named Chloe joined the family. She has also learned to hunt money, but she lacks Rikki's intensity and drive, and will never equal him in treasure hunting.

Rikki was one intelligent dog with a very productive talent and a compelling personality. He may very well be in charge of dog heaven by now, herding the new arrivals into a tidy pack and teaching them who is boss and how to maximize their rewards.

Mary Althaver, winner of the Patricia Sherman Memorial Writing Contest, is a member of the Oscoda Writing Group. She writes personal essays and will soon publish a book of Depression-era college letters written by her mother and replies by her grandmother.

Prince by David K. Anger

Almost every young boy wants a pet. I was no exception. The only thing about my first pet was that he didn't really belong to me. Let me explain. When we first moved into the Garden City house, my mom and I were pretty much alone since my dad was overseas most of the time during the war. Our location was rural with only a handful of houses nearby and most of those were farmhouses. One of these houses was behind ours and off to the west of us a hundred yards or so. It belonged to Speed. I don't recall whether it was his first or last name or even a nickname. But anyway, Speed had a big old Collie-St. Bernard mix dog named Prince.

Prince was free to roam and soon became a fixture at our house that spring when I was about seven or eight months old. He was pretty smart and fell in love with us, and we with him. My mom used to put me on a blanket out in the yard when I was starting to crawl and would tell Prince to make sure I stayed on the blanket. Well, Prince seemed to understand her and every time I would start moving toward the edge of the blanket, he would get up, move and plop down right in front of me, to block my path. From what my mom later told me, Prince would do this for hours on end. There were other times when I was a bit older and could walk and run, when Mom would come running at my screams and cries only to find Prince holding me back from the road by the seat of my pants or pinning me down with one of his big paws. Of course he would get his reward of treats or a bit of meat or something for his efforts. Some babysitter!

As a little side note, the blanket that I laid on was what we called an Indian blanket. It was soft and had bright colored designs all over it that made it look like an Indian might have made it. That particular blanket was around for years. It was used for almost everything that a blanket could be used for. It made tents or superman capes, carried leaves, formed a sail on windy days, or just laid out on the ground for relaxing. I even used to roll up in it during the crisp fall days and just lay there in the sun taking in all the smells it contained like leaves, Prince, fresh air, and other earthy smells.

While I grew, Prince and I formed a bond that I have never had since with any pet and something that I will never forget. I hope to see him again one day. We did everything together, often roaming the woods, looking for squirrels or snakes. Prince loved to go snake hunting and so did I. If we came across one, all I would have to say is "Snake, Prince!" and he would go after it. Once he caught it in his mouth he would stand there in front of me waiting for his next command drooling with a forlorn look on his face. Usually I would take the snake that had been wriggling there and put it in my pocket for safekeeping. But, sometimes I would just tell him to let it go. Man, was he happy when he got rid of the snake. He wasn't very good with frogs. I'll bet it was the taste. Now, squirrels were a different matter; Prince would tear off and chase one until he treed it and would bark and jump until I called him off. The squirrels loved the game too. They would get up in the tree just high enough to be out of reach and hang there, head down, chattering for all they were worth. I wonder what he would have done with it if he ever caught one.

We always knew when the Fourth of July had arrived. Prince would be at our door, howling and barking at the first bang of a firecracker. As soon as we opened the door, Prince would swoop past us, or over us, and head for my mom's bed and squirm his way to the farthest reaches in the corner. If we moved the bed he would manage to stay under it somehow. Once set, nothing could budge him. So, my mom would call Speed and tell him that once again Prince was wedged under her bed. The next morning, we would coax him out with snacks and treats and I would lead him home.

Our expeditions would last all summer long and before long it became standard practice for me to empty my pockets before coming into the house. I'd have stones that caught my eye, sticks, acorns, and string and just about everything you could imagine, especially the pocketknife Dad (Granddad) gave me when he thought I was old enough. My guess is when I was four or five. My mom was okay with most of it except the living things like snakes or toads or the like. I would have to trek out behind the shed and release my treasures back into the wild, all while hoping to find them again later.

It was about the time that I started school when Speed started to tie Prince up to his doghouse to keep him from hanging out at our house all the time. I guess he wanted to sell him to us, but my mom wouldn't pay Speed's price. No rope was strong enough to keep Prince away.

He would either break or chew them to get over to see us. Finally old Speed chained him to his doghouse, which was pretty big as doghouses go. Our big friend easily broke the earlier chains, so the chains got bigger and bigger until Prince could not get free. Then, early one morning in winter, Prince showed up at the back door howling and barking like he did on the Fourth of July. He was a sight to behold, half-frozen, dirty, and bloody from where the thick collar around his neck had dug in as he pulled his doghouse through the woods. It must have taken him all night. My mom called Speed and told him what was going on and begged him to let us keep him for a couple of days to treat his wounds. Speed, not being much of a dog lover, said it was all right if we didn't spoil him. Yeah! Right!

After Speed recovered the doghouse, which was no easy task, Prince was chained to a big tree next to his house. Speed always said that dogs were meant to be outside; after all, they were only good for keeping trespassers away. I was allowed to come over to his place to see Prince, but we would never roam free in the woods again. I could hear Prince howling and barking for me, late into the night, until finally I would hear Speed holler and yell, followed by Prince's yelps as Speed beat him. God was that awful! I remember crying.

The time came when I was not allowed to come near Speed's house to see that "mangy dog," as he called him. But, Speed had to go to work and I wasn't in school all the time, so we had our secret rendezvous. My mom and baby brother Tom would even come with me once in a while. We would shower him with love and treats. And in return, we would get lots of slobbery kisses.

Not long after that, my dad came home from the war. He remained in the service and reported to Selfridge Army Air Base where he worked just like any other job. In 1947, the base was renamed Selfridge Air Force Base. Sometimes he would be gone for a week or two flying missions to unknown locations around the world with some of his crew that he had flown with during the war. We wouldn't know just where he had gone until after he returned.

We were now a complete family. My dad was home, Mom was happy, and I was still free to roam around and have my sneak visits with Prince. He was starting to look old and raggedy and that only made me love him all the more. It was about this time that my mom found a small puppy that she saw being used as a football by a bunch of kids a few blocks away. She rescued the pup and gave the boys a dollar. There were happy as could be and said the dog wasn't much of a football anyway, because it kept running away and they always had to chase it. We named her Patty.

Patty was a feisty little thing, part terrier and something else. She would hide under the kitchen table and growl and snap at anyone who came near. I wonder why? HA! Mom and I received several nips and bites while we tamed the poor frightened pup, but eventually she started to respond to the love we were showering upon her. Prince didn't like her much, but he tolerated her puppyish ways. Mom thought Patty would help take my mind off Prince a little and ease the pain. It did, a little, I guess.

After a couple of years in Garden City, Dad announced that he was being transferred to Walker Air Force Base in Roswell, New Mexico. That was a shock, to say the least. What would I do about my friends and most importantly, what would I do about Prince? I was pretty upset about all this and told them that I would stay with my grand-parents in Dearborn so that I could see my friends and Prince.

All my crying, pouting, and stomping around did no good at all. Eventually, I came to the realization that I was going to New Mexico, wherever that was. We would only be gone for two years and we would come back home to my friends and Prince. That seemed to be understandable to me at the time and I agreed to go, as if I ever had any other choice.

So off we went! The "Land of Enchantment" was really flat and dry where we were in Roswell, except for a few distant mountains that you could see on clear days. Yes, Roswell, New Mexico, home of the alien spaceship crash in the 1950s. About two months after we had moved, we received a letter from our old neighbor, Mom Winnie, that Prince had died. I was devastated and knew that it was my fault for leaving him. I just knew he had died of a broken heart.

Since then, my mom and I had talked about Prince from time to time, telling the old stories about the Fourth of July, snakes, and that damned old Speed.

David K. Anger is married with two children and six grandchildren. He has been retired from Ford Motor Company for a little over twelve years. He has lived in and around Dearborn most of his life. This story is only one in a series about his life. danger123@wowway.com

Fixing Things by Mary Bandyke

A small, dark, curly-haired dog was brought into the little room. He took a long look at us—my eighty-nine-year-old mom and me—quietly walked towards us, but then hid under the bench where we sat in the visiting room of the Humane Society shelter. Mom and I smiled at each other, liking the little fellow's shy nature and that sidelong look he had given us. His amber-colored eyes had crescent-shaped borders of bright, clear white. Altogether, it gave him a most soulful aspect. These perceptive eyes looked right into our hearts, while his shy gesture of finding a safe little den underneath our bench showed a flicker of trust in us, two new human strangers.

While a quick week's time was filled with thoughts about this seven-year-old dog named Benji, phone calls to the shelter brought good answers to our concerns about his training and habits. Gratefully the shelter kept him off the adoption list while we ran scenes in our minds about how life might be for Mom and this little being whose prior life had been spent with young kids, other dogs and cats, and the two parents who had now lost their home to foreclosure. No wonder Benji looked so confused when we met him. His eyes were taking us in but he was thinking of his old family—where had they gone?

My mom has a brave and true heart. She knew she wanted a dog to share the long, quiet days with her. She wanted someone who would be happy to see her always, bringing a quicker pace to the days, and some joyful sound to her longtime house that was so often very, very quiet.

So it was decided, and Benji was brought right to Mom's house for a trial visit, with me there at the arrival. I was ready to do whatever it took to blend the lives of my now physically challenged mom and this quick-moving dog. But upon arrival, the shelter manager told us that a heart murmur was detected during Benji's veterinary exam. This little one had a physical challenge, too.

After one day and one night's stay, Mom declared Benji to be wonderful, and said the trial was over. He was staying. Two months later, at a get-acquainted visit with a local veterinarian, whom Mom chose to be Benji's doctor, the question of the heart murmur was raised. The doctor had already listened to the heart that lay beneath that sweet, curly-haired exterior. This experienced doctor decisively said, "There is no evidence of a heart murmur. None."

When the topic was discussed at some point later on, my steady mom, who had now bonded so strongly with The Little One said simply, "His heart was broken. But we fixed it." Actually, a total of three broken hearts were now fixed: Mom's, mine, and Benji's. The bond of love can heal all hearts. And so we continue, three years after.

Mary Bandyke enjoyed a career in art education that included 11 years teaching elementary art for Dearborn Public Schools. Her lifelong love of animals and nature came from both of her parents.

Jasper the Wonder Dog by Maryanne Bartles

He came to us one cold January night. Our adventure began with three boys knocking on our front door. "Is this your dog, lady?" He wasn't, but I asked what they planned on doing with him. They said they couldn't keep him – Mom wouldn't allow it. They would just leave him outside somewhere. We already had a dog so I wasn't really interested in another but leaving him in the frigid cold was just not an option. Promising my husband I would find his owner ASAP – after all, he wore a collar, someone would miss him – we took him in. We guessed he was about four months old, a long-legged black Lab-Doberman mix. Friendly and lovable, but definitely a wild man as he <u>never</u> sat still, constantly batting at you with those long legs and big paws.

Needless to say, days became weeks and weeks turned into months. No one answered our ads and the pound kept saying, "NO LADY, no one has called looking for him." My husband realized that when I named him, he was here to stay. Jasper.

In the beginning, he was high-energy, mischievous and constantly getting into trouble. We came home one evening to find newspaper strewn on the living room carpet with a potted house plant tipped over as if someone were getting ready to re-pot it. Jasper greeted us at the door with a comical expression as if to say, "My work here is done, you can clean up." Our other dog, Maggie, took the opportunity, while Jasper was re-potting the plant, to help herself to four chocolate kisses from a bowl on the end table. She was careful to leave the silver foil wrappings on Jasper's newspaper so he would get blamed.

During those first two years, Jasper continued his rampage, eating an entire tub of margarine, a pair of prescription eyeglasses (Grandma was NOT happy) and a half-dozen donuts. Surprisingly, he never got sick. And then a miracle occurred when Jasper turned two and he became Jasper the Wonder Dog. He became the most obedient, loyal companion you could ever ask for. He was never leashed as there was no need (don't tell animal control). He was my best friend, never wanting to leave my side. We would take him on vacation to our property at Hubbard Lake. There were acres and acres to run, small animals to chase and loads of really good smells, but Jasper would not leave me. He walked our property line with the precision of a surveyor, but always kept me in his sights. Although Jasper was part Lab and had webbed paws, he <u>hated</u> water. Unfortunate for him, one day, I decided to go water skiing. Imagine my surprise as I took off from the dock and I watched him launch into the water after me. He didn't get very far before he had to turn back to shore. Like I said, he HATED water. I cut my skiing short to check on him and I was positive I saw a dirty look cross his muzzle.

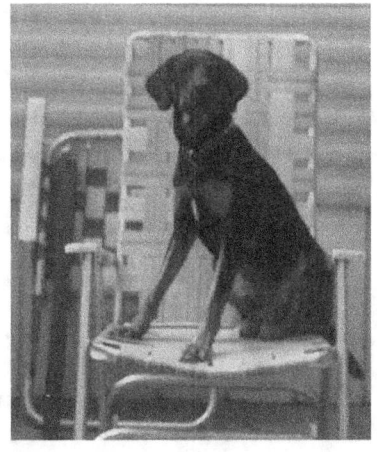

Jasper was almost always kind and patient. One day my husband's nephew and their three young children visited. Their oldest boy, Jason, took Jasper by the collar and walked him around the entire house for at least an hour. Jasper never complained, never growled, but after that long hour, he looked at me pleadingly, "Do you think you could get him to stop?" When I say almost always kind, I do remember one time when the cable repairman made an emergency stop late one evening to try to fix our cable television. My husband wasn't home and there was no way Jasper would let the guy into the house. One low growl from Jasper and our cable didn't get fixed until my husband was there to let the repairman in.

We had many more adventures, but sadly Jasper was with us for only ten short years. He was my loyal friend, always ready to lay his head on my lap, give me a sloppy kiss or just sit by my side. No matter how many pets I have had since, Jasper will always be my wonder dog.

Maryanne Bartles is a lifelong Dearborn resident and animal lover. Over the years, she has shared her life with one gerbil, two cats, three dogs, six parakeets, a Quaker parrot and two horses.

Dusty by Marge Berry

We got Dusty when I was about 10 years old. She was a German Shepherd-Collie mix, the latest in a long line of dogs that we had always had. Of all of them, Dusty was the only one that found her way into my heart. We had acquired her after her sister had been fatally hit trying to follow us to school. Unlike her sister, who was a nice combination of the Shepherd-Collie mix with the Shepherd's high-energy temperament, Dusty appeared to be pure Collie with the gentler Collie temperament.

My youngest brother was still in diapers when we got Dusty. Though Mom trusted us older children to keep an eye on him while we were playing in the yard, Dusty wasn't as trusting. If he got too close to the street for her comfort, she would grab him by the back of the pants and walk slowly backward until he was a safe (in her opinion) distance from the street. In all the times that she did this, she never once left a mark on him or walked too swiftly for his toddler legs. She also allowed the same brother to take his naps on her side. As she was only allowed in the kitchen, his head would be softly pillowed on her fur while the rest of him was lying on cold, hard tile. Mom used to say he took longer naps with Dusty than in his own crib and it was not unusual for us older children to walk in on this tableau when we got home from school.

Whether we were walking or riding our bikes somewhere, Dusty was our constant companion. If it looked like we would be staying awhile, she would find a shady place to lie down and wait patiently for us to leave. We discovered that this was true of our mom also. One evening she went to the neighbor's to enjoy some adult company and coffee after getting the younger kids to bed. Dusty had followed my mom and made herself comfortable by the back door which was open to enjoy the night air. As they were talking at the kitchen table, they heard footsteps walking up the driveway, Dusty barking and then footsteps running back down the driveway. My mom ran after them but whoever Dusty had been chasing was gone and Dusty had come back to make sure Mom was all right.

She was so much a part of the family that we even took her camping with us. On one of these trips, my sister and I were playing by the camper while my brothers and Dad had gone down by the lake. My sister was having so much fun she started screaming. Out of the corner of my eye, I spotted movement. When I looked, I saw Dusty flying at us as fast as her paws would carry her—one of her charges was being threatened. I grabbed my sister and pleaded with her to stop screaming. She must've seen the terror in my eyes because she stopped screaming just as Dusty reached us. She seemed a bit confused wondering where the danger was, but sniffed both of us completely to assure herself that we were both all right. She then found a spot in the shade to keep an extra vigilant eye on us, in case the danger returned.

Some nights I just wanted to get out of the house for a while and my parents would allow me to go for a walk after dark. I'm sure the only reason they did this was because they knew that Dusty would be my companion as well as guard dog. What I don't think they realized was that she was my confidante and due to her patient listening skills, I was able to work out a lot of my real and imagined preteen/teen problems.

Dad was a hard-working man struggling to support his family while trying to be there for them also. In her own way, Dusty allowed me to get a bit closer to him and spend some quality one-on-one time with him. He had assigned me the job, as the oldest, to make sure that Dusty's coat was always clean, brushed, and burr-free. However, when he had the time, he would help me with this job (a big one for a young girl working on a 100-lb. dog). It gave my dad and me time to bond and discuss things that were happening—admittedly, mostly in my life. These were times that I cherished with my Dad, as, other than the dog we both loved between us, I had him all to myself for a while.

We had other dogs before Dusty and others after. None of them were ever as important to me as Dusty and her place in our family. I'm not sure if anything would have changed in my life if we hadn't had her, but I'm definitely sure that her presence in it made a BIG positive difference.

Marge Berry is a Library Page at Dearborn Public Library.

The Miracle Mutt by Ellen Chene

Hello, my name is Skylar. I am lovingly called "Sky," when I am behaving; which to be honest is a day-to-day challenge for me. I am a very good-looking boy. At least I think so. I have a soft yellow coat, long floppy ears and big brown eyes which I use to my advantage when it comes to food and affection. I currently live a very pampered life, but that has not always been the case.

The day that I was scheduled to cross the rainbow bridge (permanent resting place for dogs) the Lord was with me. Somehow, I ended up in the home of the man who was to become my best friend and buddy. His name is Bob. He took in this skinny scrawny dog with every rib showing and turned me into the robust healthy specimen that I am today.

Our days are anything but typical or boring. We generally sleep in, as Bob is retired and we like to catch up on our beauty rest. After Bob has his morning coffee we go for one of many daily walks. Bob and I are both creatures of habit so our morning walk is generally to the nearby woods. Breakfast consists of anything from chicken, ham, roast beef or salmon mixed in with a little bit of dog food. I have developed gourmet tastes and Bob is more than eager to accommodate me. Then I am ready for my morning nap while Bob tends to his business. When Bob returns from doing whatever he does, it is he and I for the rest of the day. Sometimes he takes me to the dog park where I meet up with some of my old pals and catch up. If I have been really good he takes me swimming. Yes, you heard right. Bob takes me to a place called "Me and My Shadow" and we enjoy a private dip in the pool. The rest of my day includes doggie play dates and at least one other walk. Dinner is served and then it is time to hit my favorite spot on the couch and catch a few episodes of *Dog Whisperer*. What a life!!!

Now for the real reason I am writing this story. You see, I said the Lord blessed me once when he introduced me to Bob, but there was a second time that the Lord blessed me. Here is my story….

Bob and I decided to take a road trip to Florida one year. I love riding in the car, my nose out the window taking in the scents as we fly down the highway. We stopped often and I had the opportunity to see a little bit of the country. After three days on the road and spending nights in hotels (I do love staying in hotels) we arrived at our destination in sunny Florida. I thought I had died and gone to heaven: warm weather, sunshine, beaches and dog parks, where I got the opportunity to get acquainted with some of the locals. I met some great new guys and soon fit right in.

One day after breakfast we did a little sightseeing and then decided to stop by the dog park and check it out. What soon followed will be etched in my heart and memory forever. There were a few guys at the park and being the outgoing type I anxiously approached them. Gus, a regular and one of the gang, was very friendly and seemed to take an interest in me. We started the usual dog meet and greet romp but something went horribly wrong. Somehow Gus's teeth got caught under my collar and we became entangled. In an effort to free himself, Gus twisted his body which flipped me and left me on the ground gasping for air. My collar was tightening with every move Gus made. We were totally interlocked. A crowd began to gather around us but I was only aware of the bright sunshine rapidly disappearing as I slipped into the darkness of lost consciousness. I felt the strength draining from my body. The last thing I remember before everything went dark was the desperation on the face of my faithful friend Bob.

According to bystanders, a hand from nowhere reached through the crowd and with a sharp knife sliced through my collar like butter, leaving me free to breathe: but I wasn't. I lay motionless on the ground. An onlooker unsuccessfully attempted to revive me. She then began comforting Bob and offering her sympathy on his loss. Bob refused to accept the reality of the situation, grabbed me and heroically administered mouth to nose resuscitation (a skill he learned from his firefighting days). The silence of the crowd was shattered with shouts of joy as life slowly returned to my body and I began to move. The truly amazing part of this story is that nobody saw the person who freed me from my choking collar. In a crowd of 10, no one can say who did it, where they came from, where they disappeared to or how the knife could slice through a collar that was choking me and not cut or even touch my skin. It was truly a miracle. This story continues to be told today to the amazement of all who hear it.

You see, the Lord was with me when he brought Bob and me together, and once again when he kept us together. Bob and I both have been blessed. Bob's loving kindness has provided me with a wonderful life and I have filled the empty spaces in his life that only "man's best friend" can. How AWESOME is that?!!!!!!!

Ellen Chene is an entrepreneur who writes and presents Murder Mystery shows. egchene@yahoo.com

Extra Vision by Dan Colovas

Have you ever given paws (sic)
To a thought I propose,
That we can see with our eyes
What a dog smells with his nose?

Now we could view what
The breeze holds in store.
Could we really perceive
What's behind that closed door?

Would our vision be such
When strolling through a wood,
We could readily discern
Where a rabbit once stood?

Then follow its trail
Through brush ever so dense,
And find out where it
Hopped over a fence?

It seems quite amazing
We could bring back the past,
Knowing just who had walked here,
It would be such a blast!

A marvelous scheme,
What wonders we can surmise.
What a dog smells with his nose,
We can see with our eyes.

Dan Colovas is a retired mechanical engineer living in Dearborn with his wife JoAnne. He has resided in Dearborn for 72 years. He graduated from Fordson High School in 1956, Henry Ford Community College in 1958, and University of Michigan in 1962. He has been writing poetry for 20 years.

Utopia by Dan Colovas

Give me a field to roam and run,
That's where I can have great fun.
Chase a rabbit, tree a squirrel.
Watch a quiet new dawn unfurl.

Notice that chipmunk over there?
Maybe I'll dash over and give him a scare.
Then stop and listen to a meadowlark sing.
Gosh, what a spot to have a fling.

No leash tugging, holding me tight.
For a canine, sheer delight.
Following my nose from bush to tree,
Fantastic scents. If only you could see.

Now for something nice and cool,
Perhaps I might have to break a rule.
I know the sign shows NO DOGS ALLOWED.
But I don't see even the hint of a crowd.

So while you're pondering clouds above,
Meditating on a long lost love,
I'll wander away, give you the slip.
Hurry to the lake and take me a dip.

Some might think that I love to sleep and feed.
But my alternatives are few since I can't read.
So please, give me a field to roam and run.
That's where I can have great fun.

Dan Colovas is a retired mechanical engineer living in Dearborn with his wife JoAnne. He has resided in Dearborn for 72 years. He graduated from Fordson High School in 1956, Henry Ford Community College in 1958, and University of Michigan in 1962. He has been writing poetry for 20 years.

Speak Dog Speak by Collette Cullen

The son is 24. He speaks to me of passion. He wants a life infused with passion. He wants fire's flame.

Our dog was once passionate about squirrels. She lived, breathed, and bounded in the name of squirrels. In the forested yard—an Elysian Field of nuts and berries and a circus canopy of trees, an amusement park for a city block worth of squirrels—she lived her passion chasing squirrels. The adventure was further enlivened for the squirrels by the great fun of taunting the white beast whose ancestors were bred to fetch fowl from the swamp and retrieve them for the shooter. This dog named Avery (for Shug in *The Color Purple*) would course, and bay and sprint, like flashes of light through the woods in hopes of seizing that irritating squirrel.

Only squirrels enticed her. She was inured to birds or chipmunks... no sport there.

Squirrels were her passion. It made her forget heat or the traveling boy whose scent for many years lulled her to sleep at night. They made her forget the six pins that screwed her broken hip together. (She had probably seen a squirrel back when she was a 10-week-old pup and bolted into traffic; facing death in the name of her nemesis.) Ahh...that is how passion can be. (When I was scattering her ashes, I found that the crematorium had reverentially placed the pin from her hip in a zip lock snack-sized bag.)

It disturbed me how all the ups and downs of her dog life must have ailed her. Yet in spite of her age she had purpose. When I stood up, she got up. When I went to the kitchen, she went to the kitchen. If I was in the bathroom she stood outside the door often barking, waiting for me. Her purpose was to watch over me.

She watched me when I got divorced and moved from that forested squirrel habitat. She came and gave me dog kisses on the summer day upon my return from having witnessed our old land getting clear-cut. She just kissed away the tears. She stood watch when the boy left to move towards manhood, taking his smell and his spilly self (no more nibbles or half-eaten sandwiches for her). She was vigilant in her watch of me when I returned from California from the boy's bedside as he blew past a 14 blood transfusions near-death experience. Our goodbye hug, leaving behind a remnant of the boy's scent and the faint clean smell of the hospital's urgency. The dog smelled the battering to my heart.

The boy wants passion.

Just now I want to be like my dog, the way she became and remained even up to that last day. My great passion was my work as a teacher, a role lost abruptly, leaving me spinning like my dog looking to the tree tops.

I tell the boy, I want to be like my dog who on her last earth day, unleashed, followed me around the block, sniffing at a young lad and trodded forward.

On our last morning prayer/coffee time (a ritual she accompanied me for every one of her 14 dog years) she did not take her usual stance resting at my feet her paws folded seemingly in prayer. Instead on that last day she stood, her haunches burrowed into my thighs, baying relentlessly at some unseen thing. Perhaps she saw a squirrel…

So yes, I long for passion but just now I hope to be like my dog and want to move forward with some grace and purpose.

Collette Cullen: "Just a little info about me: I was a teacher for forty years and a resident of Dearborn for thirty years. My work now is as a historical reenactor. I perform as Annie Sullivan, Helen Keller's teacher.

"I do write. It is a labor of love. What I mean by this is that I am not a natural but when struck by a story I feel I must commit it to the page."
http://anniesullivanspeaks.com; collettecullen@gmail.com

Zeke the Wonder Dog by Selia Danes

This is more a story of just how wonderful our city of Dearborn really is. My daughter Charlie had just moved back home from her freshman year of college. Like many college students Charlie went to college with the belongings that would take up the space of a small sized home – at least that is what it seemed when we helped load and move her home. That was on a Saturday and my car held only the smaller stuff thank goodness. We were beyond tired and Zeke the Wonder Dog was ecstatic to have his Charlie back home to snuggle up to. That afternoon he was just in the lap of contentment, and that is why we will never understand why he was missing Sunday morning! Somehow the gate was OPEN!! Our wonder dog never left the yard – but obviously he done just that in the evening sometime.

Panic was what went through us. We searched in the car street by street in the neighborhood while Charlie ran up and down Outer Drive asking all that she saw if they had seen an Irish Setter running loose. Many people said they saw a red dog running with another big black dog but nobody could help us except to assure us that indeed he was certainly alive. After looking for more than an hour we called the police in hopes of their help. They said that they would put out an All-Points Bulletin for Zeke. The animal shelter does not have Sunday hours. We continued to look and checked back frequently with the police. Sometime after noon we were truly stymied as to what to do and returned home. Reluctantly we called the police to see if they had any Zeke sightings only to be told that they had been trying to contact us. Zeke had been found playing in the street intersection of Brady and Michigan Avenue. A wonderful woman called to the canine friends and they both came bounding into her van.

This wonderful woman took the boys home and called the police. By the time I got to her home she was gone, however. Zeke the Wonder Dog was sitting in her beautiful home giving off a stench that I had never experienced before. Zeke has been swimming in the Rouge and his lovely long feathers were tangled with all sorts of sticks and thorns along with brambles. We thanked the lady's son and wedged Zeke into my two-seat, very small car. It took much sudsing and many rinses to have Zeke clean enough to be allowed back into the house again. However, if you live in Dearborn we have wonderful people that will go out of their way to help not only people in need but also dogs. And the Police – WOW is all I can say – an All-Points Bulletin – that is just remarkable. Sometimes thank you is just not enough!!

Selia Danes is a lifelong resident of Dearborn and has been a stockbroker with the same firm for the past 30 years. She currently has and shows in the conformation ring a Gordon Setter; his name is C.H. MacGregor.

Girl by Rowden F. Dupuie

We first met at the Dearborn Animal Shelter in June of 1996. I really wasn't looking for a girl. I was engaged at the time. I had a habit of stopping by the shelter with some treats for the strays. There she was, just standing quietly, the most beautiful girl I had ever seen. Kathleen—that's the name the shelter had given her. So I gave her a treat. She took it gently between her front teeth, stepped back, sat down and spit it out on the floor. She looked up at me and I swear she seemed to be thinking, "What? a treat? really? I'm in jail here."

I wasn't looking for a pet and I guess she wasn't looking for a treat but we found each other. We left that day side by side until her untimely but peaceful passing 15 years later. I miss her.

When I first met Girl—that's her name—I owned a saloon in Dearborn called The Pelican Club. She became a big part of the place. One year, on a sunny day in July, I had a charity benefit event for the Dearborn Animal Shelter called "Critter Day," in part inspired by Girl. Her veterinarian, Dr. Caputo, volunteered to examine any pet my customers brought in. We had a horse, yes a horse, as well as fish, dogs, snakes, birds, cats and a turtle. There was a pet wash in the parking lot manned by volunteers. Girl was very satisfied with the results. We raised $1000 and I received a major donor award for the effort. After that day dogs were always welcome and Girl had many dog friends. Girl really enjoyed sitting on a bar stool by the front door munching on a bowl of ice, watching who came in.

After a few years of saloon life, I sold the place and we moved up north to a riverfront cabin deep in the Manistee National Forest, a private paradise. We had thousands of acres of forest and rivers that bordered the cabin to explore. Girl loved to chase deer and wild turkey. She never caught any but it was fun to watch her run after them, like a low flying rocket. As they disappeared into the forest, she would stop, look back at me and proudly trot back to the cabin as though she had really accomplished something. It was her cabin. She was friendly with all animals. So friendly she got a few quills in her nose from a porcupine, ouch! Fishing, hunting and hiking almost every day for 10 years. A real dog's life, unleashed.

I could go on and on about the special things my Girl did. Her habits and quirks. Everyone has stories about their pets but Girl was my friend. The best friend I ever had. If we have a choice and there is someplace we go after our time on earth, I want to be where my Girl is.

Rowden F. Dupuie is the original owner of The Pelican Club. He opened it on Friday, October 13, 1978 and was in business until October 13, 1999.

A Girl's Best Friend by Mary Jo Durivage

As I write this short essay, I can hear our dog Jack begging to be let back in from the freezing cold. His daddy (my husband) just let him in. Jack is a Jack Russell terrier my then teenaged son was "gifted" as he and his dad were looking for dog ideas at a local pet store. A woman came in with Jack explaining that her son was not taking care of the dog and was hoping that she could find a family that would give him a good home. So Jack came to live with us at the age of six months. To be honest, I was not ecstatic about having a dog in the house but I remembered how important a special dog was to me when I was a child.

His name was Jake. He was a beagle and had been given to our family by my great uncle Charlie. I don't remember how old I was when he came to join us but I think I was maybe about eight years old, maybe younger. Jake fit right in with all of us. He had his own dog house which my uncle Charlie, a carpenter, had made for him. I don't remember this but I am told that my grandfather had a stencil made for it: "11036 ½." How fun.

Jake slept and played outside during the day but at night he was definitely inside with all of us. I can just see us all watching TV and my mom cautioning us not to give the dog any popcorn. When it was bad weather, Jake would join us in play in the basement, just like one more kid. Did I mention I was the oldest of eleven? When Jake was around, there were probably "only" six or seven of us.

Even though I was surrounded by loving family members, there were times when Jake was a better listener. I can remember swinging in the back yard with Jake nearby and telling him about my latest school or family crisis, and hugging him when I needed a little extra TLC.

I don't remember how old Jake was when he came to us, so I don't know if Jake died from natural causes or whether he had become ill. I just know that I came home from school one day and my mom told me that Jake had "gone to the farm." I think I must have known that there was a possibility of Jake leaving us because I have this memory of me hugging him as I was crying and saying goodbye. What a loss for all of us, but I think especially for me.

We had two more dogs after Jake – Brownie, another beagle and Rosie, an Airedale terrier which one of my sisters brought home. My mom was really a sport about that. We loved those dogs as we loved Jake. Ask my siblings, though – Jake was always "Molly's dog."

So when my son asked me about keeping Jack, I remembered "my dog" and hoped that Jack would be as good a buddy to him as Jake was for me. He was. ☺

Mary Jo (Molly) Durivage has lived in Dearborn for thirty years and is a big fan of the Dearborn Public Library. She is the librarian at the John D. Dingell VA Medical Center and an active member of the League of Women Voters. mjdurivage@comcast.net

A New Dawn with Happiness by Zamzam A. Fawaz

Kuru was a little dog who had just come to Edward's house three days ago. Before that, Kuru was a lazy dog who did nothing but eating and playing. In reality, Kuru loved action, but there was nothing exciting to look forward to in the area he was in before coming to Edward's house.

On that sunny day of fall, Kuru was trying to discover the new place he came to live in, when he noticed a little six or seven-year-old girl trying to get up and walk toward the balcony. She, in vain, was trying to walk. Kuru was standing in the living room where he could see the whole route the girl was going in. For some reason, he did not know why he wanted to watch her. Suddenly, the little girl fell to the floor and was unable to get up again. She started crying; Edward was upstairs and it would take time to reach her. Kuru ran to the child and started sniffing her. She was utterly shocked. She stopped crying and stared at the strange dog in front of her. Kuru tried to take her hand up to his back.

"Hold on to my back and try to get up." That is what he meant to say. He had noticed that her feet were not in a good position. Her right leg was folded toward the left leg, and the left leg was folded left as well. It is normal for human beings to sit in different ways, Kuru thought, but for some reason, it did not look right. Maybe because she could not walk easily. What was wrong with this kid, Kuru did not understand.

As the child stared at him, Kuru kept trying to let her put her hand on his back to help her get up.

"I can't do that," she said. "I can't get back up, and Dad is not here." She started crying again.

When Edward arrived to the room, he saw Kuru taking the child's hand, placing it on his back, and getting up slowly so that the girl could stand up.

Lian saw her father standing.

"Be strong," he said, "Accept his help and rise up on your feet."

She held tight to Kuru's waist and Kuru stood up. She was trying with him as well.

Later that day, Lian came to Kuru and looked at him with melancholy: "Who are you and what's your name? When did you come here?"

Kuru looked in the child's eyes: Why is she so sad, he wondered. He sniffed Lian and started acting funny, trying to make her smile.

Lian asked, "Do you have friends, or are you as lonely as me, little doggy?"

Kuru decided to help Lian get out of her loneliness and sadness no matter what it took to do so.

That was the beginning. From that day on, Lian practiced getting up and walking every day with Kuru helping whenever needed. Lian and Kuru became friends. Kuru later learned that Lian had been in an accident when she was younger, and since then, she had to use a wheelchair. Doctors said the chances that she will walk on her feet again are slim. But Lian's strengths were becoming stronger by the day, and with Kuru's emotional support, she decided to show everybody that she will be able to walk again.

Kuru brought life back to a house that had long lost happiness. Since Lian's mother, Cathy, passed away, Edward also spent more time with Lian and Kuru. He managed his time to have enough time for everything. Before that, Edward took care of Lian, but also used to stay alone for a long time thinking of Cathy and all of his troubles and hardships. Cathy had passed away in the same accident, Edward remembered. In that accident, Lewis, his cousin, was driving. He had invited them to spend some time at the river. Edward was sitting in the front, and Cathy and Lian were sitting in the back. As Lewis was turning at a hard left turn, a large truck came, moved to the wrong lane, and crashed into the car. Lewis and Cathy died; Edward had a back injury that he recently recovered from after a long treatment; and Lian's legs were damaged, condemning her to use a wheelchair.

Edward had lost his beloved wife and his close friend. His paralyzed daughter is always before his eyes, suffering because she can no longer play with the other kids. And he, recently recovered from the injury, but his heart is still in pain—an everlasting pain that accompanies him everywhere.

Edward did not even want to add a new member to the family, but Kuru also has his own story. Kuru was Lewis's dog. After Lewis, his parents took care of him, but now they are too old to take care of Kuru, and they often forgot to give him any food to eat. Thus, it was

Lewis's parents who asked Edward to take care of Kuru: "He could be a friend for Lian," they said. They also thought that Kuru would help Edward forget some of his pain and hardships.

As time went by, Lian improved, and she was able to walk alone and without any help. Edward's pain was fading with time, and seeing his little daughter playing and smiling helped alleviate his sorrows. Life was gradually coming back to the house that was sad and empty for a long time. Kuru lived with the small family, happily helping whenever needed.

Zamzam A. Fawaz is a university student majoring in elementary education. Her favorite hobby is writing happy-ending children's stories. She also has a great interest in languages and is trying to learn Japanese.

Mayor Hubbard and Lassie by Shirley Foisy

As a child, we always looked forward to the annual Dearborn "clean up" parade at the elementary school in May. The whole school participated. We would line up out in the school yard and then proceed on our regular parade route. Leading the parade was our beloved Mayor Hubbard followed by a fire engine. Blaring away on the loudspeaker in the lead car, a John Phillips Sousa march bombarded the neighborhood. Truth be told, I got so I actually hated that music, as it played repeatedly throughout the entire route, year after year.

It just so happened that my childhood home was on our parade route. When the music got louder, my mother knew we were getting near and she was always out on our front porch to wave at me. Along with my mother on the porch was our collie dog, Lassie. (Due to the popularity of the TV show of that name, I think almost every collie dog in the country was named Lassie.) Mayor Hubbard was quite an amazing man and he remembered our dog. She was such a quiet and well-behaved dog. Wouldn't you know it, just as the front of the parade reached our house the firemen blasted the siren. This sent Lassie into a long, mournful howl. I never heard her howl like that for the entire 10 years we had her. Mayor Hubbard really got a kick out of that. Every year after that, he made sure the firemen blasted the siren at our house as he watched Lassie and laughed as it sent her into a long and mournful howl. He did this every year until he left office.

Shirley Foisy was born and raised in Dearborn and has spent the majority of her life there. Animals have been a large part of her life. The longest she has ever been without an animal companion is a couple of months. She has been blessed with many parakeets, rabbits, dogs, and ferrets to share life with. Currently, she has two ferrets.

Claudius the Dog by Joe Gaber

I was fifteen years old when my family adopted a dog. He was a magnificent, six-year-old Lhasa Apso with a scruffy haircut, short, stubby legs, and a generally cranky disposition. Though a sissy lap dog by breed, he looked like he didn't really fit in with the other dog show royalty. Perhaps this is why we named him Claudius, after the crippled Roman Emperor, Tiberius Claudius.

Prior to Claudius, my family had been one of dogless dog-lovers. My mother's horrific fur allergies, as well as a generally hectic schedule, had seen to that. We had fish in the past, but since you can't really get too close with grave-bound goldfish, Claudius remains, in my mind, our first real pet, and luckily, he had hair. Claudius meant something very special to all of us, since he was one pet that would surely be irreplaceable.

True to his name, Claudius was thoroughly unrefined. He was scrappy in spirit, and could not help but start a fight with any and every dog he came in contact with. I personally dislike people who can't (or don't even try to) control their pets, but my family and I were rapidly becoming such people. Despite his obvious faults, Claudius had an arresting personality, and we spoiled him like royalty. We didn't have the fortitude to properly train and restrain this creature. As we gave him more treats and human food, he only seemed to get worse.

Still, we did our best to nurture Claudius in spite of ourselves. I loved taking him for walks, out in the crisp night air, sprinting through intersections and hopping between the cracks in the pavement. Oftentimes, he would tucker out and collapse when we were furthest from the house, but I couldn't help but smile. He would lie down in the grass, prone, with his head on his front paws and his rear legs spread, so that he looked like a small, lazy rocket ship. Carrying his lazy butt back home could be pretty good exercise, after a while.

After he snapped at my parents a few times (these were all glancing blows), we finally decided to take Claudius to obedience school. The "school," an aromatic building next to a CVS, actually unlocked some useful insight for us. As soon as we entered the building, Claudius started causing trouble. The other dogs were seated quietly, awaiting instruction, when in walked my sister, my father, and I, desperately trying to restrain our ferocious Lhasa Apso. We watched in horror as our dog transformed into a whirling hairball of fury. He clashed with the Doberman, then with the Terrier, and he didn't stop until the entire room was in an uproar. As the trainer in charge of the lesson shouted, desperately trying to regain order over the tempest of barks, one thing was absolutely certain: our Claudius was the worst behaved dog in that entire "school." After a painful fifteen minutes, we left, almost as terrified as the other pet owners.

It became more apparent with each passing day that no amount of training could halt our dog's inevitable regression. Claudius gained weight, vomited regularly, and became less friendly, and more bite-y. Though he was clearly demented, I still loved Claudius dearly. I would say he only bit people because they were picking him up the wrong way. I would say anything to make it seem like Claudius was still controllable.

The final incident happened late one night as I was coming home from an after-school activity. My key was buried deep inside my backpack, so I rang the doorbell instead of digging for it. I waited, and Claudius answered first, drooling and barking in an adorable fit of excitement. My youngest sister came up the stairs, and before opening the door, she tried to move Claudius out of the way. I only heard a muffled snarl from outside, but through the back door window I could clearly see my dog bite my sister in the face. Fear came, slipping slowly into my heart. I started digging, frantically, for my key. I'd like to say I was worried about my sister's well-being, but I wasn't. At that moment, I was obsessed with Claudius' future, and worried that he was about to spend his last night at our house.

Once I was finally inside, I could hear my sister crying, no longer muffled, and my mom talking about how we need to put down our mentally ill dog. I was petrified, and it must have shown. I stared at my mom, and she looked back, and I could read on her face the truth of the situation. "I'm sorry, but we have to." She didn't say it, but I knew she meant it. I looked down to see Claudius, smiling that stupid, doggy grin. "Lunatic," I thought, tears forming in my eyes.

I have never cried for the death of a single human being like I cried for Claudius. I was fifteen, and cynical about most things, but I believed in my dog. For deciding to euthanize Claudius, I was angry at my parents for a long time. I remain the only one of my household

Claudius never bit, and though it was likely just a matter of time before I was bitten, I still held a grudge. My faith in Claudius's humanity made my connection with him so powerful that it blinded me. If I accepted the fact that he could not have been controlled, maybe the looming death of Claudius would have been easier to deal with. Easier? Maybe. Easy? Definitely not.

After we dropped Claudius off at the vet, my mom, dad, two sisters, and I went for a walk at the Henry Ford Estate. The sky was clear and blue, and it offered a brief relief from the grim thoughts about our dog. "He didn't have to die," I whimpered. "I know," my dad said. Of course the dog had to be put down, but I'm still so glad someone said that to me.

I would frequently go out at night and walk alone after that day. Sometimes I would stop at the farthest point at my route and think about Claudius before he declined. Vividly, almost automatically, I could see him in his rocket-ship pose: prone and lethargic, head resting on his front paws. He was kind of like a rocket-ship pet in the end: his time in my life burned fast and bright — and he was ultimately bound for the heavens. Coming back to reality, I would walk home, still with the weight of that scrappy, insane, and altogether perfect dog on my shoulders.

Joe Gaber is currently a sixth semester student at the University of Michigan-Dearborn, where he is majoring in Mathematics. He lives in Dearborn, and he is a "dog person."

Reminiscence for Thisbe by Anne Gautreau

A wonderful lap dog, with his improbable Shakespearean name, has been sent away, via tranquilizer and an overdose of anesthesia. It was as if he were an old car, and all the wheels suddenly just fell off. His lug nuts had simply, inexorably, rusted away and all was lost.

Last Friday Thisbe could no longer walk. He could no longer sit, nor could that sweet little dog stand without tremendous effort. He trembled constantly in relentless, unremitting pain. He has been on a downward trajectory for some months now.

Five years ago, after being hit by a car, he sustained severe life-threatening injuries; and he endured a long recuperation which included an operation to remove his right hip and create what veterinarians refer to as a false socket. Then this spring he was diagnosed with an anterior cruciate ligament problem in the other back leg. On Friday, Thisbe's lifelong veterinarian was out of town. So a new, young, highly articulate and obviously intelligent, substitute veterinarian gave him a thorough examination and diagnosed a probable brain tumor which had atrophied the muscles in his left-front leg as well as his left-upper back and left chest. Thisbe had paresis, a condition of muscular weakness caused by nerve damage. It is the stage that precedes paralysis. Also, his left eye responded sluggishly to direct light but seemed to respond to indirect light. Finally, the right-front leg was diagnosed as having tendinitis. Thisbe yelped in pain as the doctor examined him. So there he was, a dog without a leg to stand on, both literally and figuratively. The young doctor spent a great deal of time with us yet could not offer hope. He stressed that orthopedic problems can heal with time, but that there was little or nothing to be done for dogs with neurological problems. He gave us steroids and pain medication to ease Thisbe's inflammation and suffering.

After sleeping on it overnight, I decided to take Thisbe to a friend's vet for a second opinion. He was willing to see us, even though it was Sunday, for a second opinion. He did a thorough exam which paralleled the other one and said that there was not a realistic chance for any quality of life. So after anguish, dismay and agonized tears, saying good-by to Thisbe seemed to be the only humane thing to do.

I shall always miss Thisbe's warm body snuggling into mine, his soft-silky fur and his licking my feet, followed by a soft gumming-motion massage along the insteps and toes. I shall miss his frantic antics with toys, shaking them furiously as if determined to take down prey. Amazingly, when various friends would stop by for a visit, he would retrieve the particular toy they had gifted him. I was not alone in "spoiling" the boy. My sister-in-law used to bring him iced cappuccinos! The two of them would slurp side-by-side in the sunshine. I shall miss his aerial greetings behind the windows lining my backdoor. Two long, slow-motion ears would head skyward, even as his body went back down only to spring into yet another joyous leap. I shall miss his determined greeting yaps upon my return, as though he were yelling, "Hey, somehow I got left behind, and I sure missed ya!" I shall miss the pure, unadulterated delight he took in car rides. He loved the drive-up window at the bank and the blonde cashier who never failed to send him two cookies in the plastic transaction tube. I shall miss his playing bottle soccer. He adored any gallon milk jug, with convenient carry handle and cacophonous, percussive roar, to slam and skid against hardwood floors. I shall miss seeing his butt lean, like that of a little old man perched upon a toilet, against tree trunks as he defecated. Dutifully, I would stretch a newspaper-delivery bag over my hand and forearm then grab the "catch of the day." His look was quizzical as I knotted the bag and continued our walk. Was he wondering how bizarre it was that his eccentric owner wanted to save his waste? I shall miss his akimbo back leg, sans hip, slipping into "tilt" as he frequently lost balance while urinating. I shall miss his shredding promising shopping bags in search of newly purchased toys. I shall miss his sweet squeals of delight and his bossy bark when cookies were wanted. He would never touch a first treat until a second had been served as well! I shall miss cupping his ears and kissing the top of his head. I shall miss using his nicknames, Honey Bunny and Love Puppy. I shall miss his singular loyalty, love and affection. I shall miss his uncanny way of demonstrating intent by staring hard at the object of his desire after I would implore, "Show Mama what you want." I shall miss his disdainful hauteur, punctuated with snooty sniff, as we passed the yards of barking dogs. He would glance sideways and act as if he were thinking, "What is your problem?" I shall miss how he would always pause at a favorite neighbor's front walk and cock his head to discern whether or not she was at home. I shall miss how strangers took such delight upon meeting him on walks. I shall miss visiting the Caputo Animal Hospital. The women behind the counter always seemed to take genuine delight in greeting him as they cooed, "Thisbe's here." I shall miss telling strangers how my dog looked like the quintessential Disney dog. They always nodded sagely as if they instantly recognized an iconic profile. I shall miss walking behind him and watching his right-rear leg swing out and away from his body in an exaggerated effeminate motion. I shall miss picking him up from the dog groomer. He always seemed particularly proud of how fresh and slick he looked. I shall miss how he would paw at freshly laundered bed sheets and plow his snout around the bed in ever-widening circles, as though trying to create some kind of off ramp for fabric-softener freshness. Clearly, he wanted dog scent imprinted on those sheets, and he spent genuine time and effort in pursuit of his perceived olfactory perfection. Conversely, the chattering of squirrels and chirping of chipmunks, in his yard, drove him to distraction. A comical, exasperated, guttural anguish would spin up and out of him. Never once did those tree puppies empathize with his angst over their being bushy-tailed invaders.

Ironically, we were both the same age this year, that is if one divided my total years by seven. He lived his life much faster than I have lived mine, but he taught me much about savoring it and being in the moment and in tune with sensory input. He taught me much about patience. He taught me that things are just that, things. He nearly devoured the legs of my kitchen table when he was a puppy. At teething time, I wondered if he possessed monstrous genetics from a deranged termite. He repeatedly soiled a precious antique Oriental rug and cost me a small fortune in cleaning bills. He damaged hardwood floors, careening and skidding around in strong-nailed, willful delight. He taught laughter and forgiveness. He demonstrated determination and that occasionally shared decision making was a great way to maintain balance and harmony between dog and human being.

I can never thank him enough; I hope my decision to put him down was truly an act of love and not a betrayal. I miss petting my pet. How strange to realize that PET is also an abbreviation for positron emission tomography, used especially for brain scans. Life showers us constantly with its little ironies, even as life showers our cheeks with tears. But tears can become something like spring rains germinating seeds. New life, with all its attendant glorious affirmation, may take root once more.

Anne Gautreau is a retired educator and is active in the American Association of University Women, the Dearborn Library Foundation, and the Community Fund's Midwest Sculpture Initiative. Travel to over seventy countries has enriched her life.

How I Met My Dog by Nicki Goran

A bike ride in the park on a beautiful summer morning turned out to be one of the best exercise decisions my husband, Carl, ever made. As he pedaled around the paved path in the park, he approached the section nearest the street. There, on the sidewalk across from the park, stood a beautiful mahogany-colored husky wearing a chewed-through leash hanging from his collar. The dog stood motionless, his steely blue eyes fixed on Carl. Unsure of the dog's friendliness or whether he would bolt if approached, Carl slowly dismounted from his bike and called to the dog.

The husky excitedly ran to Carl with his tail wagging and his tongue hanging out. My husband was able to grab the piece of leash attached to the collar. Unable to notice anyone in the vicinity looking for a lost dog, Carl led the dog to our home several blocks away where he fed the hungry pup and then contacted animal control to report the lost puppy. After being told that an officer would not be available for about an hour, Carl contacted the Dearborn Animal Shelter to report the lost dog along with its tag number. The shelter employee asked if my husband would like to foster the dog while they awaited a call back from the owner. Of course, Carl agreed to take care of this sweet husky until the owner would claim him. He was told that since it was the Friday of the July 4th weekend, it might take a couple of days to hear any news. The weekend passed with no call from the dog's owners.

On Tuesday, Carl again contacted the Animal Shelter only to learn that the owner had been contacted and that she no longer wanted to keep this sweet dog. As she explained to the employee, she and her husband had just separated and she was left with three small children to care for. She was unable to care for an energetic young dog in addition to her other overwhelming responsibilities. The shelter employee asked if we might be interested adopting this dog and if so, we would need to wait for the thirty-day waiting period to pass before the adoption could proceed. We agreed to foster this wonderful dog for the thirty-day period hoping each day that the owner would not change her mind. At one point during the adoption period, Carl contacted the owner himself just to be sure that she intended to relinquish ownership of this wonderful pet and was told that she was happy that her puppy was going to a good home. As our good fortune would have it, the thirty days passed, the adoption was completed, and we were officially the new owners of a 6-month-old, blue-eyed, mahogany-colored male husky that we named Mochie. He has been a part of our family for almost four years now and we still feel blessed to have had such good fortune in finding him.

Nicki Goran is an employee of the Dearborn Public Library and an animal lover. She is also involved in wildlife rehab with her husband, Carl. Nicki and her husband live in Dearborn.

Smokey's Praise by Kim Heard

Don't ever leave me, I don't know what I would do,
Some people think dogs are pets but they don't know you.
I can't leave the house without kissing you first,
Making sure you have food and quenching your thirst.

As the years pass by, it's hard to find,
A human this loyal; and yes you're all mine.
In many ways, your love is better than a human,
You never lie, you never cheat, what do you think I'm foolin'?

Your love is unconditional,
Impossible to give additional.
There's nothing bad that I can say,
If you visit the trash; it's just doggie play.

Don't ever stop by uninvited just to say, "Hello,"
Because my sweetie will say to you, "Oh, no, you've got to go."
He takes his job very seriously, to love and protect;
And for those who think that they can tame, you'll get an instant reject!

So now you've heard my boast and brags, my love and adoration,
Of all the animals I see, you're a wonderful creation.

Kim Heard has worked for the City of Dearborn for 7 years, with 1 ½ years at the Centennial Library. She and her husband are the proud owners of Smokey (7 years old) and they have two wonderful children.

Geri and Me by Carol Ann Jessup

This is a true story about Geri, my service dog. He is a tri-colored male Sheltie. He was born on December 23, 2001. I have been telling this story for 12 years whenever someone asks where I got Geri.

When I was married, I lived in Livonia and belonged to the Livonia Civic Chorus. Sadly this marriage ended in 1995. At that time I had a pet Sheltie named Taffy. We moved to Wayne, and I belonged to SS. Simon and Jude Parish which had Fr. Gerry Bechard as its pastor. Taffy got very sick, and I had to put her down on April 11, 2002. Since my ex-husband wasn't paying any alimony, I had no money. So two parishioners from SS. Simon and Jude paid Taffy's $600 veterinarian bill. Shortly after Taffy died, Jan, one of the chorus members, called me to tell me how sorry she was that Taffy had died. I told her that I didn't tell anyone about Taffy's death. She said that the Levan Animal Hospital had put a picture on the wall honoring Taffy.

Later that evening her husband got a call from his sister who lived in Wisconsin and had raised Shelties for 20 years. She told him that they were making a trip to Toledo the next day with two of the last puppies from a recent litter; one Sheltie puppy was available. She wondered if he knew anyone who might want a Sheltie. Dave told her about me, and she asked him to have me at his house the next day.

The next day when we got to the house, Dave told me to go inside. He made the excuse that members of the chorus were coming over because they hadn't seen me since my divorce.

I went inside the house, and Jan yelled from the bedroom to go into the family room. I did, and there I saw a mesh playpen and thought, "Oh, good! Her grandkids are here." When I got to the playpen, I looked in and saw a fur ball sleeping in the corner and another puppy jumping like he was on a trampoline.

I told Jan that a pet Sheltie like this was going for $800 and that there was no way I could afford this dog.

Another voice spoke up. "Carol Ann, my name is Cindy Miller. I'm Dave's sister and I've been raising Shelties for 20 years. These two are from my last litter. I called Dave last night and told him that we were coming down today to take the sleeping one to Toledo and asked him if he knew anyone who might want the other dog. He told me about you. My husband has called the one Jumping Bean because he has been jumping since he was born.

"Now I've had a good life, but I'm dying of a brain tumor. I'm going to guarantee myself a place in heaven by giving Jumping Bean to you. The next time he jumps up, grab him because he's yours."

Tears were running down my cheeks and this puppy was licking them away. To this day, when I cry, my four-legged friend licks my tears away.

I changed my puppy's name to Geri in honor of Fr. Gerry Bechard.

This is how I got Geri, and I know the Man upstairs had his fingers involved in it because things just don't normally turn out this way.

Carol Ann Jessup grew up in Pennsylvania. She worked in health care in Michigan. She is no longer able to work because of physical disabilities. She lives in Southgate.

Snickers by Diane Kaye

In the hill country of West Tennessee
lived Grandpa with his hound dog Tray.
The old dog, ninety-five (in dog years)
just up and died one day.

Now Tray's death made the family grieve,
for sure it made the young'ns cry.
Folks say they saw a tinge of red
in Grandpa's sad old eyes.

So they all piled into the car—
down to the local pound they went.
They looked around to find a hound—
they found their time well spent.

For yonder in the corner pen,
with his paw poking out the door
was a smiley chocolate Lab!
Who could have asked for more?

Well, he was a big-headed dog,
his jowls loose and floppy, too.
But his tail was wagging happily—
the family knew just what to do.

Took the dog home in the car with them,
hoping their broken hearts to mend.
They took him straight to Grandpa's house
to share with him their gem.

The dog ran right into the house.
He tried to sit on the old man's lap—
fixin' to knock him off the chair,
'bout made him lose his cap.

"Git down, varmint!" Grandpa hollered.
The dog got down, proceeded to sit
smack on top of an open bag
of Grandpa's favorite potato chips!

The dog's mighty tail made chips fly
under the couch, on top of the chair
The more he wagged, the more the mess—
'tato chips flying everywhere!

"Git off, dag nab it!" Grandpa yelled.
The dog got busy picking up chips.
(Young'ns giggling wildly now!)
Big jowls flapping, licking his lips!

"Brought you a dog," smiled the family.
"I see," laughed Grandpa, "Hee, hee, hee!
Funniest thing I ever did see!
Feels good to laugh! Hee, hee!

"Old Tray won't mind, he's gone away.
Sure do miss him, feel all alone.
Reckon I'll take this chocolate Lab
and give him a good home.

"What'd they call him, where he came from?"
"They called him Spot. I can only guess why."
"I'll call him Snickers—he makes folks laugh.
He'll learn his new name, by and by."

So Grandpa had Snickers from that day on.
They laughed, they cried, they loved, they played.
Snickers got up every morning,
tried his best to behave.

Still daily pandemonium
was Snickers' claim to fame.
Though Grandpa tried to tame him,

his house was not the same.

Like the time Gramps fixed a ham sandwich,
and somebody knocked on the door.
Then, when Grandpa came strolling back,
his sandwich wasn't there anymore!

"Who took my sandwich?" Grandpa roared.
Snickers lay quietly on his mat.
"I've been asleep for a while," he yawned.
"It must have been the cat."

"Old Whiskers died in ninety-two,
haven't had a cat 'round here since then.
Reckon I got me a sleep walkin' dog—
that's the way it must 'a been."

Another time Gramps fixed his garden gate
painted the frame, put up new wire.
Sat deep in his lawn chair in the shade
his handiwork to admire.

All of a sudden, a rustling noise
pulled Gramps out of his reverie.
A small brown rabbit came out of the corn,
squeezed under the gate to be free.

Then our hero Snickers bounded out—
defending the garden without fail.
He headed straight for the gate's new wire,
Bong! Bounced right back on his tail!

This made Grandpa laugh and hoot,
he laughed so hard that he cried.
Snickers came over, licked Gramps' face,
'til every tear was dried.

Diane Kaye is a retired elementary educator. She enjoys writing and illustrating books for children, and spending time with her dogs, Lucy and Hugo.

Bark for Books by James LaRue

When he was three years old, Caiden started to stutter. A lot of children do around that age, especially the smart ones.

Most of the time, kids grow out of it. It's a synchronization issue. Neurologically speaking, learning to match brain speed to vocal articulation is a surprisingly complex thing.

The right thing for parents to do, incidentally, is to have patience. Love and encouragement is the ticket. Slow it down. Sing to and with them. With really astonishing speed, kids sort it out.

But Caiden's dad was, well, kind of a jerk. He mocked Caiden. He fake-stuttered, too, loud and long, then laughed. He interrupted and exaggerated Caiden's more difficult phrases.

Before long, Caiden's occasional stutter had turned into a serious and persistent problem.

Caiden's dad was abusive in other ways, too. Eventually Caiden's mom kicked him out.

But the damage, it seemed, was done. Caiden's stuttering isolated him all the way through kindergarten, and seemed likely to follow him through first grade, where he was just learning to read.

And he was learning fast. Caiden was so bright. It broke his mother's heart that when he tried to read out loud, his stammering frustrated him so.

Enter Cagney. Cagney was a greyhound – but not a very fast one. After Cagney failed to even place after four races in a row, his owner decided to let him go. The Colorado Greyhound Adoption people rescued him and placed him with an older and childless couple.

This couple trained Cagney in the Bark for Books program. They'd noticed that for some reason, Cagney just loved children. He'd fold himself up on his big floor pillow and look adoringly at any youngster that came along.

Caiden's mother hadn't planned to sign Caiden up for the program. But when they came into the library one afternoon, he watched Cagney with fascination as a little girl read to him.

The timing was such that just as the little girl had to leave, and before Caiden's mom knew quite what was happening, Caiden plopped down beside the dog, and opened a book. Caiden started trying to read.

The mother cringed inside. Caiden's stammering was pronounced. After a particularly painful passage, Caiden looked up, anxious and half-angry, right at the dog.

Then something wonderful happened.

Cagney, as greyhounds sometimes will, stretched out a paw and set it on Caiden's thigh. Cagney gazed deeply and steadily into Caiden's eyes, radiating calm. It was a look of utter acceptance and love.

Then, amazingly, Caiden seemed to relax. He started reading again, and this time he did much better. And Cagney seemed to like the story a lot, Caiden said later.

It didn't happen all at once. Caiden also saw a speech therapist. But that was the turning point.

Caiden is in fourth grade now. He just got the lead in a school play. One weekend, he even got to take Cagney home when the childless couple was travelling.

Caiden doesn't stutter anymore.

Recently, a library director got an email. It ended like this: "I thank the library, and that wonderful dog, for saving the life of my son."

Author's note: although all the details of this story are true, they were drawn from several families. I combined incidents and changed a few names. Here's what doesn't change: sometimes, often, dogs demonstrate way more kindness, presence, and attention than people do.

James LaRue is the author of The New Inquisition: Understanding and Managing Intellectual Freedom Challenges. *He is currently a speaker and consultant on the future of public libraries.* jlarue@jlarue.com

My Wild Life by Erica Laycock

My name is Indy. I am a Weimaraner, Bulldog, Akita mix. I grew up in the famous city of Detroit. I was abandoned by people I thought were my family, and I don't know why.

After roaming around, I found a place to rest my head. I found a tattered, old abandoned house, with broken windows, no door, and lots of holes in the walls. Kind of scary, but it gave me shelter. I lived on bugs, plants, and if I was lucky I could find something from the trash like a banana peel or a half-eaten hamburger. But I was surviving in this brave new world.

A few days later I started to notice that my tummy felt a little squirmy. Turns out I had mini-me's in there, or what humans call "puppies." Taking care of my puppies was hard work. I now had six mouths to feed, and I had to be on the lookout, day and night, to keep them safe. They became my main priority, and living on the wild streets of the city was quite a challenge!

Venturing out to explore my new surroundings, I saw bright green, red, and yellow lights floating above the road. I heard loud noises, like the sound of shoes smacking puddles of rain on the ground, and that of big trucks that go wee-woo-wee-woo rushing past, disturbing my sleep. Lots of people, lots of cars, and lots of dogs, just like me, looking for a friend, for food, ultimately, for their family. Quite an adventure.

One day, when it was nice outside, I decided to go for a stroll. I made sure my pups were safely snuggled in their bed that I had put together with last week's newspaper. I wandered, found some treats to eat, and soon was getting tired. So I found a spot to lie down. But something was different about this day. There were more people out and about, making lots of noise. There were people having picnics, there were lots of sounds…big booms and bright lights exploding in the sky. In the distance I could hear the clicking of feet coming toward me. It was a man, much larger than me. He was tall, wore black clothes with a black hat and shiny badge. He carried what looked like an over-sized phone and a scary black gun. People call him "Officer." He keeps us safe. I decided to go with my gut, and see if he'd pay attention to me. I gave it a try. I walked up to the man and clawed at his leg. He looked down at me speaking in the language people understand. I pawed at him several times and then let out a loud booming bark! I felt like a lion for a second. I wanted to see if he would follow me. And he did! My plan worked! I took him back to my house and gave him a tour. We finally got to the puppies so he could see that we needed help. He left for a minute, and returned in a shiny, black car with pretty red and blue flashing lights.

He called us, all six of us. We hopped in and went for a ride to a place he called "the shelter." When we got there I was a little scared, but soon found out there was no reason to be. The people were so nice, they gave me a bath, kissed all of my ouchies, and gave me a cozy cage to stay in. They cared for all of my pups, too. They even gave me a name. They called me Indy. You see, the kind policeman found me on the Fourth of July – Independence Day!

Life there was a little boring; not many toys, but it was comfortable. Everyday people would walk in, look around, and leave with their choice of an animal...one of us. I would get so excited, but my cage was often passed by. You see, there were lots of puppies and kittens at the shelter, and I'm almost two. Most people like the little ones. But I was patient, and I waited...

One day a nice looking couple came in. They seemed happy. To my surprise, they came straight to me! They brought me cookies and took me out of my cage. The nice man and I played together outside. I gave them lots of kisses and wagged my tail non-stop. Before I knew it, I was wagging goodbye to my puppies, and leaving the shelter behind! I was so excited, but also scared. Was I going to another shelter, or was I finally going to my forever home?

When we arrived at our destination there was a big house, with grass and trees and children! I was wagging and wagging! A little girl ran out of the house and right up to me. She had tears of excitement in her eyes! She was even calling me Indy! Her brother came and hugged me. I was filled with happiness. The girl quickly wiped away her tears and scooped me up into her arms! She snapped a leash around my neck and took me for a walk through my new neighborhood. I think I'm really gonna like it here!

Later that night, the little girl invited me into her big, puffy bed. Was this really happening? I fell asleep in her arms, and dreamt of my wonderful new life.

Finally, my forever home! Now I'm safe and have a family that I love. And they love me! Forever!

Erica Laycock: "Hello! I am a 10-year-old (5th grader) at Warner Upper Elementary School in Farmington Hills, Michigan.

"I am an animal lover, reader, writer, and artist. I dream of working with animals and sharing my writing and art when I am grown up.

"I hope you enjoy my short story of Indy, my rescue dog, who became part of our family on August 10, 2013." julielynch1968@gmail.com

Our Dog Ed by Jeff Lelek

My wife and I adopted our dog Ed from the Dearborn Animal Shelter in October of 2004. I noticed his picture on the shelter's website and something just connected us with him. Apparently he had been found on the street and was just randomly given his name, but it seemed to suit him so we kept it. I went to visit him at the shelter and he was sick with a cough at the time. When they brought him out to meet me he put his paws up on my shoulders as a greeting. We were allowed to take him home that weekend; as we were not expecting to get him so quickly, I had to run to the pet supply store and get a crate, bed, food…everything!

Some of the things Ed liked best involved the outdoors, especially chasing snowflakes or leaves blowing in the wind. He was most comfortable lying on the couch with all four paws in the air. He enjoyed his holiday platters of food when my wife and I would give him a sampling of ham, turkey, bread and potatoes and he would just clean off the plate in a minute. He also enjoyed Frosty Paws ice cream treats and his biscuits. His favorite toy was probably his squeaky rubber football.

Some of my favorite memories of him are of our frequent evening sunset walks together. I especially remember one winter's evening around Christmas when we were walking down our street and the snow was gently drifting down in big fluffy flakes. I noticed a house across the street and you could see inside its front window; people were standing around a table wearing red and green sweaters and laughing, drinking and eating food. It struck me as such a beautiful image of a holiday gathering, and I stopped with Ed and we just took it in for a second as the snow fell. I'll probably always remember that.

Gradually, we discovered that Ed had a strange aggression problem. Occasionally, out of nowhere, Ed would strike and violently bite at seemingly no provocation. I spent two Christmas Eve afternoons at hospitals, once in 2004 when he bit my mother-in-law on the face and again in 2008 when he bit my wife on the head. On both occasions the victims were simply sitting on a couch next to Ed and he sprang up and bit, seemingly for no reason. Since Ed was found on the street, we had no idea what his past history was or what might be causing this behavior; God knows what happened to him in his past for this type of behavior to develop.

We knew that, if we ever had kids, this behavior would have to be modified if we were even going to contemplate keeping him. So began a parade of behaviorists and dog trainers who would come to the house confident they would be able to tame the unruly Ed; each and every one left with his tail between his legs. In fact, I think each and every one got bit. The obvious conclusion each one reached is that we would not be able to have kids around Ed.

The issues got worse; we were not able to muzzle Ed, so we were unable to properly groom him or take him to the vet without him trying to bite. So now we had a dog that couldn't really be handled without a potential attack. We knew we would have to give him up, but who on Earth would take him?

Our daughter Jennifer was born in February of 2008 and the pressure began to intensify for getting Ed out of the house. We used gates to section off the house to keep Ed and the baby separated, but that didn't do much to satisfy the concerns of family members who, justifiably, did not want to risk the chance of the baby being bitten.

For months I searched across the country for some organization or sanctuary or shelter that would take Ed. Every single one turned me down; they were not willing or able to deal with all of the issues he had. By February 2009, Jennifer was a year old and moving about the house. I was out of options and couldn't wait any longer; I made a call to our vet to find out information about euthanasia for Ed. I remember being barely able to speak on the phone during that conversation. For all his issues, we loved Ed and did not want to resort to putting him down, but it appeared that it was the only choice left.

It was out of sheer luck that I was able to find Smiling Dog Farms on the Internet. They were a sanctuary for animals that were specifically unadoptable because of behavior or any other issues. The farm was run by Jay Hellerich and Richard Clements and was located just south of Houston, Texas. After an e-mail to them about Ed and his story, they responded back quickly with an invitation to have him come live at the farm. This was not going to be an easy decision to make; the total investment to make this happen for Ed would be north of $2,000 after van rental, plane tickets home and getting his new house and pen built at the farm. But this was an animal's life, and we felt it would be worth it to make the trip and give Ed a chance at a new life. We accepted Jay and Ricky's invitation.

We rented a van for the trip from Michigan to Texas, bought our airfare home, packed up the van and headed out in late March of 2009. We drove from Detroit to Memphis in one day; we took Ed to see Graceland the following morning. The next day, we headed out, drove all day, stopped in Houston for the night and had our last pizza dinner with Ed in the hotel room. The following morning we headed out to Wharton, a small town about a half hour south of Houston where the farm was located. We stopped at a McDonald's and shared a final lunch with Ed; he had chicken nuggets and fries, and I think I bought him a hamburger as well. We stood together in a grassy field behind the restaurant for a while, not really wanting to go and drop him off for the last time.

We met Jay and Ricky and saw Ed's new home, a cute little doghouse in a fenced yard. It was incredibly difficult and emotional to leave him there, but Jay and Ricky were very understanding and sympathetic. We had to leave for the airport so we said our goodbyes and headed out, in tears the whole way to the airport.

We continued to send Ed treats and blankets during his stay at the Farms, and I can only hope that maybe he knew they were from us. Jay and Ricky would send us pictures and updates on how Ed was doing, even sending us a picture in a doghouse picture frame. Ed was eventually partnered with a female dog named Ilse, who lived as his companion for at least a year. The two apparently got along fabulously.

In March of 2013 I received an e-mail from Jay with the subject line "Very sad news." My heart sank and I assumed the worst, and my suspicions were confirmed: Ed had passed away. He did not say if Ed had been sick or what the circumstances might have been; at this point Ed would have been around 10 or 11 years old, so old age may have likely been the cause. Apparently he lay down on the porch of his dog house and simply went to sleep. Ilse was there with him on the porch, whimpering and not leaving his side until Jay and Ricky discovered Ed the next morning.

Ed was the first dog I ever owned, and even though we had some very difficult times with him, overall he was a good dog and one that I still miss to this day, almost one year after his passing and nearly five years after we took him to Texas. I especially miss our walks. Hopefully he realized that he was a loved dog. We will always be grateful to

Jay and Ricky and Smiling Dog Farms for giving Ed the opportunity to live for a few more years, enjoy a few more sunsets and even find new companionship.

For more information on Smiling Dog Farms and their mission of providing homes and food for the hundreds of unadoptable animals in their care, check out their website at smilingdogfarms.org.

Jeff Lelek is a 9-year employee of the Dearborn Public Library with 15 total years of service with the City of Dearborn. He is married with two kids and has very little time or money to pursue his interests, which include movies, golf, writing, listening to music and playing the piano.

Rouge by Jim Miller

Since she set foot on its soil nearly one year ago, Louisa hated America. The heat and the mosquitoes in the summer yielding to the dreary frigid grays of winter that lasted half the year made her yearn for her beloved France each day. And the people, the rude, vulgar, crude colonists—the sound of spoken English and the volume at which they spoke it, made her cringe.

It was nothing at all like her beloved Paris.

She tried not to think of Paris so much now, for when she did, a feeling of sorrow formed in her belly and welled up to her lungs and eyes and threatened to swallow her whole. To even think of her gold and ivory brush sitting on her mahogany vanity, near the window, overlooking the garden would bring tears to her eyes.

"Why did Papa have to bring us here?" she asked Isabella, aged 12, two years her senior.

"You know why, foolish girl, Papa was sent by the king—he is an important businessman," Isabella answered.

"If he is so important, why did he get sent here, and why did he have to take us too?"

"Oh silly child, go play with your dolls," Isabella said, waving Louisa away as if she were one of the many gnats bombarding their cheeks as they sat beneath the maple tree.

Louisa turned to the two dolls she brought from home and whispered softly to them, "Hush precious ones, Mama will take good care of you. No one can hurt you now, just close your eyes."

For Louisa, the dolls drifted off to a deep sleep, dreaming of a picnic near a field of daises along the banks of the Seine.

Louisa too became drowsy, her eyelids weighed down from a dense fatigue, and she closed her eyes. In the shadowy world between sleeping and waking she heard a dog bark. She giggled once and mumbled, "Doggie," before falling into a deep, restful sleep.

***

"Raining in the house!" Louisa thought as she jumped awake.

But the wetness on her cheek was not from the rain, but from him—a small, curly haired terrier—a dog, licking her face!

Louisa squealed with delight.

"Who are you, little friend?"

The dog responded by wagging his tail and licking her again in the face.

"That tickles," Louisa laughed. "Oh you silly thing!" She stooped low and picked up the dog. "You are so precious, I love you already. I hope Mama and Papa let me keep you. I hope, I hope. Would you like to stay with me and be my friend?"

The dog responded with a rapidly wagging tail, then stood up on its hind legs and barked one short bark.

Louisa laughed, "I'll take that as a yes then."

Now to convince Mama and Papa, Louisa's mind reeled as she concocted plans and reasons why she should be able to keep the dog. Mama hated America too, especially here in the territories. Boston was tolerable, perhaps more an outpost than a place of culture, but tolerable. These territories by the Great Lakes, however, with the miles of dirt and dark forests, the rodents and vermin, the dangerous vagabonds—no pianoforte for miles—she deplored life here. Father was too busy with business—away for weeks at a time—and he was so loyal to the king, he would do whatever the crown requested.

After mulling it over a minute or two, no suitable plan came to her, so she pulled the dog close to her, marched straight into the small parlor and stood before her parents. Before Louisa even opened her mouth, her mother screamed, "Get that rat out of the house!"

"It's not a rat, Mother, it's a dog."

"Same difference. Michael, tell her to get rid of it."

"Louisa, now you know how your mother feels about vermin."

With that, the dog leaped from Louisa's arms, trotted to mother's feet and sat. It tilted its head slightly to the left and made a soft whimper.

Mother laughed, how could she help herself? This thing, this mutt, this creature with its soft brown eyes—did it possess some magic to melt her heart so?

"You may keep him," Mother laughed, gingerly petting the dog's head. The dog leaped onto Mother's lap and she screamed, before they all laughed.

"What shall you name him?" Papa asked.

Louisa looked at the dog and thought. The August sunlight poured through the window and upon the dog, illuminating the reddish tint of his fur, so that for an instant he appeared less a dog than a small, glowing, ruby colored orb, a thing of magic.

"Rouge, I shall name him Rouge," Louisa said definitively.

***

Louisa and Rouge had many adventures that summer. They chased birds and squirrels through the forest. Rouge was a clever hunter, sneaking quietly after his prey, before barking and jumping. But he never caught anything, not as far as Louisa knew. They spent hours splashing at the banks of the Lafayette River, cooling themselves in the blistering August heat.

Children from the village, who once looked upon Louisa as if she were a leper, now came over to play. Louisa, Rouge and the children chased each other through the fields, laughing and singing. Louisa taught the children to count in French, and the children taught her to name all the colors in English.

Rouge did not even mind when Louisa, Isabella and a few village girls placed a blue bow on his head and drank tea beneath the tall oak tree in front of their house.

As summer gave way to autumn, Louisa found herself loving Rouge more each day, her heart expanding, growing to love the colors of the trees and the smiling faces of the children from the village who now greeted her with a smile, and she returned the smile and said in soft, clipped English, "Hello."

When the rains of late autumn arrived and the air was cold and thick, Louisa hardly cared at all. The days spent inside petting Rouge and having him accompany her on her chores, or sitting by the table by the fireplace completing her lessons as he curled on a small blanket by the hearth were very pleasant days indeed.

Still, one day in early November, when the rains finally stopped, at least for the moment, Louisa clapped her hands together. "Let's go on an outing, Rouge. Let's go see the sunlight today!"

Rouge followed along, wagging his tail, as Louisa pulled close her coat.

"Stay out of the puddles," Mama warned as they passed.

"Of course Mama," Louisa responded.

"You too little Rouge—no one wants to smell a wet dog all day!" Mama teased.

Their walk quickly gave way to a trot, then a full-fledged run, like the many deer, so good to be in the fresh air and feel so free, as if they were floating above the soft ground. The sunlight stabbed through the outstretched arms of the trees, leaves shed completely, preparing for the long sleep of winter.

"We're like dragons!" Louisa said, marveling at their exhalations, tiny puffs of smoke in the frigid air.

They arrived at the banks of the river within moments. Its red brown waters, swelling over the banks from the torrential rains. Louisa threw in a stick and watched it race to the center of the river towards the large white rock, where it swirled then disappeared beneath the surface.

"That's so fast!" Louisa exclaimed.

She threw in another stick. It too raced towards the rock and it too was pulled under by the relentless undertow. Off in the distance, Louisa heard voices calling—her mother calling her back for lunch.

"Already?" Louisa said. "One more good throw," she told Rouge.

Louisa picked up a bigger stick, a branch really, broken off a maple tree, nearly as long as her leg. She stepped close to the edge of the river to get a good toss. As she stepped forward, her foot stepped on a rock at the river's edge. It was wet from the rains and the swollen river seemed to reach up and pull at Louisa's ankle. She wavered and then tumbled into the frigid, rushing current.

In an instant she was pulled under and then she popped up briefly, gasping and choking, as she was swept towards the white rock. Rouge began barking and jumped in after her. His small legs paddling after her; paddling and barking, paddling and barking, but he did not get any closer. Louisa was gasping for air, unable to scream, as she flailed her arms to break from the current, to somehow return to the safe banks.

It was futile.

At the rock, Louisa and Rouge were pulled under, as if they too were sticks, mere flotsam, void of density.

***

For days, Louisa wavered in and out of feverish dreams, reveries that danced between glorious and horrific.

When she awoke in the predawn hours of the fourth day, Louisa's mother, seated on a rocking chair, began to cry.

"Oh, my baby, my beautiful baby," as she hugged Louisa and stroked her face, noticeably cooler, free from fever.

She explained it all to Louisa: "Some men heard Rouge barking wildly, like he was mad or possessed. They knew something was wrong so they raced over. When they got to the river, they saw you stretched out on the riverbank… Rouge was standing beside you, barking and licking your face… You've been in a mad fever for days… We all thought we'd lose you… Rouge saved your life Louisa… That little dog… He saved your life…"

Mama's voice trailed off and she sat in silence, smiling at Louisa, kissing her forehead and stroking her lips and nose and cheeks.

Louisa wondered where Rouge was, but was afraid to know the answer. She paused for a moment, took a deep breath and asked, "Rouge—where is he?"

Louisa's heart sank as her mother turned away.

Louisa, crestfallen, gazed towards the rocking chair, too weary to weep. But then her eye fell upon the quilt piled on the floor. Was that quilt moving? Then the soft red fur and deep brown eyes of Rouge peered from beneath the quilt. He crawled from beneath it, hopped onto the bed and began licking Louisa's face. The fire cast a soft glow upon Rouge's fur. Although Louisa knew it was impossible, Rouge seemed to be smiling at her.

Jim Miller is a writer and educator living in Dearborn, Michigan. jmillerwords@gmail.com

We Are Connected by L. Glenn O'Kray

Perhaps it would have happened anyway. But this is how it began for me.

About thirty years ago, our daughter, Rebecca, then a snotty-nosed teenager, pleaded for a dog. She promised that she would clean up after the animal. She promised to take the pup for a walk. She promised the dog wouldn't bother us.

I was not supportive of the idea of getting another pet. My wife, Jane, and I had had one dog whom we had put to sleep. I didn't feel like cleaning up after another dog. I didn't think that a 13-year-old would come through.

But, we got a dog. Jane and I had another living being in our household. Our daughter's promises were broken on the second day.

At first I resented the intrusion of that animal. Our first dog did not nip at our legs. Our first dog did not require a daily walk. This new animal, Casey, did.

She was a pest. She was half beagle and half hound. She would howl at the drop of a hat. She would chase squirrels. She would get out of the yard, and I would have to chase her down the street.

I took her for about a mile walk almost every day. As it turned out, I found myself looking forward to the walks. At the time I was director of financial aid at Henry Ford Community College. While I found my job for the most part very exhilarating, I found it very stressful as well. In retrospect, my daily walks with Casey probably saved my life. Though stressed, I had no strokes. Though stressed, I had no heart attacks.

Meanwhile, Rebecca continued to mature. She became a vegetarian at the age of 15 and still is some 29 years later. At first our meals were meatless, if only to make Jane's cooking easier. Rebecca went to college, moved out of the home, and got married. My limited eating of meat continued. One night I dreamed I had all the feelings and emotions of a cow being led to slaughter. I began to consider vegetarianism.

Casey developed bone cancer. I took her to the vet to have her put down. Casey loved marshmallows. I brought some with me to ease her into the world beyond this one. As the doctor brought her suffering to an end, I thought about the closeness that I had developed with my four-legged friend. I thought of the connections living beings have with other living beings. I thought of how in some countries dogs are eaten. I thought of how in all countries sentient beings are eaten.

Connections go beyond marshmallows. To give testimony to our connections with animals, I have not eaten meat for the past twenty years.

L. Glenn O'Kray has been an administrator or adjunct instructor at Henry Ford Community College for 40 years. He is on the Dearborn Historical Commission. He and his wife, Jane, live two blocks from his place of birth in Dearborn. lglennokray@cavtel.net

Gypsy by Patty Podzikowski

There is a poem I have always enjoyed that really sums up how I feel about my parents called "When You Thought I Wasn't Looking," credited to Mary Rita Schilke Korzan. It has many lines, but the one that relates to this story is this: "When you thought I wasn't looking, I saw you feed a stray cat, and I learned that it was good to be kind to animals."

My mom and dad were both animal lovers and extremely kind people. Growing up, we had a very wide range of animals in and out of our house. We had the usual dogs and cats, but there were also bunnies, birds, fish, turtles, a snake, ducks, and even a rooster! Given that we lived in Dearborn, which at that time was no longer a rural area, it made it kind of difficult to keep a few of those animals. No matter what happened, though, my parents always dealt with all of the animals that ended up in our house with respect and gentle care.

In my teen years, we got a puppy for my dad right after he had quadruple bypass heart surgery. My mom read somewhere that animals were good therapy for men who underwent heart surgery. We researched and decided to get a Lhasa Poo (a mixed breed that is part Poodle and part Lhasa Apso). We were under the impression that we would be getting a small lap dog, especially since we got the runt of the litter, but that was not to be. The mother must've been a standard size Poodle, which can grow to be very large. Regardless, we all loved that dog to death! Even though technically she was for my dad, my older sister and I ended up taking care of her, loving her and just being with her most of the time.

We decided to name her Gypsy, and she was the sweetest dog in the world. As the years passed, she became a big part of our family. It seemed like no matter where we went, Gypsy traipsed along beside us, keeping us company. She acted like she was a small lap dog, but when she jumped up on her two hind legs, she reached our shoulders easily, and we were not short people! She loved to curl up on our laps, and really seemed to have a special relationship with my older sister. The two of them were inseparable for a while. Like a lot of dogs, she was sad when my sister left the house, and when she returned, was overjoyed. It really did seem like she knew when she was getting close to returning home. Some say that dogs have a sixth sense that allows them to know this, and I truly believe it. Gypsy could've been in a deep sleep, and suddenly without any prompting, she would get up and go to the door. Shortly thereafter, my sister would walk in and the joy that was evident in both her and the dog was pure and sweet.

Tragically, my sister was taken from us much too soon. She was murdered in 1994, and it was a devastating time for our family. I saw how this affected all the people, but I also witnessed grief in Gypsy. She became lethargic and no longer wanted to play. She would go to the door that my sister always entered through and wait for hours for her to return. She slept in her bed. Some argue that animals do not experience grief like human beings, but I witnessed it firsthand, and I know that they most certainly do. They might display it differently, but if there is love between a person and an animal and all of a sudden that person is gone, they must somehow deal with the loss.

This takes me back to the original point of the story. My parents, who were devastated above everyone else, also witnessed this behavior from Gypsy. This helped them in a way. They were witness to just how much my sister touched every living thing in her life, and appreciated her all the more. This came from her watching their gentle treatment of all the animals that we had in our household throughout her life. My sister learned the proper way to handle all living creatures by watching how my parents treated all animals. They let Gypsy get through her grief, and they eventually got through their grief. It never went away; it became a part of them that they didn't ask for, but that they handled with dignity and grace.

Years later, Gypsy became very ill and eventually died. I like to think that she was reunited with my sister and they once again play, snuggle, and love just like they did here on earth.

Patty Podzikowski is married and a mom of two children. She is a librarian and in her spare time loves to spend time with her family and read!

Dog: Based on a True Story by Steven R. Roberts

"What's his name, again?" I asked Bryan as he was being pulled behind a sandy colored poodle of considerable size. My neighbor's dog had been around for a couple of years but I was usually at work during the day and rarely saw the dog on his walks.

"Andy," Bryan said. "I'm trying to mellow him with a bit of exercise but I don't think it's working."

"He is spirited," I said. "I heard you were having him trained as, what do they call it, a therapy dog."

"Yes, the dogs are trained along with their owners to go into the hospitals and comfort kids and adults. We try to bring a little relief from the medical routine."

"How's that working out?" I asked, reaching down to pet Andy's head.

"Humm, Andy's done well during our hospital visits but I'm afraid I failed the training," Bryan said.

"What?" I asked. "How can that be?"

"Well, last week Andy and I met with our group of therapy dogs and owners in the hospital parking lot. There were three other dogs in our group. They were all running around pulling on their leashes and chasing each other; nipping and smelling each other, just normal dog stuff. That was until we walked through the hospital doors when they settled down and walked quietly down the hall and into the patients' rooms.

"That day we spent a half hour on the second floor. The patients look forward to our visits and the extended-stay patients even call the dogs by name. Andy and the other dogs have been trained to be gentle even around children who can be nervous and jumpy in their scary circumstances. Hugging and getting licks from the gentle, furry dogs is a welcome diversion."

"Sounds like a terrific service you are providing," I said. "What do you mean, you failed the training?"

"Well, next we moved up to the adult trauma wing. In the third room we visited, there was a lady in a coma. Her daughter was sitting quietly in the only chair in the room. Her eyes were red and she was wiping tears away with a wadded up Kleenex. She forced a smile as we came into the room. Andy sat by the bed for a moment, then moved closer and laid his jaw on the lady's wrist. The monitoring devises in the room hummed and beeped a quiet rhythm but there was no sign of life.

"I looked toward the daughter and then slowly shook my head. 'Gentle Andy,' I said, wiping at one of my eyes. Even though we've been trained to remain composed, these scenes have always been hard for me to take.

"The daughter looked up and took a deep breath. 'Thanks for coming,' she said looking up at me. 'Six months ago a truck ran into her out on Outer Drive near Michigan Avenue. It broke several bones and the doctors said we almost lost her that night.' She closed her eyes and lowered her head. I got the idea she didn't want to say more about the accident or anything else.

"Andy raised his head and started licking the back of the lady's wrist. Her hand cupped up from the wrinkled sheets and Andy nuzzled his nose under her hand, making a low purring-like noise in his head.

"'Dog,' the lady whispered without opening her eyes. A slight smile came to her lips as the room went quiet and even the monitors seemed to pause. The daughter stood, blinking her eyes wide open. She stepped to her mother's bed, petting Andy's head and putting her other hand on her mother's forehead.

"'Mother!' she said. 'Mother, are you all right?' Slowly her mother opened her eyes for a moment and blinked away at the glue that had been holding them shut since the accident. She opened her mouth to speak but only managed a smile.

"'Oh, thank God,' the daughter said. 'Dog' is the first word my mother has said in six months. It's the first word we've heard from her since the night of the accident. Thank you and thank you Andy for coming to our rescue.' She leaned over and gave Andy a huge hug and pushed the nurse's call button. Andy licked her cheek."

"By this time I was sobbing out loud sitting with my head in my hands and elbows on my knees in the only chair in the room. 'Are you okay?' the daughter asked. I nodded, speechlessly. A nurse rushed into the room and took over. She went to the mother's bed with a big smile and took the patient's vital signs.

"'Are you okay?' she asked turning toward me. The smile had disappeared. The nurse's look told me I should leave and reduce the number of problems in the room. Andy and I left the hospital immediately and I managed to drive us home. Andy had been true to his training and I had failed mine completely.

"Since then, I have been reassigned to walking Andy twice a day. Now my wife takes him to the hospital each week for licks and hugs with the patients. Andy continues to serve."

Steven R. Roberts, a longtime resident of Dearborn, is a veteran of the auto industry working in Europe and Dearborn. He is committed to a variety of community and charitable programs and currently serves as President of the Dearborn Library Foundation. Roberts has also written eight books, including action-adventure novels and a book of poetry. See www.steverroberts.com for more information. He is on board for The Big Read program.

Old Man, Old Dog by Steven R. Roberts

Old men and old dogs think the same
Of hopes and dreams that never came
They walk the streets, two ends of the lead
Shufflin', Sniffin' spent leaves, half speed.

Roaming hours on paths not there
No need to hurry back, no one to care
Show dog and show man sifting life's sand
Wet eyes meet, old dog and old man.

Rabbits fear not the chase
Fate delayed not denied, the fall from grace
Breathe in nature's juices damp and sweet
Old friends they soon will meet.

Bent in the smoky night chatting away
Bout a long ago busier day
Fought the good fight, right at the time
Last to go will drag the other's end behind.

Steven R. Roberts, a longtime resident of Dearborn, is a veteran of the auto industry working in Europe and Dearborn. He is committed to a variety of community and charitable programs and currently serves as President of the Dearborn Library Foundation. Roberts has also written eight books, including action-adventure novels and a book of poetry. See www.steverroberts.com for more information. He is on board for The Big Read program.

Speedo Can by Lisa Rose

Speedo couldn't jump like his brother who had strong legs and a sleek furry body. And he wasn't pretty like his sister who had one blue and one brown eye that Australian Shepherds are admired for. Both of them won many ribbons and trophies.

Most of the time Speedo didn't care and would rather chase squirrels all over town. He knew where everything was in the neighborhood because he went on long walks with the boy. He knew where the boy's father mailed packages that had white foam inside that he liked to play with and where the boy and his mother picked up her stiff pressed clothes that he could not play with. He knew where the bakery was that sometimes gave him a doggy biscuit and the boy a cookie. Speedo even knew where they kept the big red trucks with the flashing lights and loud sirens. Sometimes he watched them rush to help people.

One day the boy asked, "Why can't you jump like your brother and or be pretty like your sister?" That day Speedo didn't feel like chasing squirrels. He sat by the window all day and most of the night.

Until...

Speedo knew something was very wrong with the boy. He went to his bed and licked his face. The boy would not wake up. Speedo barked and barked. Still the boy would not wake up. His brother and sister opened their eyes and then went back to sleep. Speedo rushed to the boy's mother and father's room. Again, he barked and barked. But they only told him to "settle down."

Speedo knew what he had to do. He jumped out of the window and ran and ran faster than any squirrel ever could all through the town. Finally, he arrived in front of the fire station and barked and barked louder than any dog ever could.

"Hey, stop that!" yelled a firefighter out of the window.

Speedo would not stop.

Finally, one of the firefighters came out of the station house. Speedo tugged at his pant leg and tried to pull him to the boy.

"Hey, I think this dog is trying to show me something. Maybe someone is in trouble."

The firefighter got in his truck and followed Speedo as he raced back to the boy. The firefighter found the boy. He was very sick and the firefighter called for more help. The boy had to leave in a smaller truck with flashing lights for a while, but soon he returned home and felt much better.

From then on Speedo always watched the boy very carefully and never went out for long to chase squirrels. Now the boy says, "Speedo can't jump like his brother and isn't pretty like his sister, but he is the dog that saved my life."

Lisa Rose lives in Farmington Hills with her husband and daughter. Her picture book, Oh No! The Easter Bunny Is Allergic to Eggs! *is currently available through MeeGenius, with a sequel,* Oh No! The Tooth Fairy Broke Her Wing! *due to be released in March 2014. Her picture books* Shmulik Paints the Town *and* The Hungry Latke Monster *will be released by Kar-Ben Publishing in 2016.*

Fuzzy Brother by Isabella Rowan

It was May 2001 and my best girlfriend and I were hosting our annual neighborhood garage sale. It was an unusually hot day with the temperature topping out at 92 degrees. While my friend and I were baking in the sun on the driveway and waiting for customers, our five children (her three and my two) were wreaking havoc inside the air-conditioned house.

This was a particularly sad and stressful time for my children and me. I was going through a divorce from their father and my husband of 13 years. My eleven-year-old daughter and my nine-year-old son were struggling to cope with the break-up of our family and the last several months had seen a lot of emotional outbursts. It was heart-breaking for all of us.

On this hot day in May, my next door neighbor came over and asked me if we wanted a dog. For free. Apparently her sister had a new puppy—a one-year-old Cockapoo—and he was being horribly terrorized by her sister's young kids. The puppy needed a new home as soon as possible. Now the one thing my children had always asked for during their childhood was a dog. And while my husband had grown up with dogs, his answer was always "no." I wasn't really sure if this was a good time to take on a dog, but I told her to bring the puppy over so I could meet him before I made a decision.

A couple of hours later she walks over with a small ball of apricot fluff in her arms. Tigger was simply adorable. As soon as she put him down in the grass, he rolled over onto his back at my feet, four furry paws in the air as if to say, "Do what you will with me, but here I am. Take me, I'm yours." It was love at first sight and an overwhelming, "Yes! We'll keep him!"

I gathered this sweet thing into my arms and went to the side door of the house. I opened the door partway and asked my kids if they wanted to meet their new baby brother. Stunned silence gave way to peals of laughter when I set Tigger down in front of them.

For the rest of the afternoon, I sold used treasures to passersby against the backdrop of giggles and shouts of delight. It was the first time in many long months, perhaps even years, that happiness had visited my house. Who knew it would come in the form of a little dog named Tigger? He was a loyal and true friend to my kids for the rest of their childhood. He was a bed hog, playmate, secret keeper and snack stealer who loved to ride shotgun when they were learning to drive. He truly was their little brother.

Fourteen years later, my kids are grown and out of the house, but Tigger is still with me. He whiles away his days sleeping in his puffy

dog bed until I get home from work when he bounds to the door to greet me and barks and dances about wildly until I take off my socks. What is it with dogs and dirty socks, anyway?! At Christmas he gets presents, on birthdays he eats cake and ice cream, and in between he sometimes goes for a ride in the car to get a cheeseburger from the drive-thru. Always the center of attention at our family gatherings, his funny antics still make us laugh.

Tigger is a special gift that came to us at a time when we needed to be happy again. And if you look at him real close, in just the right light, and from just the right angle, you can see them—two little fuzzy angel wings.

Isabella is a librarian at Dearborn Public Library. She enjoys reading, watching movies and hanging out with Tigger.

Part of the Pack by Michelle Saad

Our first family dog had a past. Shady, spotty and definitely mixed. We picked her up on a farm when Dad found out they were giving her away and we named her Pepper on the car ride home. We were a pack of strange kids coaxing her into the house and calling her a name she did not yet realize was hers. She didn't know which way to look or what to sniff first but we did our best to make her feel at home. Before too long however her past caught up to us; Pepper was pregnant.

We were thrilled, oblivious to our parents' shock and sideways glances at one another; our dog came with more dogs! With so many kids, one dog was not enough to go around anyway. But, we had to wait. When the projected date was announced Mom saw a conflict in scheduling. We always went camping at Island Park for Memorial Day weekend. It set the summer and we were going.

My industrious mother got a dryer box and modified it for the trip. She removed the top and part of a side so that Pepper could step in and out over the half wall. We lined it with older blankets and put it in the bed of the truck for the trip.

In the '80s it was not unusual for kids to ride in the back of a pick-up, especially in the farmlands and foothills of Eastern Idaho. For a family of two adults, six kids and no back seat it was the only way everyone was coming. So we hitched up the trailer and we three oldest kids got in the truck bed with the box and Pepper, while the three younger kids rode in the cab with Mom and Dad.

After about forty-five minutes on the road, Pepper started having her puppies. My older brother tapped on the window and when Mom turned her head she didn't even need to open the slide-window to hear him shout. "She's having her puppies!"

Dad nodded that he heard when Mom repeated the news and started pulling to the side of the road. We made way for Mom to check and confirm the claim, which she did with an, "Oh, yeah." And just like that we had new seating assignments. My younger sister and I took Mom's seat and she stayed in the back with my older brother and the box of arriving puppies. We drove on.

My dad was probably the only one looking at the road the rest of the way. My siblings and I were all turned around with eyes and noses over the rim of the back window but still couldn't see into the box. Mom had taped a tarp to the top. She popped her head out and held up three fingers with a smile before leaning back in. Before we arrived at the campsite that number went up to five. By the time Dad had a tent set up for the box, Pepper was too nervous to continue. The wind had picked up and the flapping material was too disturbing for her. She would have to move into the trailer. Dad started with Pepper, carrying her into the door and setting her down while she watched him carefully scoop up each puppy and coddle them into the corner of the camper floor she would be sharing with my brother later. In the meantime, we were free to roam and play while she finally finished having her eight puppies.

The temperature continued to drop and it started to rain so it looked like Pepper would have to stay in the trailer with us. It was small for our number and we had to make use of any flat-ish surface for a bunk. The table was converted to a bed, cots in the back and the choice pick of the floor. We doubled up into them all. After the running and playing around we always did during the day it was still easy to find sleep.

While the rain tapped on the roof and peeked into the windows we took shelter together. We stuffed and stacked eight people and nine dogs into a four-person trailer. The puppies were tiny but many, every corner heaved with breathing forms and we were as happy as could be. I smiled from the rack I shared with both my sisters and laughed at how our family was already sleeping like a pack of dogs, one on top of the next.

Michelle Saad is a Dearborn resident, wife, mother of two and creative junkie. She plays the violin, writes poetic prose and draws stirring images with simple pencils.

Corky by John Sanchez

On March 18, 1994, I was returning home from a Hawaiian vacation with my girlfriend Rosalie. My mother, Alicia, asked if I could bring back a bag of Maui Potato Chips. When I arrived home, we went into the kitchen and talked about our vacation. I left the bag of Maui Chips in my carry-on luggage which was now sitting in the living room. While we were in the kitchen, Corky grabbed the bag of Maui Chips and proceeded to my mom's bedroom and ate all the chips. Corky took the empty bag and placed it back in my luggage. When we returned to the living room, Corky was sitting on the couch with his front paw hanging over the armrest. He acted like nothing had happened. I soon discovered what he had done and found leftover crumbs in my mom's bedroom. My mom never got her chips that year. We still laugh about this even after 20 years. Corky passed away on May 13, 2009. He was 19 years old. He was a great companion.

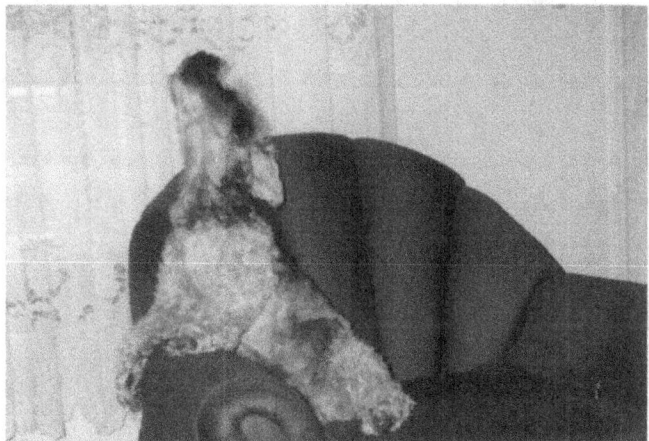

Author's note: When the City of Dearborn started testing the emergency warning system the first Saturday of each month at 1:00 p.m., Corky started jumping on the chair and began howling like a wolf. This would continue until the siren stopped. The included photo is Corky at his best.

John Sanchez has been the owner of the Alan Sanchez Landscaping Company for the last 38 years. He has landscaped over 3,400 homes in that time. He is an award-winning artist and owns Artistic Woodcarving. He specializes in marquetry paintings. sanchezart@aol.com

A Love Story Starring Jack and Zelda by Susie Duncan Sexton

"Some people don't understand why we help animals in need. We don't understand why they wonder." - Lucky Dog Rescue Blog

"Where do I begin to tell the story of how great a love can be?" Well, now…that assignment is easy as pie! Most folks who rrrreally know and understand me realize that I respect other species so deeply that I cannot ever find the appropriate words to express that pure reverence for dogs, cats, horses, bumblebees, alligators, swans, whales, cows, deer, pigs, sheep, duck-billed platypuses, ad infinitum. I am not ornery about this affection, but any living beings who breathe in and out, who have eyeballs, who possess hearts, and who feel, hear, see, sniff, touch, and taste…sure, allllll "creatures great and small" DO count and matter. I can honestly state that I was born believing that way…and thanks to gentle guidance along my path, from my favorite empathetic humans, my initial instincts have become doctrines of "successful living and letting live" which I recommend highly.

Keen observation of family pets, farm animals, zoo prisoners, circus entertainers, documentary stars, Walt Disney's animated mammals, storybook characters, and wildlife I happily have crossed paths with lead me to one conclusion. Human beings peacefully must share this globe with all living beings…we are just one species of so very, very many. For the moment, I'll focus on  my regal *Great Gatsby* Dingo-type mongrel whom we named Jack because a dozen years ago his intensely bright yellow color conjured up an image of recently deceased movie star Jack Lemmon, but this majestic canine also resembled Michael Caine who portrayed "Alfie," so the proper label remained up for grabs for a couple of days. Jack? Jay Gatsby? Michael? Alfie?

His "Bonnie & Clyde"ish, eventual-roommate Zelda and he, who got captured on the lam by the local cops while both mutts joyously veered back and forth between McDonald's and Wal-Mart, landed in jail near the water plant in C.C.'s once-upon-a-time rather makeshift "shelter" several years back and were scheduled for euthanasia after their mug shots got featured in the local newspaper prior to the July 4th holiday. The Modus Operandi for ages! I, reminding myself of Al Pacino/Michael Corleone in that glorious scene in the *Godfather* Trilogy (where Al hides in a hospital to protect his gravely injured papa Marlon Brando from further harm at the merciless hands of disgruntled Mafia guys), lurked behind one of Dr. Mike Mawhorter's pillars in his new facility as the two gaunt, wayward vagabonds were delivered by pick-up truck for the "final solution" for stray, wandering, and over-reproduced living beings whom nobody wants.

I extended to Mike an offer he "could not refuse": I would "spring" for neutering (Jack!) and spaying (Zelda!) in addition to the battery of shots for each "convict" plus de-worming—the entire nine yards— rather than the doc receiving the obligatory, paltry euthanasia fee that would have transferred from city government to veterinarian. My bill totaled over 400 bucks...and that was a dozen years ago!

I brought post-operative "patient" Zelda "home" first. She had an endearing quality of utter submission, rolling onto her back and lov- ingly gazing at humans while batting her seriously Ginger Roger-ish eyes. Charming! However, during her first evening on my back porch, she disassembled every board game, lamp, padded chair, and window treatment within her grasp. Vandalism at its very worst! I decided to teach her that the opposite of "submissiveness" is NOT a rampaging romp by Attila the Hun, via my instruction and encouragement NEVER to roll over again. I felt like a "dog whisperer" extraordinaire. At the height of her bipolar behavior, I decided to name her "Schizophrenia" which my friend JoEllen advised against. Thus, "Zelda," the sadly nutty wife of F. Scott Fitzgerald, stuck as the perfect nom de plume...the perfect designation under which she would write L-O-V-E into our lives and across the sky for a dozen years to follow! She developed into an amazing ALPHA dog worthy of a novel! Like her namesake, our girl jumped into a series of backyard kiddie pools throughout the years just as drunken, party-girl Zelda Fitzgerald once frolicked repeatedly in gushing water fountains of public squares around the globe!

In a couple of days, strapping, muscular Jack and clueless Susie left the vet's never really having ever been officially introduced to one another...I might as well have been Santa Claus being dragged across the heavenly horizon by Donner and Blitzen and Rudolph and all of them there reindeer combined with a team of huskies as well! He positively sailed once we exited the door, and the two of us careened allll over the parking lot...me at one end of the flimsy leash and he—in all of his massiveness and his happiness to be "free at last"—at the other! I soared across the pavement absolutely airborne! My hairdresser Yvette, departing for home from the nearby Northern Highlights Beauty Shop, assumed incorrectly that I enjoyed power-walking my energetic dog, and she gleefully honked as Jack and I flew alongside her passing car which then disappeared into the distance. Help?

Long (happy) story short, Jack and Zelda enjoyed a dozen years joined at the hip. Together they formed an exquisite Remington sculpture...they HAD to share vet appointments—none of that "one at a time" stuff—or they would sulk and pout and whimper. They were so strong that once Don and I were pulled across the vet's office floor while sitting in our respective chairs in the lobby. Iditarod, here we come! They were one. LIFE was good.

Gorgeous Zelda, the Alpha dog with the schizoid name, impressed us as a model of graceful serenity as the years fled by...then one sad day, she indicated that her life was nearing its conclusion. I gave her a gentle bath, and we petted her and scratched behind her still perked up ears. She could no longer stand. We lifted her into our car, listened carefully to the veterinarian's advice, knelt down on his tiled floor on either side of her, and held her and kissed her as the needle injected whatever chemical concoction it is that terminates life forevermore. The "rainbow bridge," a man-made concept for coping—IF one buys into it—does not, for me, describe the hereafter but the NOW, in other words, the "bridge" being our gift in real time of many quality years of nurturing and of being nurtured by a beautiful being. All that is left of Zelda would be her paw print in cement courtesy of the veterinarian's staff, her collar with its jingling tags, a container full of her Shepherd/Collie mix fur, photographs, and our memories of having made a difference, of having saved a precious life, of Zelda having enhanced ours. Unconditional love all around. HOWEVER....

Whenever rain falls upon our roof, or thunder rumbles, lonely Jack paces the length of the back porch, quietly whines, paws at the door alerting us that Zelda may still be outside in the dark…that we forgot to bring her inside to sleep alongside her companion of so many years, her playmate, her best friend. I pat his head and offer him a soft blanket and a pillow and speak to him with assurance that Zelda sent me to spend some time with him and to make sure he is comfortable. Her name on my lips calms him. Now, how about that? But I don't refer to this process as me becoming a "dog whisperer" but rather a "dog listener"…other sentient beings in addition to humans speak to us and have done so since the beginning of time. I share that belief with a fellow who rescues horses from slaughter. His name is R. T. Fitch, author of *Straight from the Horse's Heart: A Spiritual Guide through Love, Loss, and Hope*, one of the loveliest and most important books which I have enjoyed in my lifetime.

Fitch dedicates his powerful stories to the memories of his mother "who always laughed at my jokes, greeted me with a smile and a hug while teaching me that it was okay for a man to cry" and to one of his exceptional horses named Ethan, "my teacher and mentor and guide who taught me to slow down, keep quiet, and listen. He was the voice of the herd."

Susie Duncan Sexton grew up in a very small town, Columbia City, Indiana. After graduating twelfth in her class at Ball State University (winning the first ever John R. Emens award for "most outstanding senior"), she returned to her hometown where she has worked as a teacher, a publicist, a museum curator, and a health lecturer.

Dylan and the Birds by Donald G. Smock

The gentlest dog that I ever had live with me was my buddy Dylan. He came into the shop where I was working and a young guy named Andy took him home that night. (Many guys there wanted the pup.) He was just a puppy about four months old, a good-looking little Collie mix. I told Andy that if for any reason it did not work out, I would gladly take the dog. I had had dogs just about my entire life and at that time I was with a lady who was depressed and I thought that having a puppy would help. Andy's parents would not let him keep the dog so I got him the following day, took him home and named him Dylan. The lady and I eventually broke up but the pup became my best friend and I lived with him for about 13 years.

I've never seen a more gentle dog (with the possible exception of little Lena, a Brussels Griffon who is with me now — but that is another story entirely). When I ended up with a miniature lop-eared rabbit that I could hold in the palm of one hand a few years after Dylan came to live with me, I would let the rabbit in the backyard with Dylan and he would watch over the little bunny and I never was afraid that anything bad would happen. (Later when I went to the Dearborn Animal Shelter and took home a little terrier who I called Mary to keep Dylan company, I knew that I could never leave Mr. Rabbit for a minute with her because she had a fierce hunting instinct, a heart of a lion — she was not afraid of anything!) But the gentle Dylan was special in that way. In 13 years he never bit anyone or any other animal to my knowledge and he had a very gentle disposition even with feisty little Mary.

One of the first indications of his gentle nature is the example of Dylan and the little bird that awed me when it happened. It was summer and sometimes I let him stay in the backyard while I was at work, with the gate padlocked of course. As I walked up the drive that day I saw Dylan in the backyard intently looking down at something as he lay on his belly in the grass with his ears all perked up. As I neared I saw the movement of wings or something and I thought initially that he was inspecting a butterfly; as I got closer, I could see that he had his front paw on the tail feathers of a tiny bird but was not harming it in any way. He very gently lifted his front paw and the tiny bird flew away. I was amazed by the incident and I still see it vividly in my mind whenever I think about him.

Then years later my friend Dylan died and of course I was heartbroken. At the end when I saw that he was ill and took him to the vet he had some kind of severe infection and died a few days later on October 4, the feast day of gentle St. Francis, who loved animals. The fact that he died on St. Francis' feast day seemed in some ways auspicious to me.

At that time I had a couple of pigeons who had lived on my roof for several years. Their "droppings" were often on the tarp covering my deacon's bench near the back door. It used to puzzle me and irritate me that when it rained for some reason the dirty rainwater on the tarp attracted Dylan and he would lap it up—even though I always had fresh water for him! "Crazy dog," I would think as I chased him away. It was only after his death that I learned that apparently pigeon droppings carried a lot of diseases. So it was that almost exactly a year after his demise when I was thinking about Dylan as the one year anniversary of his departure came, I had by then convinced myself that those pigeons with their filthy droppings had killed my dog. I was working on some repairs to my garage and as I went in the back door towards evening I muttered something to the effect that I "ought to kill those pigeons" (which I would never really do, but sometimes a person says something or thinks something that they don't really mean).

The next morning I had to go to the store to get some things to finish my work on the garage and when I returned home, instead of parking on the street—there was a city truck there doing something— I pulled in the driveway. I sat in my car for a minute to see if the truck was going to move. Out of the corner of my eye I caught some movement on the ground inside the gate to the backyard. As I looked, to my immense surprise, it appeared to be a rather large hawk! I thought that maybe he had come to drink some water from the dog bowl outside (Mary was still with me at that time; she too died a few years afterwards to the tune of the sacred Ave Maria sung by Andre Bocelli as I held her in my lap, but that too is another story), but then I saw that he had something in his talons and whatever it was fluttered. A moment later that hawk slowly took flight and I saw clearly that he was firmly grasping one of the pigeons. Even though it is a natural event, I felt sorry for the poor pigeon. I had actually always enjoyed their presence except for the droppings and the newly found knowledge of the disease associated with them which may have made my dog sick.

When I went in the backyard, the other pigeon's rib cage was lying there in the grass picked clean to the bone. It spooked me a little as I thought that I had somehow cursed those pigeons. It is the only time in my life (63 years) that I had ever seen a hawk in the backyard of anyplace that I lived. It was almost as if that hawk was avenging the gentle Dylan's death, he who would not even harm a little bird. I've never seen another hawk again in the backyard—and with little 7 ½ pound Lena, I am careful (she's not much bigger than a fat squirrel)—and I've never had any more pigeons take up residence at the house either. And for the record Lena is just about as gentle of demeanor.

Don Smock is a lifelong dog-lover who currently has a little Brussels Griffon (Lena) living with him as well as a recently adopted cat named Donny. His activities/jobs have included mechanic, tour bus driver, water wells driller, author & poet, folksinger, press operator, men's clothing salesman, agricultural extension worker, agricultural machinery researcher and Peace Corps volunteer in Africa.

Mr. X. by Kathryn Takach

My name is Xavier, but those closest to me like to call me Mr. X. I answer to both, though, so it just depends on how well you know me and how much I like you...but I digress. I was going to tell you a little bit about my adventures in this world. Like most stories, things did not start off the way they "should have" but as my owners tend to say—"such is life."

I was born the runt of my Bichon Frise litter, but everyone fawned over my good looks. They said I was as perfect a purebred as anyone had ever seen and that I'd make a great show dog! Imagine that? Even though I was on the smaller side, I was beautiful in every way! It was an exciting prospect! People would look at me and admire me for years to come... My owner was thrilled and had me tattooed, cleaned up, and ready to go. However, once I was old enough to compete, my owner got some bad news. Something about me not being able to create offspring and the show world turned its nose up at me... Whatever. Human speak can be confusing.

I'm not really sure what happened next, but my owner decided he needed to take a trip somewhere and that his family could watch me. So, I went to my owner's family's house. It was a bit overwhelming at first—they had these little humans called "kids" and they loved playing with me and petting me and feeding me! It was very different from my owner's house, where I only had other dogs to play with. I became especially close to the littlest human. She called me her baby and even made a special place for me to sleep!

My owner came back for me. He talked with his family and then the humans decided I should stay! So the owner's family became my owners...I told you humans can be confusing!

That summer, my little owner taught me how to play soccer! All I had to do was take the ball and run it around the yard and everyone was so impressed. Apparently it doesn't take much to amuse humans either...

There are times when humans get pretty angry though. Like the one time my little owners were selling these yummy smelling things called "chocolate bars." I followed that scent straight into my big owners' room and found an entire box under their bed. My big lady owner yelled at me and told me she couldn't believe I ate 10 candy bars "wrappers and all" (whatever that means). All I know is that I enjoyed them.

Then there was the time when my little girl owners left their beads out and I ate a bunch of them. My big owners yelled at me about having to watch them pass or something. Come to think of it, the majority of the time that someone yelled at me, it was because I ate something that they said I shouldn't have...

Whenever someone yelled at me, though, I always found a way to let them know I wasn't happy. My favorite tactic was to *growl at them when they tried to touch me*. Of course, they figured this out and learned that I would just give in and be nice again. Or there was the *sneak into one of the owner's rooms and make a mess* tactic, but then I usually just got into more trouble. Or I would *stay up late or wake up early and bark and bark and bark and bark until someone couldn't stand it anymore* and they'd let me out of my room. All in all, you can say I've had a good life.

Kathryn Takach is the teen librarian for Dearborn Public Library. She found inspiration in this story from her childhood family pet.

Greyhound by Dennis Underwood

I

He curls in the back
Of the newly bought crate.
All he's ever known
Until now has been
A crate, a muzzle,
Food and racing

How do I give him
His freedom?

II

He sleeps on the bed
Where the crate used to be.
A blanket (his very own)
Over him.
Scattered dog toys all around;
Little pieces of his heart.

How do I give him
Surety of Love?

III

He's racing in circles
Where I had a backyard.
He's chased his "squeakies,"
So now he just runs
For pure joy.
He knows he's loved
And in return, so do I.

How did he find
So much love
To give to me?

Dennis Underwood is a 69-year-old Vietnam veteran. He began writing about three years ago. He is married with four adult children and two grandchildren. He and his wife live with four rescued cats and one greyhound rescued from the track in Florida. dennisu@umich.edu

No by Dennis Underwood

No! Puppy, puppy, please don't go.
Puppy, puppy, I love you so.

Puppy, my puppy, don't lie down.
Puppy, good puppy, get up from the ground.

Puppy, come and play with me.
Please good puppy, don't leave me.

You were just playing "run puppy, run."
You mustn't stop, you can't be done.

Who will meet me at the door
When I come from the puppy store?

I'll keep the rugs that made me trip.
We put them down so you wouldn't slip.

You loved your toys, see, here are some
We can play, if you will come, puppy, come.

Dennis Underwood is a 69-year-old Vietnam veteran. He began writing about three years ago. He is married with four adult children and two grandchildren. He and his wife live with four rescued cats and one greyhound rescued from the track in Florida. dennisu@umich.edu

Pesky Pooch by Jane Vos

We are blessed with five children, a son and four daughters. When our son, Daniel, finished high school in 2000, he left that fall for university. He moved to Lexington, VA to attend Washington and Lee University. The transition was a bit of culture shock as this middle class young man embarked on his studies at this prestigious place which attracted wealthy southerners.

Each fall, the whole family (Doug, Jane, Charis, Priscilla, Talitha and Promise) would drive down for Parents' Weekend. One year, to save some money (and embark on a memorable adventure!?), we decided to camp near the university. Mind you, it was the end of October. I remember arriving late on a Friday night; we were shivering as we walked to the bathroom and most of us took a hot shower to prepare to set up the tent.

The next morning, some of us woke up and scurried to the bathroom to take care of ablutions. Seemingly out of nowhere, this little furry creature appeared. It looked like part dog, part wolf, if you know what I mean. Terrified of stray dogs, I tried my best to ignore this, this thing. But, to no avail. Yes, you guessed it, this mangy creature followed us from the bathroom back to the tent. And, wherever we went on the campground, we were followed.

We went to some of the events at W & L, then returned to the campsite on Saturday night. By this time, a motorcycle couple who was camping allowed this mutt to crawl into their tent. Aghast, we just giggled and then made a quick run for the bathroom! We also came up with a name for this creature: Pesky Pooch!

On Sunday morning, we woke up early to get ready for church. And yes, you guessed it, Pesky Pooch was up and running around. We were followed to the bathroom. He stared as we packed up the tent. He sniffed around for some table scraps as we loaded the cooler and picnic basket. He chortled when we put the dirty laundry bag into the trunk.

To this day, we have many good laughs when we think about our camping trip for Parents' Weekend and our adventures with Pesky Pooch!

Jane (Jones) Vos has lived in Dearborn most of her life. She is a wife to Doug (33 years), mother to five children plus two son-in-laws and a daughter-in-law, grandma to several grandchildren, bookkeeper, but most importantly a Christ follower. She has essays in volumes I and III of Dearborn's Best Stories *and wrote* Cherry the Cello, *a children's book.*

Chapter 7: Fish Tales

Bitter Dolphin by Alfred Brock

The country of Haiti is a study in stark contrasts. The blue swells of the Atlantic clash against the dark rocks of the coast. The last of the greenery in the highlands is a tempting sight from the dry and ravaged lowlands and hills that have been denuded of forest and in many places even grasses.

The border between Haiti and the Dominican Republic is guarded ferociously by both sides. The verdant fields and jungles of the eastern part of the island, under control of the Dominican Republic, are coveted by the poor and estranged of Haiti and selfishly kept empty by the Dominicans. It is said that the Dominicans do not even have to guard the border because the Haitian Army does an excellent job of keeping people in – you see – hardly anyone gets out.

Many people still visit the place, however, despite the poverty, ignorance, and tragedy of the place. Ruled by a succession of bloodthirsty dictators who were as inept at ruling as they were practiced in torture and killing, the population does not easily trust government.

Founded in revolution as a nation of slaves risen up in revolt against the French Empire, the revolution in Haiti can be said to have never ended. Just taken on a different form.

The visitors to the island are sometimes 'care' workers – that is United Nations soldiers, doctors, nurses, or administrators. Visitors include businessmen intent on exploration or exploitation or both as the island has some unique mineral deposits that are cheap and easy to get to. Often all the capital that is needed is the money to pay day laborers and an equal or greater amount to pay the corrupt officials who are supposed to protect the islanders from just that sort of thing.

The real danger is in the violence on the island because it is true that if one of these 'care' workers or business persons rubs someone the wrong way they might end up dead – and the investigation into their death will be just as thorough as the process that allowed them into the country. It is safe to say that many people who go there are never seen again.

The majority of those who do return are vacation travelers. They go to the island to certain small areas set aside for them by the government and enjoy themselves at first-class world resorts. They arrive by air or by cruise ship and to them Haiti is an island paradise. The only contact they have with Haitians being the few workers lucky enough to land a job at one of these places. The reality of the disease, poverty, despair, crime, and violence just across the heavily guarded ridgeline is never allowed to break through the air of wealth and leisure that is an imprint at these resorts.

It is the events surrounding one particular meal at one of these resorts that this story takes place.

The main character is Leema. She is a middle-aged woman who worked at the Slipstream Resort for nearly twenty years. The Slipstream Resort is one of the smaller hotels clustered around one of the larger resorts and marinas. The larger resort can be reached by bus and the clouds of poverty and despair are still secreted away across the hill in the direction no motorized traffic goes.

Leema walks to work each day. Six days a week she cleans and takes care of the rooms for the guests. She has a staff of three girls that work for her. She only hires clean girls who do their work and won't mix with the guests. She had one girl one time who was a little loose and she had to cut her off. She was sorry about that especially since the girl contracted tuberculosis about two years later and died shortly thereafter.

On the seventh day Leema would work in the kitchen as the restaurant was well known in the area and the larger resort would sometimes send guests there for a taste of 'authentic Haitian cooking.' The cook was actually from Somerset, New Jersey. In all the time that Leema had worked at the hotel only one guest had asked to see the cook to compliment him. The headwaiter sent out one of the dishwashers who could not speak anything but Haitian Creole and the conversation was soon over with lots of backslapping and a confused dishwasher walking away with an American twenty-dollar bill clutched in his hand.

The dishwasher did not appear at work the next day as he was killed the same night over the twenty-dollar bill after showing it to a friend and asking him what he could do with it. The friend did not kill him but an acquaintance of both. The killer was never arrested and it was rumored that he worked as a bell captain at the main resort. No one bothered to check.

Leema had been in the habit of cooking up a sweet sauce from the few local fruits and yams she was able to collect during the week. This sweet sauce was regarded by the cook from New Jersey as extraordinary, not only because it saved him hours of work, but because it was the one item that he knew actually was authentic Haitian cuisine. Leema was able to make a few extra dollars each week just from providing the sauce.

There being no banks in the area, she used the extra money to buy supplies for the women and girls that worked for her and also provided needed things, quietly, to neighborhood children.

The balance of her pay was used for her own care and anything left over she gave to the church.

Leema was generous to a fault.

She had grown old in her work. There was no healthcare to speak of. After the last earthquake, she visited a clinic that had been set up by the United Nations and a visiting dentist from Detroit had pulled one of her teeth and told her to brush every day and gave her some floss.

She received inoculations for various diseases caused by contaminated water and so survived the wave of death that followed the earthquake and was also allowed back into the resort compound to stay until the crisis was over.

The crisis was never really over in Haiti. It is just that after a crisis the steps taken to combat it are slowly put aside or ignored so that when the next crisis comes along the same problems must be met again in a whole new way.

It was one month after the earthquake that a devastating wind blew over the island. Leema could not collect her fruits and yams to make her sweet sauce. The chef was in a real stew about it. He normally drank himself into a stupor each day, but without the sweet sauce he did not know how the guests would react.

Leema had spent the week helping friends and neighbors collect whatever they could from their ravaged homes, and acted as interpreter for some of them with the visiting care workers. She had attended the funeral of one her workers – indeed the funerals of that woman's entire family as their house had collapsed upon them. She had spent time at the local school caring for the children who could not find their parents because their parents were missing, killed, or had run away and left them behind. She had seen the marauding soldiers and held her tongue as the police, rather than helping, had herded the people into filthy tent camps and started a new wave of disease, violence, and death.

She had cooked for her friends.

The cook did not know these things and had he known them he would not have cared. He put himself into a high state of worry and considered quitting – but twenty years at the Slipstream and drinking nearly nonstop had made him unfit for nearly any other life than the one he was living. Even he could see he might be overreacting.

The evening came that Sunday after the earthquake and the sweet sauce was nowhere to be found. Leema was in the kitchen and the cook was shrieking at her.

She took the matter calmly and looked at him with the diffidence of a Haitian for a non-Haitian. Everyone in the kitchen knew that the cook was walking a thin line. Talking down to a Haitian at any time, especially in public, could make one a marked man. The one true vestige of their revolutionary fervor that still existed on the island was an insistence that no one ever be treated like a slave again – at least out loud.

The island groaned under pain and sickness – but it would not bear a demeaning word. The cook was asking for help, though, so the others clustered around in the kitchen listened with interest.

A pair of visiting doctors from Switzerland had ordered the dolphin. This is not the air-breathing creature I am referring to but a beautiful, long, rainbow-colored sea fish which is very popular in the Caribbean. The chef normally broiled it, spiced it, and glazed it with Leema's sweet sauce, however, he sobbed, there was none about. What was he to do?

Leema looked out to the tables and saw the two men from Switzerland sitting with their wives. They were clean-shaven. Dressed perfectly.

The chef was asking her why he should keep her on if she could not meet her duties.

She turned to look at him and in her mind ran back over the last thirty days in her mind.

She recalled the heartache and sorrow, the blood and the pain. The incompetence and uncaring attitude of mankind she had witnessed and lived through for the last month was detailed in the face and the sound of the voice of the cook standing before her.

She reached down to the plates of food before her and scooped up the two upon which the dolphin steaks had been carefully arranged.

She turned to one of her workers and said, 'Take the rest and follow me.'

The chef was beside himself and did not know what to say.

The headwaiter stiffened as he saw Leema enter the dining room. He was unsure about what would happen next.

Leema walked up to the table and presented the dinners.

She turned to the woman following her and took the plates as offered and provided them to the wives of the doctors. The wives were not so adventurous as their husbands and had ordered Jerk Chicken.

After she served the plates, she called to a waiter to come and serve the wine.

The wine was poured, sampled, and approved.

One of the men took up his fork and was about to taste the fish when Leema held up her hand motioning him to stop.

The eyes of all the workers in the kitchen rested upon her back. The headwaiter stood at the top of his toes and tried with all his might to keep himself calm and poised. They all knew that their jobs and so their lives depended upon what Leema would do next.

Leema said, 'As you may know, gentlemen, the fish here is of the finest sort. The chef sends you his compliments and would like you know that this fish, freshly caught and prepared today solely for you, has been cooked in a stone oven over a blazing wood fire. It was finished with charcoal flavoring and brought to you now as it is with the need for one last finishing touch which I can provide for you.'

She reached behind her to the tray the woman following her was carrying and took from two halves of a lemon. One she squeezed upon one of the fish and across the vegetables and potatoes besides and the other she took and squeezed upon the other doctor's plate.

She stood back then, both hands streaming juice from the crushed lemon halves and said, '*Bon Appétit, Monsieurs et Madames.*'

The men slowly sampled their fish and murmured approval. The wives cooed and told the men they were very brave and had made a wise choice.

Leema turned to go and started ushering her helper back to the kitchen when one of the men asked, 'Tell me, what do you call this delicious fish dish?'

Leema turned and said, 'Bitter Dolphin.'

Alfred Brock enjoys the old woods. alfred.brock@gmail.com

Dreamworld of Water by Alfred Brock

In the dreamworld of Water
Comes a fancy
The fins in languorous motion sweep
Rays of light in columns
Colored gold and silver white
Green and white
Blue and lined
The blackness below
Whitened bubbles on the surface grind
The wind above in jet stream line
In the dreamworld of Water

Sirens sound in silent deep
Echoed voices
Faint light
Rocks without shape
Stones without faces
Deepening water forever spinning
Slowly wound currents from one top
To one end below
The clouds in perpetual motion
Above the languid depths
Sirens sound in silent deep

Winter chill and summer heat
Have no motion here
The perfectly chilled water
Far below freezing and approaching perfect zero
In slowest motion holding tightly onto itself
Clinging in atomic minutiae
Perfectly formed water
Bound in watery mass
The planet lit from deep within
No star or burning comet to light the ebon night

Winter chill and summer heat

Beneath and then within
The frozen arc of sky
The water hosts a lively set
Of creatures both behemoth and sly
In fractured beams they live their lives in seconds counted
While others their brethren of old
Will live and thrive within the cold
Its part and being told
A million years or more
The simplest motion leaning into walls of water hard and gravity
Beneath and then within

In the dreamworld of Water
Far beyond the light of clustered stars within a galaxy
Nigh
Close
Nearby
The glide of signing sphere
In empty space
Velvet blackness enwrapped on salty face
The sound not heard but known
In space span infinite
In the dreamworld of Water

Alfred Brock likes to travel. _alfred.brock@gmail.com_

Mother's Day by Alfred Brock

Doctor Webster stood in front of the Red Sea tank with fists clenched.

The morning custodian passed by and asked if there was anything wrong.

Doctor Webster's face was reflected in the glass of the aquarium and it was as tense as her hands.

She breathed, 'No!' barely audibly and marched loudly away.

At the other end of the aquarium, Professor Bottel looked with grave concern into the sea urchin exhibit. His mouth produced a frown that resembled the beautiful markings etched on the shells of the scallops that were nestled deeply in the rock crevasses.

He likewise turned on his heel in a huff and marched off.

As the day began at the aquarium the windows were washed and the doors flung open. The pure white light that fell down all over Puget Sound rushed into the aquarium and seemed to fill the building up.

Soon the visitors and tourists would arrive.

Both Doctor Webster and Professor Bottel independently calculated the time and distance to the Director's office. It just so happened that they arrived both at the very same time and with very much the same sour attitude at the Director's door.

As if the serio-comic incident had not gone far enough they both raised their hands to the door and knocked at exactly the same time and with the same force and speed. The resulting sound was much louder than either one of them had expected and their angry state of mind was temporarily scattered.

The Director had been taken by surprise. She had just started to enjoy her morning coffee when the loud rapping came at her door. A brief, wry thought of Edgar Allan Poe's 'Raven' popped into her mind as they had lately been laboring at the aquarium to include shore birds in the exhibits – at least in photos – and the large ravens that frequented the shores along with the seagulls had been included in one set of photos she had been preparing.

She looked at the door and by the sound of the silence outside she quickly determined who was knocking on her chamber door.

She called out, 'Margaret, Steve? Is that you?' She waited tensely, hoping for the word, 'No.'

The door opened and in walked Doctor Margaret Webster and Doctor Steve Bottel.

Director Patricia Bourgeois indicated the seats before her desk.

The two academics were already sitting down, eyeing each other suspiciously.

The Director asked, 'What is it this time?'

Then Webster and Bottel pointed at each other.

'Okay, Webster, you first.'

Doctor Webster stated, 'The Red Sea.'

Director Bourgeois waited for more but there was no more. Doctor Webster was sometimes very much like the clams she studied. You couldn't get anything out of her.

The Director turned to Professor Bottel. 'And, you?'

Professor Bottel became animated and half-stood as he gesticulated widely with his arms. 'The urchins, Director! The urchins!'

Director Bourgeois asked, 'What about the urchins?'

'They're gone!'

'So are the fish in the Red Sea tank!' said Doctor Webster – now very much a clam on the move. 'There are three prize fish missing! I'm sure he's got something to do with it! This is going to ruin my chances of completing my grant let alone getting a new one!'

'Why would I destroy my creatures AND your creatures if I wanted to grab your grant? Wouldn't I just destroy your creatures?' asked Professor Bottel, proud of his logic.

'I don't know,' said Doctor Webster. 'That's just it. You must be hiding them somewhere!'

'Hiding my sea urchins?' asked Professor Bottel. 'Where could I possibly hide them?'

'There's an ENTIRE ocean right outside the door!' began Webster in a strident tone.

Director Bourgeois stood up.

'That's enough! I agree with you. There's something fishy going on around here!'

Both Webster and Bottel glanced at each other quickly at the reference to fish but said nothing and both sank into their personal stew over the matter.

The Director went on. 'I don't think either of you had anything to do with the other's creatures or problems for that matter, so let's put that aside. You may be aware that several other researchers here have reported missing creatures from the displays. Something is going on.'

'What are you going to do about it?' both Webster and Bottel competed to ask.

Director Bourgeois said, 'I am going to get to the bottom of this.'

During the next week, the aquarium was locked up tight each night. Still, each day, some creature or creatures were missing from the tanks. Even some of the salmon in the ceiling display case were missing. On more than one occasion their holding tank had been drained very low.

On Saturday of that week Director Bourgeois decided to spend the night in the aquarium to see for herself if she could detect what was happening. She made her plans in strictest secrecy and set her cot in a room off the service area on the roof. Due to the design of the place the overlook where she would be allowed her to view nearly every part of the aquarium but she would not be visible.

The night came on. There was no untoward activity. No strange noises. No odd occurrences.

Against her better judgment she prepared to sleep. Her concern about what was happening was very real. The main problem with the disturbances was that nearly all of the researchers were at each other's throats. They were all sure one or the other was sabotaging their research. Not much work was getting done and that which was being completed was in danger of getting sloppy.

Director Bourgeois lay down to rest. She gazed up at the stars through the wispy, misty night and was just about to drop off to sleep when she heard a sound.

Of all places, she realized the sound was coming from just a few feet away from her near the salmon holding tank. She then felt a pang of fear and wondered if it was a good idea to be up there alone.

She quickly regained her composure and slowly moved her folded arm from off her face.

Still, slowly, her fear giving way to curiosity, she turned her head to the right.

There in moonlight spilling across the deck on the roof she saw a small shape huddled next to the salmon holding tank. At first she thought it looked like a little person. As her eyes adjusted to the dark she finally made out what she was seeing and let out loud yelp of surprise and joy!

The next day she held a meeting in the aquarium cafeteria. All of the researchers had been summoned in to work on Sunday for the great announcement concerning the culprit behind all the fish rustling.

As they settled down in the cafeteria looks of distrust melted away into interest and excitement as they all perceived that one of their problems was going to be solved. They were all, to the Doctor and Professor, all sure that one of them was guilty of this underhanded activity.

The Director stood on a table and called for their attention.

'As you all know here at the Seattle Aquarium our water supply is brought in directly from Puget Sound. Also, when that water has been circulated through the aquarium and made its way through tanks and systems it is discharged into the active fish ladder that lets wild salmon return to these waters and spawn right here in downtown Seattle. Well, ladies and gentleman, fish are not the only creature that has been using our fish ladder.'

Director Patricia Bourgeois was handed a poster board covered with a towel.

'Meet the Terror of the Deep here at the aquarium.' She removed the towel to reveal the smiling face of a sea otter.

'Mother Otter has been coming up the fish ladder each and every night and has been raiding our tanks. She has moved freely from tank to tank taking whatever she wanted. She even used her dexterous paws and wonderful brain to open the valve on the salmon holding tank to lower the water so as to make it easier to catch one of her favorite foods.'

One of the attendees raised his hand. He was a docent and had been working as a volunteer for some time.

'But Director – how could one otter, even a big one, eat so much?'

'Oh, she wasn't alone,' said the Director, 'she had help eating all that food, it is true. As it turns out she has twin pups she is keeping up under the aquarium pilings. We will need to let her raise the babies before we can move them. Many of you have made a life of studying the wonders of the sea and now, each one of you can say that your studies have helped to create life.'

And the babies grew big and strong and went off into the crystal waters of Puget Sound to raise their own families.

Alfred Brock has recently launched an effort known as a 'Fish Rescue.'
alfred.brock@gmail.com

Fishing with Dad by Hank Czerwick

My dad was a fisherman for all of my life. I don't know who he inherited the interest from. My grandfather had no interest in fishing. I do not know if Dad fished before he married Mom. But I do know that he fished for as long as I can remember.

The one really good thing about Dad was that he wasn't a solitary fisher. He always loved having someone along. Luckily that someone was me! Even when he would go fishing with some of his friends from work, he would take me along. I really loved that because his friends let me call them by their work names. I didn't have to say mister, just "Ace" or "Slim." It made me feel grown up and like one of the boys. And that was just the way they treated me.

Our fishing venues were usually somewhere along the Detroit River, once in a while on or near Lake St. Clair, and other times near Lake Erie. Sometimes the "boys" felt fishing was better on the Canadian side so we went to Mitchell Bay. Other times Detroit Beach held an allure.

The fish we were trying to catch were walleyes or perch, but we caught mostly white bass. These were considered too bony and were kept on our stringers until something better came along. If not, they would be kept. Dad would like to come home with something for our efforts.

My dad was a good cook, as well as a good sportsman. Whether it was pheasant, duck, rabbit, or fish, he would clean and cook them. If the catch happened to be the lowly silver bass, then he would de-bone them as best as he could and finely grind them into fish balls. The deal was, that we always ate what was brought home.

One of Dad's peculiarities was a fishing psychology that I could never figure out. It was that you had to be on the river or lake before daybreak. I guess that he thought the fish would be sleeping and that when they woke up, we would be there serving them breakfast on the ends of our hooks. Meeting this "get there early" requirement took advance planning so there was more to it than just going. First, the car had to be packed the night before. In went all of the fishing rods, which were first checked for tangles and their reels lubricated. Then the tackle boxes were examined to make sure that any trash put there from the last expedition was removed and the equipment, especially the harnesses, were in good order. Dad never threw any trash over the side of the boat, but always stowed it in the tackle box to keep it from blowing away. Also, in went our venerable one-cylinder "Caille" outboard motor and a can of gasoline properly mixed with oil. The Caille outboard motors were once a popular Detroit brand. Included with this equipment might be a trolling box that Dad made from the works of an old wind-up Victrola. Once the car trunk was loaded, the next step took place in the kitchen. Here Dad made the sandwiches which we were to eat the next day. These might be made of kielbasa, pork chops, or just bologna. An apple was usually included and hot coffee was poured into our plaid Thermos bottle. That evening this was all assembled near our back door in preparation for the next mornings early departure. It included a variety of clothing for either the warm or cool weather conditions which might occur.

It seemed like I had barely fallen asleep when Dad would quietly and gently be shaking my shoulder and saying, "Wake up, it's time to go." I would just make it out to the car and would fall asleep again until our arrival at some boat livery. It's my guess that the proprietors of liveries never slept.

No matter what time we arrived, there was someone there to take our money and direct us to the clunky flat-bottomed mini-barges that were called fishing boats. Each had a crudely hand-painted number on it. The anchors varied from actual anchor-like devices, to small buckets filled with cement attached to a fuzzy, water-soaked rope. The two oars were just as beat up as everything else. The attendant might also furnish buoyant pillows in case we didn't have our own. These were considered to be life-saving devices before the advent of life jackets. Then moving things from the car to the boat proceeded. First the motor and fuel, followed by the fishing gear, placed handy to where Dad would sit and operate the motor. The livery usually sold bait. Dad would buy some worms and some minnows, not knowing what would be the fish's desired food du jour. The minnows would go into our bucket with the perforated lid and the worms would be in a cardboard cottage cheese container mixed in with moist moss. These, too, went into the boat. Last in would be our food and the plaid Thermos with an extra plastic cup. Strangely, I was allowed to drink coffee from an early age.

I remember on one occasion, we were on an inland lake. The skies were indicating that a storm was approaching. Dad pulled in all of our lines and the anchor. He slipped a piece of rope around the flywheel on top of the old Caille outboard and gave a pull to start it. As he gave it a sharp pull, the acorn nut on top, which fastened the flywheel, came off. The nut danced around on top of the flywheel and bounced to the floor of the boat. Whew! There was a 50/50 chance that it could have gone into the lake! It was lucky. That old outboard motor never started on the first pull. Dad took out the pliers from the tackle box and re-affixed the nut to the top of the motor. Then he started it and we made it safely to the dock before the storm.

On another occasion, I remember the liveryman asking Dad what kind of motor we had. When Dad told him it was an old Caille, he told us to paddle out of the canal until we got to the lake. He didn't want us to waken the residents along the way with the clatter of that old motor.

We used that old outboard motor until the early '50s when my mom surprised Dad with a new Evinrude motor. Soon after, Dad purchased his own new boat. It was an all mahogany Clyde Craft, a Detroit brand manufactured at a factory on Livernois Avenue. It was there that Dad and I went to pick it up.

Dad would own a succession of fishing boats; a pontoon, when he moved to Lake Ogemaw near West Branch, and an in-board boat later when he moved to Florida. He fished and cooked for as long as he could.

I never became a fisherman. For a while, it looked as if my son would take up where Dad left off. Although my son had a boat, a motor, and a good deal of gear (mostly Dad's), he did not continue to fish after moving to Upstate New York. He has, however, continued to honor his grandfather's legacy…by becoming an excellent cook!

Hank Czerwick is a 66-year resident of Dearborn and product of its schools. He retired from Ford Motor Company as an engineer and from Henry Ford Community College as an educator. His writing has been published in many magazines.

Chapter 8: A Frog Tale

Peepers by Beaufort Cranford

These latitudes have all sorts of small, unobtrusive harbingers of spring. Nubs of skunk cabbage, or snowdrops, or buds on trees. But in early spring, small and unobtrusive don't always travel together. And nothing breaks that pairing with more vigor than the spring peeper. If spring is closing in, the peeps of peepers usually announce it sooner than anything else except for the snorks and quacks of their cousins the wood frogs, who in some years begin to call even while there's ice in the water. Starting in mid-March, listen for spring peepers if you have any standing water nearby.

They're Michigan's most abundant singing frog, according to the DNR. Male peepers make a note usually called a whistle and described as "bell-like" or "piping," ascending at the end. Some people think these slippery little singers actually say *peep*, but to me it's more like *wheat*. What's absolutely certain is that a bog full of spring peepers, all saying *wheat* over and over as loudly as possible at one-second intervals, makes a stupendous racket.

Science knows the spring peeper as *Pseudacris crucifer*; my generation learned it as *Hyla crucifer*, which labeled it a tree frog. But DNA analysis has since determined it to be a closer relative of the chorus frogs, and thus the *Pseudacris*, which comes from Greek words meaning "false locust," referring to the peeper's call.

It's not something I'd argue with. Despite having a tree frog's standard-issue sticky toe pads, peepers aren't avid climbers and seldom go very high. The *crucifer* comes in because peepers have a well-defined X, like a cross, on their backs. A line between their eyes is also an identifying tool should you ever see one, which isn't likely unless you take pains to go looking for them.

They're only about 1 to 1½ inches long, for one thing, and their coloring, which varies from brown through gray and shades of olive, tends to keep them camouflaged. This is probably a good time to mention that a pair of Michigan tree frogs (the almost identical *Hyla versicolor* and *H. chrysoscelis*) takes this talent to the next level by actually changing color in accord with their environment—although the one I found hiding under a friend's toilet seat several years ago had been unable to match the pale blue of its surroundings.

I'm told that once upon a time the sort of rural folk who believed in leprechauns and cockalorums also thought frogs generated spontaneously in water. Some water I've seen, I almost could believe that. And old-time Germans are reported to have thought frogs somehow were caused by spring rains. The fact that few, or no, hearty souls apparently leaped forward to say, "Wait a minute, maybe all these frogs are just *attracted* to water" tells you something about the general and inexplicable lack of attention most people have paid to the natural world since we moved out of caves and into houses.

Happily for peepers, temperate evenings and rain do make a lot of places hospitable to them in spring, drawing them out of the torpor in which they've weathered winter in protected places. In early spring, any calm water surrounded by a few trees or bushes is almost certain to have a stock of *P. crucifer* males waiting for nightfall so as to begin calling *wheat* to beat the band. But, and I recall being completely surprised the first time I heard this, they don't actually call from the water but from nearby branches and trunks.

They're *wheat*ing for love, of course. In fact, only the male peepers peep and females listen for a voice that appeals to them. After mating, a female peeper will lay 700-1,000 eggs in the nearby water, and you know the rest: Tadpoles hatch out and, if not eaten, dried up by drought or buried by a strip mall, gradually develop into tiny adults.

The need for water in which to lay their eggs is what makes spring peepers and all frogs amphibians, along with the toads and salamanders. It also puts them at some risk, because we humans have an aggravating tendency to allow pesticides, fertilizers and other chemicals to run off into the pools, rainwater or otherwise, that are essential to these creatures' survival.

After mating season cools down, the chorus of peeps and wheats gradually dies away, though sometimes a few particularly vocal or bewildered individuals will sing even into autumn. Also, sometimes early hibernators fooled by unseasonably warm late fall days will come out and start singing again.

Frogs may be squishy and pop-eyed, but they're also durable creatures. It's one thing to sit on a limb and peep in the moonlight, but another thing entirely to drop into a pool of 36-degree water clad only in your skin and still keep love on your mind. Luckily, peepers and their pals don't have much in the way of minds to worry about.

Mature spring peepers eat various pesky invertebrates from gnats to mosquitoes and other bugs, but probably not enough for us to notice. Their primary value to humans – in case you think they have to have one – is spiritual uplift, because when the peepers start to sing around here, it's almost time to throw off the overcoats and let the good times roll.

Beaufort Cranford retired from Wayne State University in 2013. *beaufortc@gmail.com*

Chapter 9: A Goat Tale

Nannyberries by Arty Grins

Nannyberries was the best word that our mom would let us use to talk about the small, round, dark droppings that our goat left everywhere she went. We weren't allowed to swear, and the word poop sounded silly, so nannyberries was the best word we had.

"Watch out for nannyberries, Caleb," my older brother Roy said to me.

"I know, I know," I replied, looking down at my timeworn shoes as we stepped from our backyard, through the gate, and into the goat's yard.

Nanny, our off-white goat, stood at the far end of the yard and looked up from a clump of grass. She looked us both in the eye, back and forth. She yelled, "Myaaaa," before dipping her head back down to the earth and ripping off a piece of grass.

We stood by the gate for a moment, hands in the pockets of our faded blue jeans, looking at the goat's yard. The grass and leaves in Nanny's yard were missing wherever they were within reach. Even the grass in the yard, just outside the fence, and the leaves of trees that hung beside the fence, were missing. Nanny ate leaves and grass and even the bark off the tree trunks. It didn't matter how much we fed her. Nanny was hungry.

"This time for sure," Roy said, clapping his hands together and rubbing them. He looked at me, smiling.

"I wish you wouldn't, Roy," I said, almost begging. "It's not right to ride her now, not anymore."

We loved to ride Nanny. She was very large, larger than any dog we had. When we sat on her, our legs didn't reach below her belly. Her spine stuck up into our rears and was a bit bony and uncomfortable, but it was still fun. She had long horns which curved backward from the top of her head until they pointed back at her neck.

I had ridden Nanny plenty of times, too, but now it was different.

"Just leave her alone, Roy," I yelled.

"Shhh," he said, but there was no reason to be quiet. Nanny was looking at us out of the corner of her eye as we approached.

Nanny was smart. We would get on her by getting close enough to grab one horn. She didn't like that, so she would try to move away. All we had to do at that point is throw one leg over her back, roll on top, and hang on to both horns as tightly as we could.

But, like I said, Nanny was smart and she didn't like that. She knew her own yard, too, and she would head straight for a pair of trees growing close to one another. She would charge between them, barely fitting her body through. The openings she chose were only big enough for her. Whoever the rider was would have his knees sticking out the sides; there was no way to pull them in. Nanny would emerge from the other side of the pair of trees, riderless.

"I'm not listening to you, Caleb," Roy said. "I have been waiting a long time for a good ride and now Nanny is too big to fit between those trees."

He was right. Nanny had babies in her belly; kids they were called. Her belly was larger than it had ever been before. When she went into her shed for the night or when it was time to eat, we could hear the coarse fur on her sides bristling against the door frame. There was no way she was going to fit between those trees where she always used to dump her unwanted riders.

"It's just mean," I said, one last time. I stood on the other side of Nanny from Roy, arms folded across my chest, frown creasing my face.

Roy smiled and crouched low. He reached out for Nanny's horn but she jerked her head away, yelling at him, "Myaa!" He smiled wider, showing his teeth. He stood up straight and sighed. He shrugged.

"It's no use," he said to me. "I give up." He took off his jacket.

"Thank you," I said, relieved.

"Here," he said, tossing his jacket over Nanny's head. "Hold this."

Nanny followed the arcing jacket with her eyes at first, then with her whole head. The sleeves fluttered behind the jacket as I caught it and I pulled it toward myself. Nanny turned her head and then her whole body until her horns were pointed at Roy. He grabbed onto Nanny's horns, and swung one leg over her back.

They were off! Nanny yelled, bleated, screamed at Roy. Roy just laughed, holding onto both horns. Nanny ran, bouncing through the yard. She ran toward the gate and turned sharply along the fence. Roy hung on. She ran along the fence and then turned inward to the open yard. She charged first at one group of trees. She turned sharply at the last minute. Roy hung on, knuckles white from the strain. She charged at another group of trees but veered away at the last minute. She stopped at the far end of the yard. She breathed deeply, turning toward the front. She yelled.

"Myaaaad!"

Nanny started into a trot but gained speed quickly. She turned gradually around groups of trees, never slowing. She kept gaining speed. Roy stopped smiling. I could hear the worry in his voice, which was broken by the bouncing of the angry, charging goat.

"Oh-o-o-o-o-o-oooh!"

Nanny was running faster than I had ever seen her run, faster than I thought a goat could, faster than I thought a horse could. She pointed her horns toward the open door to her shed and dropped her head. She ran even faster.

"Nooo-o-o-o-o-oo-ooo-oooh!"

WHACK!!!

Roy's hands and arms were ahead of him and he was leaning forward when his knees stopped short against the door frame to the shed. He slid backward off of Nanny, past her short, wagging tail. His hands and body turned in the air, his legs and rear pointing up, driving his screaming face hard into the ground. He didn't have a chance to stop or slow himself.

I laughed. I couldn't help it. I laughed hard and loud. Maybe I took it too far when I crouched low to the ground and started slapping my knee. I slowly calmed down and stopped laughing, though.

Roy wasn't moving.

I ran as fast as I could toward the shed, toward my big brother, who lay motionless on the ground before a goat. The goat, Nanny, smiled.

I shouted, "Roy!" He didn't respond.

I got up to the shed and slid along the ground to my brother's side. I grabbed him by the shoulder and shook him. He moved!

He groaned, low and quiet at first, as he started to stir. He pushed himself up and propped himself on his elbows. He turned to look at me and groaned, much louder this time.

"Myaa." Nanny smiled even wider, showing her teeth.

Roy spit out a mouthful of the ground he had landed in, face first. Small, black balls fell out of his mouth and hit the ground.

I asked, already sure of the answer, "What is that?"

He spat and sputtered, "Nannyberries."

Ryan Grinwis is a husband, a father, a food plant inspector, and a student of Secondary Biology Education at Ferris State University. While he mainly writes fairy tales as Arty Grins, he occasionally enjoys writing stories about growing up on a hobby farm in West Michigan.

Chapter 10: Grab-bag Tales

I Want a Magical Unicorn by Zeinab Elhourani

I want a magical unicorn to make my wishes come true.

Image from a 17th century Dutch print

Zeinab Elhourani is a student at Lowrey Elementary School in Dearborn, Michigan.

The Beavers and Little Bunny by Sarah Kalmoni

In a beautiful forest, far away from civilization, lived three beavers along the Grand River, in Michigan. The beavers—two of them were brothers, while the third was their sister—worked hard everyday to make sure the river was safe and their home well built. Chubby and Tubby were the names of the brothers. Moody was the name of the sister. Spring was coming soon and the beavers couldn't contain their excitement, as they couldn't wait to see the trees have leaves again, and to see the other animals roam around the forest.

While the beavers started to play by the riverbank, the wise old owl sat in his tall oak tree, gazing upon the horizon. "What a wonder of beauty," thought the owl, and closed his eyes to resume his afternoon nap. The deer and moose returned to the forest with their young fawns, grazing on the freshest grass of the new season. While the animals were happily returning to their daily routine, danger was brewing in the west. Lake Michigan was enduring heavy rainfall in April, and the river was starting to rise.

The wise old owl awoke from his nap and decided to fly and look for food. As he was flying, he noticed that further up the forest, the animals were starting to run away from both sides of the river. The river had high rapids and the water was gushing against the rocks everywhere. "Who, who, oh, no! I've got to get back and warn the others!" exclaimed the owl. The owl frantically flapped his wings together, gliding as fast as he could. He was almost out of breath when he reached his old oak tree. "Animals, calling all animals!" the owl cried. The beavers, the deer, the moose and all the other animals gathered around the wise old owl's tree. "The river is rising and it's headed this way. We must leave this area at once!" The animals looked at each other in shock.

A little bunny next to his mother said, "Mama, it's our home, we just got here. How can we leave now? There must be something we can do to keep our forest safe." Mother Bunny looked at her little one and said, "The owl knows what's best for us. We need to go so we can be safe." Chubby, Tubby and Moody huddled together. After a brief moment, they turned to the owl and the rest of the animals. The beavers in unison, squeaked, "We have a solution, oh wise owl and friends! We beavers are great at building dams. We will build a big dam strong enough to withstand the water from coming into our forest. Little Bunny is right. It's our home and we need to protect it." The beavers got to work right away. They gathered as many tree branches as they could and worked with the mud along the bank to build their dam. The other animals got involved too. A bear pushed a huge tree trunk towards the beavers. "Will this help?" she said. "Yes!" the beavers smiled. The birds gathered some hay with their beaks and brought it to the beavers. "Some hay might help the mud stick better," said the birds. "Perfect," said Moody. The moose kicked some pebbles in a pile next to the dam. "The more rocks the better," said Chubby. With all the help of the animals, the beavers built a magnificent dam to protect their forest from the river's rapids that were closing in. Now that the work was all finished, there was nothing else they could do, but wait.

And so the animals waited. And waited. Little Bunny snuggled next to Mother Bunny as they rested in their burrow. The wise old owl kept watch as the other animals, exhausted from the day's labor, tried to rest and sleep. The beavers, though very tired, inspected their work, looking for any weak spots. "Everything's in order," Tubby said. Chubby and Moody nodded in approval. A large rumble sounded. "The rapids are here!" hooted the owl. "Brace yourselves. Don't be afraid. We'll make it." And the rapids came. And the rapids couldn't break through the dam the animals had built. The rapids calmed, and with the cleverness of the beavers, they had built small holes at the top of the dam to allow water to flow a little at a time. It looked like a shower, almost like a water fall as the rapids passed through the river's dam.

The wise old owl sat in his tall oak tree. "What a wonder, it is. Three beavers put their heads together and came up with a solution to save the forest. All the animals worked together for one goal. What a wonder," he thought. Chubby, Tubby and Moody sat by their beautiful dam and gazed at it in amazement. "Aren't we lucky animals to have friends that help us when we need it most?" said Moody, with a smile. Chubby and Tubby nodded in agreement. Tubby said, "Why don't we call this dam 'Little Bunny's Dam'? It was his idea for us to be brave and not leave our home." "Oh, yes!" said Moody and

Chubby. In Mother Bunny's burrow, Little Bunny was sitting next to Mother Bunny. "My brave Little Bunny, I'm so proud of you. You had the courage to speak up for our forest," she said, and gave her baby a kiss on the head. Little Bunny looked up at Mother Bunny and said, "I'm so glad that I made a difference. We all made a difference by working together." And so all the animals rested and went to sleep, looking forward to the next day's adventures to come.

Sarah Kalmoni is an aspiring writer. She enjoys writing short stories, poetry, essays and minibiographies about her favorite musicians in her spare time.

Animals and Me by Marcel Pultorak

I grew up around animals on the east side of Dearborn during the 1940s. My dad grew up on a farm in northeastern Poland. His dad died when he was a small boy and so he and his brothers had to help take care of the family farm. When he was a teenager, his mother remarried. My dad had his own ideas about how the farm should be run and did not get along well with his new stepfather. Long story short, he was sent away to the United States to begin a new life.

There's an old saying that "You can take the boy off the farm, but you can't take the farm out of the boy." And that was true of my dad. He was amazing at growing things, even though we lived in the city. And he always had animals around.

I am the youngest of six children and was a mid-life "surprise," coming along fourteen years after the rest of my siblings after my mom had been told she could not have any more children. Before I came along, the family had had a German Shepherd named Maggie and I heard tales of how she guarded the house while my dad, a WWI U.S. Army vet, was away in a veterans' hospital during the early years of the Great Depression.

Some of my earliest memories are of playing with my dad's pigeons in the backyard. He had a pigeon coop in the garage and raced his carrier pigeons as a hobby. (The slow ones got eaten.) Almost every Saturday in spring, summer and fall, we would go to the Western Market in Detroit to buy fresh produce and often, live poultry. The chickens, ducks or geese would be penned in our backyard until they were needed for our table. Once WWII started and food rationing began, Dad turned half of the garage into a chicken coop with an adjacent outdoor pen and we began raising our own chickens for eggs and meat. My jobs were helping to feed the chickens, collecting the eggs and helping to pluck the feathers off the slaughtered birds when harvested for meat. Dad always took good care of his animals, making sure they had clean shelter, food and water.

We also had Victory gardens on one or two entire vacant lots nearby to grow vegetables, and several fruit trees in the backyard for fresh fruit.

As I grew older, the Lassie movies, based on the novels of Albert Payson Terhune became popular. Still later, television came along with reruns of old Rin Tin Tin movies about a heroic German Shepherd dog of the same name. I begged Mom and Dad for a dog, especially a Collie like Lassie. By this time, my brother Tony was home from the war and he and my parents took me to a kennel to pick out a Collie puppy. I was in seventh heaven!

The puppy was six weeks old and cost $85, a huge sum in 1947. I don't know exactly what my dad was paid then, but based on what I've since learned it was likely about two weeks' pay. I picked out a male puppy and named him Laddie. Laddie was a beautiful pup, but soon became sick and within a few days he died. I was crushed! We were told that he died of distemper. The breeder gave no recourse to my family. We were out the money and I was to have no more dogs until I was an adult.

I adopted an occasional stray cat or kitten, but was forbidden to have them in the house for long. Later, when recovering from polio, I had a pet parakeet named Joe, who turned out to be a Josephine after we found eggs in her cage one day. During my recovery from polio and several leg surgeries that followed, I read many animal stories and books, including all of the "Lassie" tales. In my heart of hearts, I still wanted a dog.

Years later when I met my wife to be, I found that her family had a dog, Duchess, a friendly Fox Terrier mix. A few months after we married, we both decided we would like a dog, but it had to be a smaller dog as we were living in an upper flat apartment. We wound up getting a West Highland White Terrier from a pet shop in early 1965 and named him Frosty since his fur was all white. We were to have Frosty for fourteen years, and he was a great companion for us and our two children. It turned out that Frosty was a little larger than most Westies and he had the bark of a much larger dog, which made him a great watchdog. Unlike many small dogs, he was not yappy and only barked for a good reason. He was great with children and loved retrieving a ball that I would throw all the way down the stairs to our upper flat. Frosty went everywhere with us. We began camping and Frosty loved it, especially lying next to the campfire on a cold night. His main bad habit was occasionally walking under our car to scratch his back. The result was a reverse skunk appearance: all white with a black stripe down his back. Bath time! Eventually, Frosty got too old and sick, so we had to put him down.

All of us missed having a dog, so after some months, we decided to look for another, settling on a Cairn Terrier from a local breeder hoping for a dog similar to Frosty but with a brown coat that would look cleaner. My wife wanted a female this time so we brought a new puppy home and named her Dusty. Dusty turned out to be much yappier and not as easygoing as Frosty, being more excitable. Still later, our son (then a teenager) wanted a dog of his own, a German Shepherd. After some weeks of discussion, we found a breeder in Algonac that had a female German Shepherd pup that likely fit our needs and also fit our budget. She was named Brandy for the tan in her black and tan coloring. She grew into a beautiful dog with a gorgeous tail. People often remarked on her beauty. The two dogs eventually reached accommodation with one another. In the house, Dusty ruled. Outside, Brandy was dominant.

Both dogs went camping with us. One night, camping out of season in a largely empty state park campground, our son started to howl at the moon and Brandy joined in right away. I joined in as well and that became a family tradition. We regularly had a howling good time, letting off some steam with a good howl. Talk about Call of the Wild! Brandy loved it!

Since Brandy was growing into a fairly large dog, we enrolled her in obedience school at the German Shepherd Club of Detroit. After two semesters, she failed to graduate, but did win an award as the most improved dog. She learned to behave when on a walk or run, so when our son enlisted in the U. S. Army after high school, I was able to exercise her on my bike if I was careful to watch for squirrels or other small critters. Brandy was to become our dog after our son married soon after returning from the army. Soon after, we gave away Dusty, going back to a one-dog household. No one dared approach our door without a warning from a very wolf-like, fierce looking German Shepherd which my wife appreciated when I was often at night-time meetings or away on business. Sadly, after 13 years, Brandy too got old and sick and had to be put down.

During this same time, while we had Brandy, we adopted a stray cat that had been hanging around my mother's house next door after my mom passed away. We named him Shadow, both for his dark gray color and his tendency to "shadow" us as we moved around the house. We had him for a few years, but he died of kidney disease about the same time as we lost Brandy.

For a short while, we had no pet, and our kids were both on their own. Some say freedom is when the kids move out and the dog dies. Well, we were torn about this and missed our pets. In the spring of 1997, my daughter asked me to go with her to the Animal Shelter so she could adopt a couple of cats, as her cat Pepper had died. While waiting for her, a long-haired black cat with a white blaze on his chest reached out of his cage and tapped me on my shoulder. The attendant asked if I wanted to hold him and the rest is history. We adopted that cat, named Hyacinth by the shelter staff. When we got him home, we discovered that he was an exceptionally vocal cat, so much so that we seriously considered returning him! Fortunately, he proved to be an extremely affectionate and friendly cat, so we kept him, but renamed him Mr. Mau both for his vocal proclivities and our opinion that Hyacinth was no name for a big male cat. Mr. Mau is still with us today, nearing age 18!

Soon after we got Mr. Mau, a tragedy struck our extended family when one of our nephews, Jeff, died suddenly at the young age of 39. He had just remarried about a year before he died and had a young female yellow Labrador he had named Spike. Spike was an exceptionally well-trained and well-behaved dog, so when Jeff's widow asked us a year later if we would be interested in adopting Spike, we immediately agreed.

We were to have Spike for ten wonderful years. Spike was known throughout our neighborhood. At first, we still lived in east Dearborn and many of the neighborhood children were not used to dogs. Spike became a favorite playmate, as she loved to retrieve tennis balls thrown by the kids using a Jai-alai-style thrower I bought to save my sore throwing arm. About four years later, we moved, wanting a one-story house as we aged and Spike again became a neighborhood favorite. Both Spike and Mr. Mau traveled with us as we took a long two-month trip to California and returned with our then new RV and went on many subsequent shorter trips. Spike traveled in the truck, while Mr. Mau had the fifth wheel to himself with all the amenities.

After we had to have Spike put down, we were again "dogless" for about a year after which I began looking for an adult dog to adopt. Surfing the net, I saw that the Dearborn Animal Shelter had an older black Lab mix, Baron, looking for a home. I went to see him and we connected immediately. Baron was seriously overweight, likely due to lack of exercise and the Lab's tendency to overeat. He had been returned to the shelter six months after his first adoption when his second master died unexpectedly.

Baron and Mr. Mau were kept apart by baby gates for the first few months, as the cat tended to run when Baron approached and dogs like to chase running critters. They reached a peaceful truce in about nine months. As winter approached, we turned on a new gas fireplace insert and encouraged the animals to enjoy the heat. They did! Mr. Mau decided he would stand his ground and stay in front of the fire and Baron decided he was O.K. with that. They've been fine together ever since. Both animals are black with a white blaze on their chests so we joke that they are wearing their tuxedos.

It turned out that Baron is really what I call a Labrador "Deceiver" in that he does not like to retrieve. He has no interest whatsoever in a thrown ball, but he will retrieve a stuffed animal two or three times after which he apparently decides that if I am dumb enough to throw it away again, I can go get it myself.

Baron is also an omnivore in that he loves fruits and vegetables. As a result, veggies are a regular part of his diet and he stays close by when I am cleaning veggies or fruit for some tasty morsels. Green beans, broccoli and romaine lettuce are regular treats. People are amazed at how he relishes veggie treats. Thanks to exercise and a diet of regular veggies, he is now at a normal weight and looks great!

Both Baron and Mr. Mau help keep me warm on these cold winter days—Mau on my lap and Baron at my feet, often resting his chin on my foot. He will nudge my legs with his snout until I raise them for him to become my footrest. At my age, I can no longer cope with a puppy or kitten, but found that an older adult dog or cat can make a wonderful companion. We have learned to communicate non-verbally and to enjoy each other's company.

With the exception of a few pets, like parrots or tortoises which are long-lived, most of our pets have relatively short lives, so we must endure loss when they die and we must go on without them. I especially mourned Spike, as she had been such an exceptionally good dog as well as a constant reminder of my brother and his son, both of whom were taken at too young an age. My pets helped me to learn that death is part of life. I adopted the philosophy that it is better to have shared their company and affection than not to have known it at all, especially my dogs. Dogs and humans have a special connection that I have been privileged to experience.

Later this year, we will have been married for 50 years and have enjoyed the company of our dogs and cats for almost all of that time. Should we survive Baron and Mr. Mau, it's likely we will adopt a new furry companion, as long as we are able to care for them. I can feel myself relax when my guys share some affection, especially on a cool morning as we all enjoy the morning quiet by a warm fire. Try it!

Marcel Pultorak's family moved to Springwells, later Fordson and now present day Dearborn around 1926. He lived on the same block for his first 62 years seeing the area around Warren and Schaefer transition from a neighborhood with many vacant lots and fields to the built-out city we see today. No more farm animals, but plenty of pets. He likes to camp in northern Michigan where you can still hear the call of the wild.

Mammal House by Angela Scott

When I was outside,
I saw there was a goose on the loose,
I went inside to tell my mother but she had turned into a moose!

I knew it was her because it had her apron on,
I went to find my little brother but saw he had turned into a fawn!

Then my father was nowhere to be found in the house,
I went looking for him but I was cut off by the cat chasing my dad,
the mouse!

My sister could not be seen from anywhere,
But I noticed in the backyard there lay the brownest biggest bear!

I knew it was only a second before I turned into something myself,
Then suddenly my legs made me leap on top the highest shelf!

I held my hand in front of my face and was suddenly in awe,
For instead of my hand there was a big gigantic paw!

On the shelf was a mirror and I looked in it to see,
There was a furry face with a mane looking back at me!

I leaned back my head and roared out to sing:
"There's no messing with me, in this mammal house I am king!"

Angela Scott lives in Canton and is currently working as the Youth Services Librarian at the Inkster Public Library. In her spare time she likes to write silly poems and stories that make people laugh or at least let out a chuckle or two.

Pet of My Dreams by Phyllis Tippett

I once had a
chameleon
for a pet

One day he
turned green and
disappeared into the grass

A garden snake or
winter probably got him
Poor baby!

My mother presented
me with a young chick
for Easter

She put it into the oven to
keep it cozy and cooked it
Poor baby!

I had a white rat for a while until
he disappeared into a basement trap
Poor baby!

We got a small brown
dog named
Baron Munchausen

I sought the reason
for the name: the baron was
a mythical adventurer

We fed Baron Munchausen taffy
and laughed as he smacked

Poor baby!

Now I have a pet named Horace
if it's gender correct
doesn't even matter

Horace doesn't need walks
nor litter box and can't turn green or
disappear or get baked

I could have named him Baron
Munchausen as he is something
of a mythical adventurer

He has all the attributes of
a live hamster without
any of the work

No water bottle to fill
nor pellets to resupply
nor litter to clean

Horace lives in his box
on a home page equipped
with water dispenser and running wheel

He is always running his wheel
investigating his space or
simply sleeping

When I click a pellet
falls then he eats the
pellet and follows the cursor

When I tire of my virtual pet I send the
pet of my dreams into cyberspace
Poor baby!

Phyllis Tippett's favorite pursuit in writing is haiku, the diminutive Japanese form that celebrates the natural world. Recently, she published a book entitled Alphabet Critters *which is available on Amazon.com.*

Tuck and Stockins by Eleanor Vallie-Floetke

The rain was dense, heavy and cold and suddenly, in our driveway, he was there: small, soaking wet, shivering with the cold. As I approached the little dog, he jumped, gratefully, into my lap and immediately became part of the family. That is, except for our one-year-old calico kitty, "Stockins" (so named for her four white paws). It was Stockins' practice to come into the house just long enough for breakfast, lunch and dinner. She wasn't too pleased about this "stranger" who dove into her food dish with a vengeance. Each time that the little intruder dove into the food, we pulled him back with a firm "NO!" It took only a few times to convince him to practice better manners and once we purchased real dog food and his own dish, we were able to put both dog and cat dishes side-by-side and each animal ate the appropriate food and accepted the other's meal partner.

What to name this intruder into our life and heart? Since we lived in a forest, we decided on a formal "Friar Tuck" and a more appropriate "Tuck." Tuck was eager to please us and he was soon answering our commands to "roll over"; "speak"; "sit" and "say please" for food. Tuck's biggest accomplishment was as a messenger. We each stood at one long road and commanded: "Go get Daddy!" and "Go get Mama!" It took several times to get our message across; we could then send Tuck for Daddy or Mama, whichever one was needed. There were times, too, when we put a written message on Tuck's collar and he faithfully delivered the message, even waiting, at times for a written answer.

There was the time when Tuck was required to have minor surgery. The vet told us: "Put him in the sun for a couple hours and keep him quiet." Tuck obliged, while Stockins lay nose to nose with him for the required time.

Tuck kept Stockins a kitty and Stockins kept Tuck a puppy even as the years went by. At age nineteen, Stockins was attacked and injured severely by a groundhog on our property. We rushed her to the vet who didn't give us much hope for her recovery but seeing our concern, gave us antibiotics and "special" salve for her injury. Despite following the doc's orders and special attention by ourselves and our faithful Tuck, Stockins put her paw on "Daddy's" hand and died of her injuries. Shortly after a tearful burial service, we became aware that Tuck began to abandon his "puppyhood" and seemed to age quickly (he was eighteen years old). Tuck developed many "old dog" ailments and a year after Stockins' death, the vet gave us the sad news: "The only humane option for Tuck is to put him to sleep." It took us several days before we could decide to follow the advice of the vet but we knew it had to be as we watched him stumble and struggle to walk; leave his food and water untouched and turn his sad eyes toward us as if to beg for mercy. "Give me time to dig his grave, next to Stockins, before we take him to the vet," my husband said. We stayed with Tuck while the vet administered the lethal injection. We all cried, even the vet, as Tuck gave a slight moan and (we're certain) joined Stockins in Animal Heaven.

Not many kitties beg for the door to relieve themselves but Tuck had taught Stockins to do that! She came in to eat and to sleep at night but thanks to Tuck, we never had a litter box for our kitty once Tuck became part of the family.

"Never feed chocolate to a dog!" Or so the saying goes but Tuck begged for a chocolate treat each time someone in the family had one. He thrived on it!

Grandchildren, young nieces and nephews could play (sometimes pretty hard!) with both Tuck and Stockins but neither ever snapped at or bit a human being.

Both animals rode, proudly, with Daddy as he drove his golf cart around the property.

Tuck and Stockins are long since departed from our family but they will live on in our hearts and memories forever.

Eleanor Vallie-Floetke became a resident of Henry Ford Village three years after the death of her husband of fifty-plus years. She's busy all the time, as are most of the residents! She met a wonderful man there. They began singing together and have now been married for five years.

Chapter 11: A Hamster Tale

The Experiment by Zahra Seblini

Hamsters are more like lab rats than you thought.
A child asks for a hamster,
Asking for a cuddly pet
Who they can feed and
Watch run around in a plastic ball
And a parent buys them a living, breathing, peeing time bomb.
The Experiment begins.
Hamsters barely live two years,
So it is guaranteed the child will have a taste of grief.
A "Real World" emotion.
How something so alive one day,
Small and warm in a child's hand,
Can be gone the next, and
No "I'm sorry" or "I'll do anything, I promise" can bring it back.
The finality of death dawns upon the child
And the experiment is over.

Zahra Seblini is an eleventh grader who has a soft spot for animals in the rodent family including but not limited to: hamsters, squirrels, and bunnies. She aspires to become a traveling interior designer. seblini2015@gmail.com

Chapter 12: Horse Tales

If *Gaze* Were Real by Zain Alsayad

If *Gaze* were real I
would use my spiky spurs to
ride the steel horse fast.

Zain Alsayad is a student at Lowrey Elementary in Dearborn, Michigan.

Statue by James Oleson / Photo by Leslie Herrick

Horses by Linda Choo

Tails gently swishing
No particular design
Easy and joyful

Linda Choo is a librarian at The Henry Ford. While walking in Greenfield Village one day, she saw some horses resting outside and was inspired to write this haiku. Watching animals often reminds her to relax and not take life too seriously.

Gorgeous by Nourah Sinahi

gorgeous
amazing
zantancular
extraordinary

Nourah Sinahi is a student at Lowrey Elementary in Dearborn, Michigan.

Remembering Dan by Dennis Tino

Growing up as a boy in Troy, Michigan, I lived on a 13-acre parcel of land that was about 300 feet wide and a half-mile deep. My father liked to do a little farming and used our workhorse Dan for tilling the soil, mainly for vegetable gardens and strawberries. Dan was a typical broad-shouldered workhorse, white in color, not too tall, and very mild-mannered. It was not a problem for me and my brothers to ride him bareback with just a set of reins to get him to go wherever we wanted to go.

Dan was kept in a shed-like structure attached behind the single-car wooden garage in our yard. While there was room for him to lie down, I don't remember ever seeing him off his feet, even at night while he was sleeping. I always assumed that this was typical for workhorses.

Near the rear of the property there was a large oak tree, known as the "Big Tree" that was well suited to climb, and which had an outstretched branch that was just right from which to hang a swing. Oftentimes in the summer, we would ride Dan out to the Big Tree and spend the afternoon swinging and playing around there. When we went into the nearby woods to play, Dan was satisfied to be tethered near the Big Tree, munching on grass, or just patiently waiting for us to come and ride him back home.

As time went by, my dad had less interest in farming, and Dan was "reclassified" as our pet. He lived to be nearly 20 years old before passing away, the only time I saw him lying down. What a great old pet was our Dan.

Dennis Tino retired from Ford Motor Company as a mechanical engineer in 1994 and has been a Dearborn resident since 1976. He enjoys reaching out with the Gospel through personal interaction such as International Student Ministry (ISM) at Wayne State University and prison ministry through Crossroad Bible Institute (CBI). He and his wife Norma are blessed with and enjoy their five married children's families with sixteen grandchildren, and one great-grandson.

Chapter 13: Hunting Tales

Law of the Wild by Syed Mustafa Akbari

Day after day, the baby bison began to grow weaker, and no matter how hard it tried to keep up, it had slowly begin to lag behind in the herd. Several days ago, a rabid lone wolf had attacked the herd. It had pounced upon the baby bison and was going for the final blow when the rest of the herd drove it off, but the wolf didn't leave until it left a nasty wound on the bison's leg. Sadly, the baby bison's mother had died last month when a hunter had illegally shot it, so now the herd was the only one taking care of the baby. Being injured, motherless and a baby can be a dangerous combination for a bison...

A massive blizzard was approaching the Yellowstone National Park; consequently, the bison were out, finding all the food they could before the storm hit. In Yellowstone, a blizzard could last anywhere from a few hours to more than a day. The herd was grazing on a snow-covered field but most of the delicious green grass was under the snow. Only a few patches of grass were visible and they were spread out far from one another, so the bison had spread out. The baby bison suddenly noticed an open patch of luscious green grass. Unfortunately, it was slightly far from the group, but food was food. The baby bison hobbled over to the grass and began munching down. As it ate, it thought it felt something was off... Something was not in its right place... Then, as it listened, it realized everything was quiet— too quiet. Even the birds had stopped their melodious singing. He slowly looked up. Thirty feet away, where the field ended and woods began, he saw something move, something fast, lightning fast.

He gave a loud warning call and slowly began to walk back to his herd, not moving his eyes from the woods. On the left! He saw another flash of fur. The rabid wolf attack suddenly replayed in his mind... Those horrible, razor-sharp claws... Those giant, needle-sharp teeth... Except this time, he was facing not only one wolf, but a pack of wolves set on eating him... He quickly turned his head and sprinted for the herd, or basically hobbled as fast as he could, because the herd was his last hope. Unfortunately, the herd deserted him and turned tail and ran. He heard a long howl coming from behind him, and then he heard yelps and snarls. He mooed in terror as he doubled his hobbling speed. All of a sudden from his left a wolf burst out of the woods. It closed the distance between it and the bison within seconds and with a snarl it sunk its teeth into the bison's healthy leg. His leg felt like fire, but with his previously injured leg, he kicked the monster's jaw. It reeled back in pain, but just a few seconds later, it struck again, this time on his previously injured leg. It bit, and then using his own body weight, the wolf pulled back trying to bring the bison down. The bison gave one last desperate call to the herd, but his cry fell onto deaf ears... His leg felt as if thousands of red hot needles were being thrust into it. After a few more steps, he lost his footing and fell. Moments later, the rest of the pack arrived. Most animals as you probably know kill their prey before eating them, but not wolves. They eat the animal alive... The pack descended upon the bison tearing into his flesh and ripping giant chunks of meat off. The air was filled with their yelps and shrieks as they made quick work of the bison. After all, in the wild, only one law prevails: survival of the fittest.

One of Syed Akbari's dreams has always been to be a published author. He absolutely loves reading, and people at his school who don't know his name call him "the boy who reads" because he reads even while walking to classes. He is also very fond of archery, playing soccer and swimming.
smustafa.aakbari@gmail.com

Hunting with Dad by Hank Czerwick

Unlike fishing, my dad did not let me go hunting with him until I was at least 10 years old. At first, he allowed me to carry my Daisy BB rifle. I had to handle it like a real rifle, uncocked, muzzle pointing either straight up or towards the ground. Also, unlike when we went fishing, on these occasions Dad never let any of his friends accompany us. As we walked the fields on my grandparents' farm, or those of a neighboring field, if we saw other hunters, my dad would hail them and then we would move in an opposite direction. Dad was always super cautious of having anyone within gun range of us.

As I got older, Dad allowed me to carry a real gun. It was a Stevens .22 caliber rifle. It was not loaded the whole time I carried it and the very same safety rules applied. When we stopped to eat the sandwiches that Dad carried in the same pouch of his vest that any game might go into, he would hand me a cartridge and allow me to shoot a can or twig. This was always placed against a tree or steep embankment. A rifle should never be discharged into the air like a shotgun. Eventually, I was allowed to carry a single shot 16-gauge shotgun. Dad would always walk to my right as I was right handed.

I was taught to have a profound respect for firearms from an early age. Hanging in my grandparents' living room was a mounted deer head on an ornately carved backboard. At the bottom were two deer hooves pointing up. It was here that my dad's 12-gauge Winchester Model 12 shotgun always rested. It was always loaded though not cocked. On a farm, there might be an immediate need to have a gun in hand. It might be a chicken hawk, a weasel, or a fox threatening the barnyard. And there was need for security during the dark nights when my grandmother and I were the only ones at home.

Like our fishing expeditions, if we went hunting somewhere other than on neighboring property, we had to leave early in the morning to be in the field, so that at the stroke of eight, we would load our guns and start hunting.

Certainly it was thrilling to have a pheasant jump up and to have Dad, in a split second, determine that it was a male ring-neck and to down it in a single shot! I always enjoyed the scent remaining after a shotgun shell was discharged. We would walk over to the downed bird and Dad would pick it up with one hand and gesture as if he were approximating its weight. He would then examine it to see where most of the shot had gone. He was always hopeful for a head shot and that a minimum of lead BB's would need to be picked out later when cleaning the bird.

More than the thrill of getting a bird, I always enjoyed the walk in the fields. I wore galoshes because hunting boots were too expensive to put on growing feet for a single season. Thus I had to be careful where I stepped. But Dad always seemed to pick the higher, drier ground as we looked not only for game but for mushrooms or an old apple tree. If a spot where mushrooms called "stumpers" grew was found, the trip might still be considered successful even though a pheasant was not to be had. However, that late in the year, most mushrooms were buggy. Not always so with apples. An abandoned tree might still have a few hangers-on. If there were bugs, Dad would cut out the good parts with his jackknife. Then, we would sit under that tree and if it was near noon we would enjoy our lunch with an apple dessert.

Hunting without a dog was difficult so there were only a few times, when Dad was between dogs, that we hunted without one. The first dog that I remember was an Irish Setter named Red. He was my dad's absolute favorite dog. Red lived on the farm with my grandparents while we lived in the city. On weekends, when we went to the farm, Red was always the first to greet us as we turned into the driveway.

Once, when Red developed a large tumor on his head, Dad took him to a veterinarian in the city. After his surgery, he convalesced on our enclosed back porch. During this time, Dad was very concerned, but soon Red was back to his old self.

In time, Dad's extreme concern for safety, especially mine, was to prove itself true. One sad day, when Dad and his good friend "Doc Stan" went to the fields with Red, there was an accident. Doc shot Red. I remember Dad carrying Red cradled in his arms up the driveway, tears streaking down his cheeks, with the remorseful Doc behind them carrying Dad's gun. That day, we buried Red near a big tree in the woods.

Doc tried to make it up to Dad by bringing over a succession of dogs for dad to try. Some were Irish Setters. None had the rapport with Dad as did old Red. Eventually Doc gave up and Dad was to find a reasonable substitute for Red.

We had a Beagle named Penny. She was a bit overweight. Dad always kidded about Penny. It was hard to tell whose scent she was on. It could be a rabbit, a pheasant, or even a deer. Dad called her a "county" dog because she always seemed to be in the next county from where we were!

During the dog drought, we tried hunting without one. In desperation, Dad took our Dachshund out one day. He reasoned that the dog was, after all, a hound. It worked! Figaro really could instinctively hunt. But Dad was embarrassed as heck if there were other hunters nearby and Dad had to call Figaro, Figaro! The final blow for Figaro as a hunter came one morning when he just refused to perform. All he would do is walk behind us and slow at that. Later we discovered why. Being our pet, he rode in the back seat. Dad had also put the brown bag with the sandwiches in the back seat. Unnoticed by either of us, Figaro was dining on our sausage sandwiches while we drove. We discovered the reason for his lethargy when it was our time to eat lunch!

Dad finally settled on a Brittany as the best all-around dog. Not too big, not too small, and certainly one that focused on pheasants and hunted in the same county as Dad. Dad also bought 40 acres of woods bordering the Huron National Forest near Rose City. Here he installed a trailer and built an outhouse. He had finally achieved the nirvana of all hunters: a good dog and his own piece of Paradise!

Hank Czerwick is a 66-year resident of the city of Dearborn and product of its schools. He retired from Ford Motor Company as an engineer and from Henry Ford Community College as an educator. His writing has been published in many magazines.

Hunting Trip by James Knapp

This account of a hunting trip in Montana is both a tale and a confession. Not having hunted large mammals before, I'd embarked with friends partially for the experience of field dressing a kill. That sounds callous, but I think it's important to grasp where meat comes from.

A hunting trip is a finite event, in this case five days. As time wore on without success, I and others began to feel... *anxious*. So on the fourth day, in the dim dawn light I bailed out of the truck as a herd of pronghorn antelope (they're called "goats" out there) slowly walked single file into the distance. This was an opportunity, as pronghorns are the fastest distance runners in the hemisphere. Hurriedly, I pulled my borrowed rifle from its case and fumbled rounds into the magazine and chamber. I then went prone in the scrubby dirt and decided to make a shot. Having a rough idea of the bullet's likely trajectory, I aimed five feet ahead and four feet above a horned male. When I pulled the trigger, the scope impacted my eyebrow which immediately began to bleed. While not a rare occurrence among hunters, I nevertheless felt the wound was the badge of a foolish amateur, and perhaps it was.

Oddly, I didn't know if I'd hit anything and I walked downhill unsure what I'd find. What I found mortifies me to this day. Goats blend into the terrain and I didn't notice him until he was fifty yards away, but there – limping – was that male with most of its left hind leg destroyed and dangling. Disgusted and almost nauseated, I closed with the goat, chambered another round and quickly dispatched it. I later ranged the initial shot at 340 yards.

So I learned lessons in large animal anatomy that day as I gutted the goat and smelled thick blood and took warm goo up to my elbows. And I saw the goat's eyes slowly change from life to waxy death.

In retrospect, I would have better acquainted myself with that rifle before using it, and I would *not have taken that shot*. Better opportunities came later, but not knowing that, I *still* should have held out for a better opportunity to make a clean kill. These lessons learned, I left for Michigan with a cooler full of meat.

James Knapp is a librarian for Dearborn Public Library who explores Michigan via its roads, waterways and trails – and loves every minute of it.

Local Encounter by James Knapp

I've had a Michigander's share of "up north" animal encounters, but one of the weirdest happened here in Dearborn.

On a rainy Easter Sunday morning about ten years ago, I was walking off-trail among the then-leafless hardwoods that thrive west of the Henry Ford Estate. I began to hear insistent barking in the distance and noticed it getting louder. And it was clearly coming from more than one dog.

I froze – astonished – as a panting, wild-eyed deer bolted past me. It appeared to be making a run for deep cover, or perhaps the river. Charging close behind were two dogs: yellow brutes of indeterminate breed. Lagging behind, but still in the chase, were a third ... and then a fourth dog. One of those looked like a German Shepherd.

They vanished from view, but not before I'd found a stout stick at some point, to arm myself. The barking slowly grew faint, and then stopped.

I later read in the paper there was a pack of feral dogs that was using the Rouge corridor as a hunting ground. They were exterminated by authorities.

James Knapp is a librarian for Dearborn Public Library who explores Michigan via its roads, waterways and trails – and loves every minute of it.

My First Deer by Nathan Nourie

Once I was hunting with my grandpa. About 3:05 p.m., he saw a buck and I couldn't see it. I waited for it to step out, then it stepped out and BAM!!!! I hit it. The buck jumped 3-5 feet in the air. It took off quickly. We waited about an hour then we went to track it. We were walking and walking in the woods and we eventually found it. It was dead laying by a tree. It was on opening day and it was my first deer I shot.

Nathan Nourie is in fourth grade at Nowlin Elementary School in Dearborn, Michigan.

Chapter 14: Moose Tales

The Moose by Alfred Brock

I came to Canada in search of moose.

A friend of mine had put a picture on Facebook of a moose and I realized I had never seen a living moose.

I went to the Toronto Zoo and I saw two moose there. One man moose and one lady moose.

They both seemed to be a little under the weather.

I went to eat at a place called Montana's.

Across from me, above the fireplace, now not in use, there was a beautiful painting. It showed a forest of maturing aspen, trembling aspen and birch. In the far back was an ice mist and so the view of whatever was out there was gently obscured by the white icy air.

Standing behind the trees was a dark shape. I could just make out the head of a moose. Towering above the perspective of the center of the image. It was so well done. I could feel the quiet of the forest about me. The white ice fog suspended in the air. The creature of mammoth size itself frozen in motion in order to hide from my seeking eye.

I recalled the places in the wild forests where I have been. The rocks covered in freezing sweat, the water unable to fully turn to ice but unwilling to flow. The evergreen trees bedecked in snowy blankets and holding suspended and dusted upon them crystals of intricate design and delicacy born and placed there by elements whose power is beyond my ability to comprehend.

Winds from the night before had left their blowing icy breath upon the trunks and branches of the trees. Blown so hard that in places the leaves left fallen on the earth from the previous autumn were exposed and themselves painted in yet a different kind of frost.

Still the moose stood still. A painting, I know, but the sound of the wind high above the trees and blowing through the bare branches sleeping in a cold that would freeze my blood and crack my bones came to my ears. Not howling as you might imagine but the heavy and mighty breathing of the air itself. The heavy wind bearing down upon the trees like your hand upon grass in dewy springtime day.

The moose stood stock-still. Knowing me and my place. Watching me with pools of dark water sitting high upon a face of long thought.

The moose in the painting and the moose in the world and in the zoo – they know savage thoughts as they have felt it inflicted on them. The moon's light brings the wolf across the range. Seeking food and safety for hearth and family. The moose in giant aspect enjoys repose in empty valleys and kirks filled with wood. Places where one or two wolves might find their way but places where the pack is useless.

The moose sees me and stops to stare – but the word "stare" is not of use here because the creature so giant among the wooded slopes and far-reaching space beyond it, behind me and around us also fills its eyes. Reflected from their shining surface are tens of thousands of trees gently moving in the wind and upon the land.

An adult moose moves through its landscape but no one knows even till now how far they range while walking for food. They walk – for life – for pleasure – for some other reason known only to them? Known only to each one of them.

It is a mystery to me.

As you can see.

I finished my meal and as I waited for my waitress to bring me the bill I turned around to look out the window. There was no window there. Upon the wall though was hung the head of a moose fully as big as me.

Its face long drawn and powerful.

Even stilled as it was his visage was beautiful and something to gaze upon. It was only as I turned away that I felt the sadness of the end of that one particular great creature. I looked again and noticed that even though it is called a giant deer its face more closely resembles that of the pronghorn antelope of North America.

I ate some donuts shaken in a bag with white powdered sugar. They tasted like zeppolis.

Alfred Brock likes animals. *alfred.brock@gmail.com*

Moose on the Loose by Teresa M. Lousias

While visiting Yellowstone National Park ten years ago, my two friends and I noticed a female moose drinking from a pond. It was almost sunset and what a wonderful site to behold.

As a photographer and lover of wildlife, I pulled the car off the road and got out to take some photos of our discovery. I invited my two passengers to join me but they declined.

I got out of the car with my camera hanging from my neck and walked to the pond down an incline. I was about 100 feet away from this awesome creature. I was on one side and the moose was on the other. She would put her head down to drink water and chew greenery from the pond. Miss Moose just kept doing this many times. While lifting her head and looking my way, she seemed not to mind me clicking my camera rapidly.

After a few minutes I decided to return to my friends. I thanked her and started walking back to the car.

All of a sudden my friend Cheryl rolled down the car window and started yelling to me to hurry up. I said, "I am coming." She said, "I mean right now!" I thought, "She is very anxious to leave here." She yelled again and started pointing to where the moose was. I looked back and as I did the moose had left the pond and was running up the incline towards me. Wow, I then too started running and made it into the car just in time. The window was down somewhat and as I slammed the car door the moose tried to put her nose into the window.

Whew, my heart was beating so hard and I was out of breath. All ended up well but I certainly learned my lesson about wildlife. Do not turn your back and we all need to heed and respect "The Call of the Wild" and yes I did "Hear the Call!"

A former banker, now a freelance photographer, Teresa Lousias has traveled the world and all 50 states of the USA. She loves nature and wildlife. They give her peace and happiness. *coolphotogirl@aol.com*

Chapter 15: A Mouse Tale

It's Me, Rachel by Mark Somers

Full Title: It's Me, Rachel: A Moonlit Introduction to Someone Particularly Special

"Got it!"

It was three days ago when he first caught a glimpse of it out of the corner of his eye. It ran across the floor along the wall so fast it was hardly more than a little blur. Whoosh! Under the door and into the room where Christmas decorations are stacked in boxes and the furnace quietly waits for winter to arrive.

Now, trapped in a box, his prize was in hand. And so it is he who stepped victoriously into the wild beyond the front door with the mouse.

It was a cool evening. Not so much as to need a jacket, rather more like the first time in the fall one thinks to oneself it might have been better to have worn long sleeves. The air is clear. The moon casts soft shadows. Leaves of oak and maple lie still on the grass.

It's a coolness you notice halfway down the block. You pause, but then go on, unhurried.

That's the very sort of evening it was when he placed the box on the lawn, expecting her to scurry into the shadows faster than his eyes could follow. Catch and release. Flip the box over, lift it up and . . . and there, perfectly still, not a blink between them – their eyes meet. Hers glisten. Shiny, black gems set in soft grey fur. Her nose twitches. Silently she speaks – "Rachel."

"My name, that is. My name is Rachel."

Silently, curiously, he stares.

She continues: "I think Rachel is a good name. That is, I think Rachel is quite the very best name for me. It rather suits me, don't you think? Right down to a tee. How very fortunate – my mother thought so when she named me. It saves the whole tiresome trouble of having to change it, though I am most assuredly and competently capable of choosing a name for myself.

"How entirely awkward would that have been anyway? I mean, how does one explain to one's mother that she has made such an obvious and silly mistake as to have given you the wrong name in the first place? Courtesy and consideration should hardly allow one to casually raise the point at dinner somewhere in between 'Would you please pass the carrots?' and 'Thank you, but I shouldn't care for any Brussels sprouts today.'

"Perhaps one might start a note on rather nice stationery with 'Dearest Mummy,' but had she named me Clareece, just how then would I have signed it?

"That is, I couldn't very well have actually signed it 'Clareece' or I should seem quite insincere to insist that I am 'Rachel' – and 'Rachel' is most certainly and truly a sincere name as I am most sincerely and truly confident that you must agree.

"If I were not Rachel, then quite frankly I just wouldn't be myself, now would I?

"In fact, if I were not Rachel, then whom might I ask would I be – or, should I say, then just whom might I ask would be me? I cannot begin to imagine anyone else being me. I am far and away the very best candidate for the position.

"Why, who could believe that Josephine or Margaret – as perfectly lovely as they may be, to be sure – why, who could be so distracted as to believe them to be me, Rachel? It defies logic and reason. Rather unscientific. That is not to say that the application of scientific principles is required in this situation. Anyone who knows me is perfectly well aware of who I am. Otherwise, they should hardly be heard to claim they know me at all. Why, if I weren't Rachel, the monogram on my sweater would be all wrong!"

She pauses, still looking at him. He returns to the house.

"Honey, you wouldn't believe it, that mouse just sat there looking at me as if to say 'Why are you putting me out, don't you know who I am?' It's the funniest thing!"

It was a cool evening. Not so much as to need a jacket, rather more like the first time in the fall one thinks to oneself it might have been better to have worn long sleeves.

Leaves of oak and maple begin to rustle gently on a breath of air across the lawn. The moon casts soft shadows. Rachel peers back toward the house on the corner – the one with the little hole between the brick. There, just beneath the water faucet.

For Cora and Luke – from Pop-Pop

Mark has lived in Dearborn over 30 years and is a judge of Dearborn's 19th District Court. msomers@ci.dearborn.mi.us

Chapter 16: Nature Tales

The Wild World of Levagood Park by Judy Altesleben

I have been a resident of Dearborn most of my 68 years, living in the Levagood Park area for 42 of them. Levagood has been a big part of my life and the lives of my children, with picnics, swimming lessons and Adray baseball.

Now that I am retired, I walk as often as possible on the track at Levagood with my friend Barbara. Recently we were surprised that our regular exercise turned into a nature walk.

A few months back, we were walking along near the swimming pool when the woman walking about 30 feet ahead of us stopped still. As we wondered why, we saw a doe dart across the park from Silvery Lane to Denwood. I feared I would hear screeching brakes but thankfully did not. I had no idea where the doe escaped to, but I hoped she was safe. About a week later, my husband saw a buck in the middle of the street, near Bryant Middle School, early on a Sunday morning. The deer have really come to "Deerborn."

A few weeks later, as again my friend and I walked the track at Levagood, we spotted a large bird on the ground near a picnic table sitting on something. Before I could see what it was, the hawk flew off with a squirrel in its talons. I have never seen anything quite like it – a truly amazing sight!

So, Dearborn residents, you don't need to go to the North Country to experience nature. Look to your own neighborhood park.

Judy Altesleben and her husband have lived in Dearborn their entire lives and raised seven children here. She taught Home Economics at Divine Child High School for 18 years and is now enjoying retirement.
judygingerbread@gmail.com

Waves by Joseph Bongero

The waves keep coming,
they never seem to stop.
One after another they advance
like soldiers into the line of battle.
They crash onto the beach
in a relentless volley expressing
in a final act of torrid sound.
Where are they born
no one really knows.
But their mother is the wind
and their father is the sun.

Joseph Bongero (1938-2011) was a United States Postal Service Letter Carrier and an English major in college. He loved being out-of-doors, observing nature and its constantly changing phenomena. He endured Parkinson's Disease the last 15 years of his life but even as the last five years meant limited mobility, he loved nothing more than being able to sit on the porches of his vacation home in Greenbush, Alcona County, Michigan, watching the ever-changing Lake Huron and landscape and searching for whatever birds, waterfowl and wildlife he could see, making records of them in his journals and often writing short stories or poems. His wife, Agnes Bongero, sent in this poem.

Woods by Joseph Bongero

A lonesome twig
struggling to survive
like a marble sparrow
at a winter's handout.

Adolescent leaves strain
to catch a single ray
of the summer sun
breaking through relenting clouds.

Autumn paints them, then
wipes the canvas clean
before winter's breath
brings frost-coated hibernation.

The spring's nourishment awakens and
the leaf damp floor gets further away
as arms slowly reach
then finally touch the all day sun.

From the last page
to the first
until that day
when the woodsman makes his choice.

Joseph Bongero (1938-2011) was a United States Postal Service Letter Carrier and an English major in college. He loved being out-of-doors, observing nature and its constantly changing phenomena. He endured Parkinson's Disease the last 15 years of his life but even as the last five years meant limited mobility, he loved nothing more than being able to sit on the porches of his vacation home in Greenbush, Alcona County, Michigan, watching the ever-changing Lake Huron and landscape and searching for whatever birds, waterfowl and wildlife he could see, making records of them in his journals and often writing short stories or poems. His wife, Agnes Bongero, sent in this poem.

Indian Head by Alfred Brock

I was living in New York at the time. The greatest city on earth. Yet, still, I felt that I had not a single solid idea what I was to do with my life. I was asking in my heart and soul for some solution to a problem I could not understand.

Simply – it came down to my wondering if there would be some sign that would answer my question as to whether or not there was something special for me to do in this world – or if there was any reason I was here other than to live and breathe. As if that were not gift enough.

Day after day I went to work. I worked with my hands. I worked hard. I left my house early in the morning and came home late at night. I worked six days a week. Each day I started out fresh and clean with laundered clothes and when I returned, I was tired, weary and covered with grime and filth.

It was a rather hard life. I took to it at first, but it began to wear on me. I sought an answer outside myself but could not find it. I began to learn as much as I could about animals. Taking my Sundays to read or visit museums. Always wondering, always asking questions.

Being in New York there was not often time to be in tune with nature. The local squirrels offered chatter and the birds, pigeons and starlings mostly, were communal and avoided close contact with people. The few songbirds that sojourned or passed through did not stay long. Leaving one song or a few notes on the air before charging out of the metropolis as fast as they could go.

One day while I was looking at maps I came across the name of a mountain in upstate New York that was not too far from New York City but far enough to be considered 'in the country.' It is called 'Indian Head.' It is seated deeply inside a public park, a nature reserve, and it seemed like a goodly destination for an 'expedition' into the wilds of North America.

In any case I set myself one Saturday night and determined I would head out the next day for the 'wilderness.' In picturesque opposition to the small town rube or country bumpkin, my preparations for this journey were very much those of a city boy who had very little experience with nature outside of that great human preserve of city and suburb. I packed a lunch of peanut butter sandwiches, four apples and a banana.

The next morning I awoke and had a small breakfast of coffee and donuts. I then drove north out of the city and headed to the mountain.

Indian Head is a Devil's Path range of the Catskill Mountains. It is 3,573 feet tall.

I arrived at the base of the mountain late in the morning. I parked my car at the trailhead. There were just a couple of other cars in the parking lot. I went towards a small building and saw a stand that had a book in it that hikers were supposed to sign in order to let the rangers know who was on the trail.

As I looked at the book and searched around the compartment for a pen or pencil to sign the book, a ranger came out of the building.

She asked me if I was going on the trail.

I said, 'Yes.'

She asked how far I was going.

I said, 'To the top.'

She looked at me with a quizzical look and said, 'Some experienced climbers find they cannot make it all in one day. Do you know when we can expect you back down?'

I said, 'I am not camping. I am going to the top and coming back down.'

She said, 'Okay. Do you know how tall the mountain is?'

I said, 'No.'

She told me and then said, 'Sign the book.'

So I did.

I then busied myself while she gave some specifics about the mountain including staying on the trail. I told her that if I encountered a difficulty I would turn around and come back. I told her I did not anticipate any difficulty. I added that I was there looking for animals and birds.

She told me of some animals and birds I might look for.

I thanked her and she cautioned me to be careful once again. I assured her I would follow her advice and I then bid her adieu and began my hike up the mountain.

The climb quickly became steep and difficult. I was not in the best shape. I decided that to make it I would need to periodically rest on some likely rock and just take it one step at a time.

As I advanced up the mountain my hike became an outline for the type of life that I might find appealing. I started to form an outline of how I could make an exit from my present difficulties, if I would just rest when weary and take things one step at a time.

Though the climb was arduous and steep, it seemed as if the more difficult it became the better it was for me and my soul.

I kept close to the trail. I saw all of two chipmunks – well, one chipmunk and the rustling leaves left in the wake of another scurrying through the forest floor – and one brown bird. That was the extent of my wildlife observations as I climbed the mountain.

To give you an idea of the slowness of my ascent, a retired couple wearing hiking gear passed me at fairly good walking pace. They left me behind in no time.

As I climbed and I formed my plan for the future I still wondered if there was any real reason for me to be doing what I was doing. It had dragged on me for two to three weeks that I must climb Indian Head but I had no idea what for.

As it was I was glad I had finally found a way out of my difficulties, or at least a way to tolerably live with them without having them crush me to dust.

The day was balmy and though the sky threatened rain at one point, thankfully, it did not.

I continued climbing slowly and surely. Eventually I came upon the retired couple sitting by the side of the trail. The man looked in pain and his wife worried. Apparently he had overexerted himself. I stopped to ask if I could be of assistance. I was told that they had decided to cut their climb short and were returning to the base.

I stayed nearby a while until they started back down. The fellow seemed okay and they waved me off so I turned back up the trail. Walking slowly and resting at every likely rock.

I travelled like this through quiet woods – the only sounds being a light breeze above the high trees once in a while and the sound of my shoes on the trail.

Because of the thickness of the woods I could not determine how far up I was or even how far I had come. It occurred to me that perhaps I was making a mistake. I checked my watch and determined that if I had not reached the summit by a certain time I would go back down no matter what. Though I had not retrieved what I was seeking, I already had been given far more than I anticipated.

The path began a tortuous circling. The trail nearly disappeared as it was necessary to begin ascending rock ledges – some of them four feet tall or higher – using whatever hand and foot holds were available. Still, I scaled ever higher.

I then heard a voice up the trail. As I climbed further and got closer I could hear someone – apparently a guide – explaining some of the dangers of the mountain. The voice told about extreme weather, unsure footing, remoteness and other things including the necessity of wearing the proper clothing. Still, I climbed on. I climbed one ledge about eight feet in height and after dragging myself over the edge of it I found myself in the center of a half circle of hikers whose attention was upon their skilled leader. All of them were dressed in hiker's gear and had extensive equipment.

I said, 'Hi there!'

I was met with faces as silent as the woods around them. I became intimately aware of my dress. Tennis shoes, tube socks, green checked cotton shorts and a button shirt.

I stood stock-still for a few moments and not getting any response I said, 'Excuse me,' and passed through the group. I climbed the next ledge and went on.

As it was I had a few more ledges to climb when I walked out on a plateau of some size. I immediately found the remains of a fire and some spent shotgun shells that appeared to have been discharged there or thrown into the fire for 'fun.'

I reflected that the folly of humankind was not restricted to city limits.

I walked around a large granite outcropping and walked along a ledge. I realized I was on the very top of Indian Head Mountain and I was atop the brow of the granite Indian Chief.

I sat down in exhaustion. In the warm sunlight I gazed out upon the forest extending down the valley to the very horizon. I went to sleep.

I awoke some time later and looked in amazement at the beauty before me. Still I wondered why I had come there. Was there some reason? I lay my head back with eyes closed and prepared myself for the journey down.

I gazed into the sky and saw a small dot. It moved. I thought it to be a jet plane far away but there was no contrail. Then, as it approached, I thought it to be a small passenger plane but it flew erratically. As it approached I thought it might be a bird and counted myself lucky to see two birds after all that travel. Still it approached but it was not a bird. I could not tell what it was but it was travelling extremely fast and headed right for me!

In a flash the thing was upon me and struck me with a force full in the chest that felt like someone had poked me with their finger. I was frightened and shocked. I looked down and saw in my lap an enormous Monarch butterfly. It wasn't moving.

Still ignorant in the face of all that had come before this, still doubting, still full of myself, I thought, oh, great, I came all this way to kill a butterfly – one of only four wild creatures I have seen today. I looked at the perfectly shaped thing lying motionless in my lap and then I saw it begin to breathe. Laboriously and slowly, its abdomen moved. After some time it righted itself and stood upon its legs. After some more time it cleaned itself and showed other signs of life. For all my reasoning the insect appeared relieved, if that could be the case.

Slowly it climbed up my shirt and stopped on my chest above my heart and spread its wings to the sun. It stayed like that for some time and then continued to my shoulder. Facing me it sat as I gazed down at its sequined eyes and intricately formed and brightly colored wings. As the breeze died down and the wind stopped it leapt into the air and flew into the woods behind me, disappearing into the woodlands.

I looked back over that wide expanse of wilderness and thought of how that creature had vaulted and arced through the air in a dance with death that sped it ever onward at greater and greater speed towards its ultimate destruction and doom on the face of a craggy rock thousands of feet above an uncaring forest until it happened to bump into me.

Then I went home.

Alfred Brock likes to hike and photograph animals. alfred.brock@gmail.com

Queen Anne's Lace by Beaufort Cranford

Most people wouldn't know Queen Anne if she came up to them riding a rhinoceros. But you've got to keep your eyes shut tight to miss Queen Anne's lace, and most people who know a daisy from a doughnut know its name, too.

Some folks say Queen Anne, the bride of James I of England, insisted on bringing this graceful white wildflower into her garden, and since she was a notable lacemaker the connection was natural. Others say the queen was posthumously honored by the naming, and that a tiny dark flower in the center of a large white cluster represents a drop of the royal blood produced when she pricked her finger while making lace.

One thing we know for certain about Queen Anne's lace is that it's in the parsley family, otherwise the *Umbelliferae*, in that those familiar flat groups of flowers are called umbels. The family includes parsley, anise, caraway, celery, chervil, dill and fennel. But by far the most famous player in the umbel-o-rama is the carrot.

Queen Anne's lace is sometimes called wild carrot, for it and our table carrot are both *Daucus carota*. Some people make garden carrots the subspecies *D. carota sativa*, with sativa implying cultivation. The roots of Queen Anne's lace are white and slender instead of orange, and not nearly so mild as their domesticated relatives, but people have eaten them since people have eaten.

In fact, Queen Anne's lace came to North America with early colonists who ate it. In turn, it thought the place was wonderful, and dug in and prospered. Now it's common in fields and on roadsides from sea to shining sea. In summer, freeways throughout this area are prettified by hillsides painted in Queen Anne's lace; in vacant lots all over town, its white flowers pair perfectly with the blue of chicory, which blooms a little earlier but hangs around most of the summer.

Queen Anne's lace starts with a low bunch of leaves that look like a carrot's, as you might expect, then usually in its second summer throws out 1- to 3-foot stems with umbels on top. No one seems to know what that little purplish flower in the center is for, but there it is.

When the flowers are finished, the umbel closes up, probably to protect the maturing seeds inside. Eventually the umbel opens again and the seeds escape.

Obviously, this process is marvelously successful. It's also lovely; certainly one of the Midwest's most striking warm-weather sights is a field of Queen Anne's lace, its thousands of tiny parasols gleaming white in the sun.

On the other hand . . . Queen Anne's lace is a ferocious colonizer, and if left alone will crowd, shade and virtually obliterate most everything around it. If you don't want them but have a couple anyway, just mow them down before they bloom; if you have a meadowful, better hitch up the mules next year and plow them under.

Long ago, farmers who knew that appearances can be deceiving gave this mild-looking wildflower still another of its names: devil's plague. To black swallowtail butterflies, however, it's anything but. If you're around a field of Queen Anne's lace, you may see these large, dark butterflies looking for a place on which to lay their eggs. A couple of weeks ago I watched four fat black-swallowtail caterpillars do violence to the tender foliage of a carrot garden, and they love wild carrots just as much.

Most of us don't have to worry about the plague aspect of Queen Anne's lace and are simply free to enjoy it. So we should thank whoever mows the roadways in this part of the world for often passing it by, thus upgrading corridors that otherwise would be mighty uniform and grim. Its flowers are the clearest signal of high summer in the Midwest—and quite unlike another white blanket we'll see on those same roadsides in a few months. For now, anyway, I'd prefer my scenic gems to be measured in carrots.

Beaufort Cranford retired from Wayne State University in 2013. beaufortc@gmail.com

Three Days in Mid-Atlantic by Mohamed Fawaz

My dream had come true. But I was not enjoying it in the least. I have always wanted to seclude myself in an isolated spot in the Atlantic for days at a time, sip some hot, hot coffee while meditating, relaxing, thinking, and maybe reading or writing science-fiction. The water was not too cold. Not nearly as cold as I ever thought it would be mid-ocean. It was my third day like this. I was stranded in the middle of nowhere. I was somewhere in the Atlantic Ocean, and with nothing to eat or drink whatsoever. I was drinking the ocean's salty water, and salty water keeps one alive, but it does not quench thirst. I was a big fool. Yes, a big fool. I had left my quiet Michigan town of Ludington to spend a nice vacation in Virginia Beach. It was a beautiful place, everybody said, and I was immensely delighted to be in my little rented canoe in the Atlantic Ocean. It was so beautiful and so relaxing. I was thinking of nothing—absolutely nothing when I fell asleep. And when I woke up, I found myself here. But where is here is the good question. The waves had swept my canoe from near the beach to some spot in this vast ocean. And yes, I still have my canoe, and that is something to be grateful for. But the little canoe did not prevent the ocean's waves from soaking my entire body. It was foggy, and I could barely see a few feet ahead of me. The air was so humid, and I could feel my lungs aching with every breath.

I was being pushed by the waves in every direction. I thought about using my paddles, but what for, I thought. I was totally disoriented, and I had no means of knowing where to go. Even the sky was difficult to see, and if I saw it, I did not know which direction to take. I did not know where the shore was anyway.

Part II: The Whale.

I looked at the huge and wild fire in the middle of the ocean, and I could hardly believe it. I recollected the movie that people once talked about. It was called *2012*, or maybe it was called *Doomsday*, I cannot remember. My canoe was still sitting on the back of that huge whale. I was so worried the whale would throw me into the water along with my canoe. The fire was vast, and it was expanding every second. It was a wild fire in the ocean, and amongst the waves. But the whale was still calm. He was not evil. I knew that. I feared him so much when he (or she) first approached me, and raised my canoe on the top of its back. But whales do not eat people, I hear. Yet still, hearing and experiencing are two different things. Several other whales had assembled around me, and they all appeared to be watching the huge fire. We had moved a little, and, luckily, the wind was pushing the smoke to the opposite direction. A large bird fell right into my canoe, and it appeared sick and struggling with death. I could not even tell what kind of bird it was. It may have been an eagle or something, but I could not be sure. I reached to the water and washed the bird's head a little. But the bird only needed to rest. And within minutes, the bird recovered strength, and it flew away. I looked to my side, and the book that I was reading was still sitting next to me. I had placed it in a zip lock bag, and had connected a thick string to the bag and then to the seat in the canoe. How ironic, I thought. I was reading *Moby-Dick*—the classic novel about the whale—and here I was sitting in my canoe on a whale's back. But Moby-Dick was only defending itself, I thought, and in this case, this gigantic whale only wanted me to see the huge oil spot within the ocean. There were lots and lots of dead fish floating in and around that oil spot, and it was killing the marine life there. The only solution I could think of was to set it ablaze using my lighter. I lit a sheet that I extracted from my *Washington Post*, wrapped it around a dead fish that I grabbed from the water, and threw it, as hard as I could, toward the oil spot. And yes, some may wonder how my newspaper was still intact, and that is because I had placed several books and this newspaper inside a large sealed bag, and put them with me. I was planning to read them all while relaxing in this little canoe.

The fire started to shrink, and the oil spot was shrinking as well. Seven whales were still watching from a distance, and my whale, or, in other words, the whale that I was riding, was also quietly floating in the water. Fatigue was drowsing my eyes, and when I woke up, I was roughly 50 yards away from the shore. The whales had disappeared, but a few of the eagle's feathers were still in my canoe. My torn *Washington Post* was also still sitting next to me, and I could but weep with anguish because we are causing all of this destruction and pollution in the ocean and in space, and we never take a second to think what harm our actions are causing to the wildlife. I am so glad we have oceans; and am so glad because we have fish and whales; and am all hope that this treasure will always be there. I just pray that this ocean will not ever become a memory of the past.

After getting his bachelor's degree in psychology and creative writing, Mohamed Fawaz is now attending law school and wants to become a public prosecutor. He loves nature, and his writings reflect this passion. His writings have appeared in the Grand Valley State University Student Reading Series, Vinette, Long Story Short, *and elsewhere. He also has one book in press. fawaz.moe@gmail.com*

The Call by Anne Gautreau

Call of the Wild

Call of the Wind

Call of the Wondrous

Call of the Wanderer

Call of the Wish

Call of the Willow

Call of the Wisdom

Call of the Winner

Call of the Winsome

Call of the Wolf

Call of the West

Call of the warm wolf wisdom worrying wrongs

Call of the wrathful wrinkled-woolen woodsman

Call of the wondrous-wish wanderer

Call of the west wind

Call of the wild

Anne Gautreau is a retired educator and is active in the American Association of University Women, the Dearborn Library Foundation, and the Community

Fund's Midwest Sculpture Initiative. Travel to over seventy countries has enriched her life. This is an example of an echo and recurrence poem.

Pine Tree by Sarah Kalmoni

Pine tree, pine tree
So tall and green
Branches spread out
So strong, so lean

Springtime has come
Pine cones in bloom
Squirrel, won't you come down
It's half past June

Pine tree, pine tree
Getting taller each day
The shade is glorious
On a hot summer day

Summertime is so fun
Pine tree feels so good
Why can't days like this
Stay forever in a kind mood?

Cooler days ahead
Fall season is here
Pine tree makes a nice bed
Squirrel sleeps near

Snow falls on pine tree
Wintertime around the bend
Pine tree weathers the storm
Eagle finds a friend

Pine tree, pine tree
No matter what time
Life is beautiful
And nature sublime

Sarah Kalmoni is an aspiring writer. She enjoys writing short stories, poetry, essays and minibiographies about her favorite musicians in her spare time.

Love of the Wild by Veronica Susalla

I think it was stories like *The Call of the Wild* that made me come to appreciate nature and respect the wild. I have always been at home in the wild; fishing with my father, hiking, camping. Generally, wild animals are content living side by side, but for food and protecting their families. If you do not seek them out, most animals can sense you mean them no harm. They may even come close enough to see what you are all about.

When I'm in my yard, it is not unusual to have squirrels, chipmunks, birds, and butterflies all hovering close. It is a lovely feeling to know they trust you enough to come close and act natural. They can be quite entertaining at times. I have a pair of ducks that visit my yard every spring. I have had the excitement of watching a family of raccoons, Mama and four cubs, splash and frolic in puddles left after a heavy rain. I have had similar experiences walking in the woods. And while I never forget and respect that wild animals are wild animals, I will always treasure time spent sharing nature with my wild friends.

Veronica Susalla is a lover of animals and nature, enjoying every minute she spends in the wild. She has written two books: A Twist of Fate *and* Come Back to Haunt You. *She also writes reviews for TripAdvisor under the name Chammy13. She has over 10,000 followers on Google+.*

Dusk by Claudia Taniguchi

The lone hyena pads along the bank,
his skulking moves him toward the drinking pool.
The night hawk follows where his paw prints sank,
his eye: a silent, watchful, golden jewel.
The restless lions stand and stretch their spines
to wait the absence of the sloping sun.
A beetle wakes upon the dusty vines,
its nightly quiet quest for food begun.
This stealthy scarab's scuttle quickens swift,
escaping past the rhino's roaming nose
and fits himself within a narrow rift.
The sky displays its grays in mottled rows:
as Day concedes her shift of golden time
to Night who gleams with vigilance sublime.

Claudia Taniguchi loves her job as a high school English teacher. In her free time, she enjoys reading, traveling, and spending time with family. claudiamud@yahoo.com

Wild Dearborn by John Toohey

When I was growing up in Dearborn during the 1960s and early '70s, I don't recall ever seeing any deer, black or grey squirrels or martens while spending most of my spare time in the woods behind our house on Long Boulevard. These relative newcomers to our natural environment add to the already wildly diverse variety of animals that helped make my childhood so enjoyable. There were plenty of raccoons along with opossums, skunks, rabbits and woodchucks, and a small pond where tiny spring peepers would sing loudly in early spring. I had a Have-a-Heart trap which caught animals live and unharmed and I used to catch raccoons that were sneaking into the garage to raid our garbage cans at night. My Dad would release them somewhere along Edward Hines Drive but there were always more to take their place. One night I caught two baby raccoons at the same time and kept them for a couple days in a spare cage I had for my pet rabbits. There was plenty of other wildlife as well and I remember one summer when a huge snapping turtle buried itself in the dirt behind my next door neighbor's house. A friend of mine from down the street and I dug it out and then had our picture taken with it by a photographer from the city. A few days later we each received a copy of the photo signed "Best wishes from Mayor Orville Hubbard." Then there was "Clean the Rouge Day" every spring when we would walk down the middle of the river with the water up to our waists pulling out all kinds of trash and debris, everything from shopping carts and tires to old mattresses. I was always on the lookout for turtles sunning themselves on the banks or hiding in the water. I also loved to explore the nearby woods and the swamp behind the First Presbyterian Church on Brady Street. In the summertime there were always plenty of frogs, toads, turtles, salamanders and garter snakes to catch. I would release most of them, but a few I would keep as pets for a short while before letting them go. It was always such a thrill for me to see all the wildlife in their natural habitat after reading about them in schoolbooks or seeing them on television.

In 2004 I moved back to Dearborn after living in Colorado for 20 years. I brought with me my two Shih Tzus who also love to go hiking

in the woods and observe the wildlife. Their favorite thing to do is chase the deer and the squirrels although they're never quite fast enough to catch them. It's always funny to see the curious expressions on the faces of the deer as these two hairy little pooches run towards them. I ran into a hiker one day who told me the deer are descendants of a small herd that Henry Ford used to keep on his Fairlane estate. That made me wonder why I had never seen them while I was growing up. They seem to have formed a sort of deer highway that runs along the Lower Rouge River and stretches from the Ford Fairlane estate down to Dearborn High School and back. I've seen herds as large as a dozen deer which amazes me considering Dearborn is in the middle of such a well-developed urban metropolitan area. Each spring I still enjoy watching tadpoles in the swamp develop into frogs and toads and seeing all the young animals with their mothers. I've noticed a huge increase in the number and variety of turtles living in the pond at Ford Field, thanks in part to the completion of the CSO project. The cleaner water has also attracted a large assortment of fish aside from the carp that are so plentiful. One of my favorite of the recent changes in Dearborn is the walking and biking path that goes from Andiamo's on Michigan Avenue all the way to Hines Drive. The views you experience in autumn are some of the prettiest examples of fall foliage I've seen, and the deer running through the woods are an added bonus.

I'm so glad to see that things really haven't changed very much with respect to Dearborn's wildlife population. It was a wonderful place to grow up all those years ago and it's still a wonderful place to explore and observe nature today, although I really do miss the sound of those spring peepers.

John Toohey is a longtime Dearborn resident, environmentalist, and animal lover. He supports many animal related causes and charities.
toohey1@wowway.com

Chapter 17: A Panther Tale

The Fall of Me by Byan Al-Qalyuby

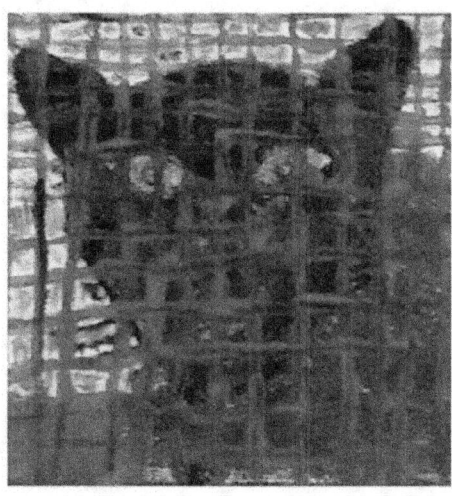

I run as fast as I can, and nothing can hold me back. I am wild and free. I feel the wind touching my fur and brushing over my head. I feel powerful and fearless and nothing can stand in my way. The smell of fresh air inhaled makes me think of the flying birds up high. Peace surrounds me from every side. Color green everywhere, red I hunt and blue I drink. I am the king of my home, I rule my empire and I stand alone. Black fur and crystal blue eyes is what I wear. At night, I sit and stare at the clear skies with the bright shining stones. The moon talks to me and protects me from every side. Nothing but me, myself and I.

I wake up after a long twinkle fall. I hear strange sounds. My heart beats; I feel something. I feel something never felt before in my own home. I feel fear. My body is speaking to me, intending to protect me but I simply ignore it. I hear heavy footsteps but I am not clear on what it is. I see a shadow, actually eight shadows. Two-legged creatures with long hands, some had black hair and some blonde. They hold some strange machines in their hands. The smell of their bodies displeases my nose and the flying birds are now falling. Surrounded I am, confused as my body won't move. I command it to move but all I hear is my heart pounding even louder. I am pushed, pinned down and stabbed by four. I feel worthless, I feel lost and the question I ask is why? I am held down and I am numb. I see blood dripping from my legs. They hold me down so tight that I can no longer breathe. My body once again tries to help, but this time my mind is forced to protect me by taking me to a far place with many beautiful flying birds, dancing stars and moons that wear beautiful smiles. On my knees, down I fall hard, and forever broken.

I wake up in a big cage. I have no room to run. I don't see blue or green. Just see tall repulsive buildings with a lot of two-legged creatures wearing fake smiles. I can't smell anymore. I can no longer hear the birds because they are now dead. I have a strange feeling but this feeling is just a new one, a scary one. I feel dark, hate and destruction. I have lost my mountain and power. They don't know what they have done to me. I can no longer sleep or feel. I am so cold with no heart. My boat is no longer sailing and is anchored with more weight than I can bear. I am stuck in reverse with no direction. My empire has lost its king…

Byan Al-Qalyuby: *"The silence of the night tends to bring out a special side of us. A side that we ought to protect and show the daylight more often."*

Chapter 18: A Possum Tale

Pete, the Possum by Barbara Sophie Hansen

Once there was a possum, named Pete, who lived by the Rouge River. He had many possum friends, and they could usually chase each other and find food when they were hungry. However, Pete was getting bored with the same old food and the same old routine every day. That's when he decided to venture forth from his usual habitat. Moreover, he had heard from raccoons that there might be some good people food, further down the river. "Why not go for an adventure?" he thought.

Thus, Pete took off in the morning and decided to explore the neighborhoods where people lived. Maybe he could find a nice, warm, cozy place to stay. He could also get out of the usual possum world and watch everything from the people's views. He had left without even saying goodbye to his possum friends.

As he was travelling, he noticed these big strange things on smaller rounded objects, moving. He didn't know what they were, but he somehow avoided them. Eventually, he found some houses and poked his nose around as much as possible, looking for something he could eat. "Where is the food? Where is there a place to stay?" He wondered about what was happening. Did he really make the right choice to leave his possum friends? Well, Pete wandered through the yards of several houses, before he became tired.

Just when he was about to give up, he spotted one of those big things with the rounded objects on the bottom in a backyard. Since it wasn't moving, he decided to check it out. He ran under it. "Hmm, no food, but I could stay and keep warm over here. Maybe I could bring leaves and food to this place." So Pete decided to climb up from underneath and explore. He got under what was the hood of the car, and he was so comfortable that he fell asleep.

All of a sudden, there was a thundering noise that repeated itself over and over. It was so loud that Pete woke up. What was that noise? Why did he have to be disturbed? Pete was very upset and nervous. Even worse, it turned out that a human was trying to start that contraption that he was so comfortably settled in. This human was sitting in the contraption, not too far from him, but, at least, he was away from the human and unnoticed. Pete did not know that the human was trying to start a car and would soon be looking under the hood. Just then, his beady eyes came face to face with those of the human. Pete was scared. What was he to do, now? "I know! I'll just play dead." So that's what he did. Eventually, there was no more human. He thought that he had won the battle and solved his problem. Now, he could go back to sleep.

Well, little did Pete know that something else would happen. He was sound asleep when he heard noises and looked up. A big looping rope was swinging, or was it a hook? "Oh, oh," he thought, "I'd better do something." Unfortunately, it was too late; he felt himself being lifted up in the air. He panicked: "They're grabbing me! I've got to get loose! I'll try to wiggle and keep at it." Lo and behold, Pete wiggled free and scampered down the driveway. He was still scared, so he headed as fast as he could, away from the place.

Pete decided that his idea was not so good, after all; and he headed away from the neighborhoods. He kept telling himself, "There's no place like home. There's *no place* like home." Soon, he found his way back to his surroundings, and he was ever so happy to see his friends. As he was telling them about his adventure, he was telling himself that he would never leave his home, again.

Barbara Hansen is a retired teacher and also a retired historical presenter from The Henry Ford. This story actually happened, many years ago on Roosevelt Street, and she decided to tell it from the perspective of the animal in the story. barbarasophiehansen@hotmail.com

Chapter 19: Rabbit Tales

A True Story: The Baby Rabbit by Haneefa Mahmood

Have you ever attempted
To rescue a rabbit?
If you don't know how to
Then don't make it a habit

So let me tell you
A story with suspense
About a little rabbit
It really does make sense

It all started one day
When I saw a small bunny
Stuck in a fire escape
With a coat the color of honey

It looked ever so scared
Its nose was twitching
Ears up straight
Eyes barely blinking

So I raced up the stairs
Ever so quickly
To cry out for help
For once I wasn't picky

And help came at once
And raced quickly outside
Carrying a box
To trap the bunny inside

So we could get him out
Safe and sound
So he wouldn't be
Lunch for a hound

As soon as he saw us
He filled with sorrow
He didn't know we were trying to help him
Get back to his burrow

My grandma went
Down the ladder
Carrying a box
This made the bunny sadder

She tried to get him cornered
By using the box
She had to get him out soon
So he wouldn't be eaten by a fox

And soon
He was caught
Trapped in a box
What fight he had fought

So we let him go
He ran neither with fear nor glee
But the good thing was
He was finally free

You might have thought
The outdoors was boring
But now I hope

Your imagination is soaring

Haneefa Mahmood loves the outdoors and Jack London's The Call of the Wild. *She loves reading and writing poems. She loves all animals, especially cats and rabbits. She hopes to have one of her own someday. She is 11 years old and lives in Dearborn, Michigan, with her parents and little brother.*

The Straw Filled Room by Anita Polzin

Leah was seven. It was spring and the walk home from school to her family's small farm was refreshing. She could not wait to see the bunnies! She had discovered little white fluffy bunnies in one of the two back rooms of their garage. What a nice surprise that had been.

"There are so many! Let me count them! One, two, three—please stop hopping—thirty nine, forty! They are so cute! They all look alike. How can I tell them apart?"

The old room had two doors. One was leading into the garage and the other outside. Straw was spread across the room and a small stack of hay was in the corner. Every day at school's end, after checking in with her mother, Leah would visit the bunnies. She would spend hours petting and paying attention to each of them. A special bunny had one pink eye and one purple eye. This one she could definitely tell from the others. After she named him Pinky Purp, this bunny was always first to be noticed. Leah would sit on the hay pile with Pinky Purp on her lap. Pinky Purp would get so comfortable he would fall asleep. Not wanting to disturb him Leah would sit very still and observe the other bunnies. She began noticing that like the seven dwarfs in Snow White they had different personalities. Sometimes she would sing to them:

> Here comes Peter Cottontail
> Hopping down the bunny trail
> Hippety hoppity
> Look at Peter go

A peaceful, serene contentment was experienced by Leah daily in the small straw filled room.

One pleasant sunny day Leah, as always, ran to visit the bunnies. As she stood at the threshold of the room she saw none of the bunnies were there. "Where are the bunnies?" she thought. She heard her father's voice in the garage. She ran through the entrance. "Daddy, where are the bunnies?"

She stood frozen in shock. Around three sides of the garage, hanging on nails, were bloody, headless, skinned bunnies. With tear filled eyes she looked at her father. He told her, "I thought you knew. They were like chickens—not pets."

"But not Pinky Purp!"

"I'm sorry. I did not know about Pinky Purp."

She ran from the garage, shock still numbing her small body. "No! Bunnies are not like chickens! Chickens are ugly and unfriendly. Bunnies are like kittens. You don't eat kittens!"

No one consoled her. She grew up a lot that day.

Anita Polzin is retired as a court clerk at the 36th District Ct. in Detroit. She has been a Dearborn resident since 1997. This story is based on a childhood experience growing up on a small farm in what is now Southgate, Michigan.

Chapter 20: Rescue Tales

Of Heart And Karma: Petey Jefferson's Story by Walter Lamb

There is a feeling I have harbored for as long as I can remember that the concept of karma is righteous. Jesus touched on it in his "Sermon on the Mount" without verbalizing the word. Confucius did likewise with his "Golden Rule." Sayings such as "that will come back to haunt you," "God will reward you for that," and "things have a way of coming around," etc. also touch on the concept.

I also feel you can stockpile karma over the course of a lifetime onto the positive side of your ledger when Judgment Day arrives and that is where you will be able to find this story when my friend Brian presents his resume.

Brian and I are surveillance and protection specialists that for years have plied our trade at an infrastructure alongside the Detroit River near downtown Detroit. Brian and I both served in the Marine Corps and have spent our entire adult lives doing this type of work. Brian worked in a private sector military capacity in Kosovo and elsewhere during his career. In spite of being a boot-leather-tough jarhead, he possesses an affinity for disenfranchised animals that rivals all I have heard about the renowned St. Francis and during the course of our years at the infrastructure I have become cognizant of his big heart and amazed at all the karma he is surely harvesting. Photo: L to R: Yours truly and Brian.

The area where we work is a decaying urban center that nudges aside the conventionality of city living as wildlife has reclaimed the area long thought to have been relinquished. There is a jambalaya of animals, i.e. red foxes, grey foxes, coyote, and occasional deer, raccoons, rats, mice, squirrels, possum, ground hogs, hawks, pheasants, alley cats, ghetto dogs, etc. Brian and I would provide food for the animals that were struggling to survive or when they were hungry, and I have witnessed foxes, cats, and raccoons eating side by side from a pile of dry cat or dog food on many, many occasions. The foxes, cats, and raccoons all came to trust Brian to the point they would take the food from his hand.

There was a female fox that Brian named "Mama" in recognition of the two litters she raised in the last five years. Mama and a two-year-old runt are the only red foxes left as all the others were spotted on a voyage aboard a huge chunk of ice headed to the Canadian side and were never seen again.

On two occasions Mama and her runt developed severe mange which destroyed their beautiful coats and crippled them to the point they could barely walk. We scoured the internet and found a home remedy herbal solution therein which when mixed with cat food allegedly could cure mange. Like magic within a month the two foxes were sporting beautiful coats again and running without a limp.

Throughout the years Brian has rescued at least ten cats from certain death at our assigned area. They varied in age from kittens to the elderly. Each cat was provided a trip to the vet for complete examination and treatment for all ailments. The cats live/lived in bliss with Brian in the warmth and comfort of his home. One male cat Brian named "Smokey" and not just because of his all black fur. The vet advised Brian that his paws were maimed from fire. Two weeks ago while Brian was sleeping on his couch, Smokey was batting him on his head and then jumped down and stared up at Brian's face. Smokey then bolted out the back trap cat door (specially made) and up onto a shed facing kitty-corner from Brian's house. When Brian followed his gaze he was stunned to see a neighbor's house on fire.

Yet, it is the tale of an American Bulldog/Pit Bull mix puppy that is the star of this document. His name is Petey Jefferson, so named because Brian first observed him on a swath of Jefferson Avenue that looked like a dried up river bed in the Amazon, covered in weeds and trash. He also possessed similar markings closely resembling his namesake Petey of "Our Gang" fame.

Petey came rambling down Jefferson one morning so emaciated it was possible to count his ribs. Petey for weeks ran at the mere sight of Brian or me but would be observed eating the meals left for him at various times. The photo immediately below shows Petey's appearance as we first observed him.

Petey was covered with large black ticks and fleas and winter was rapidly approaching. It took weeks but eventually Petey came to trust Brian as much as the other animals and allowed Brian to pet him and pick him up to be examined.

One night I arrived to relieve Brian and he said, "Take a look in my back seat." I was not surprised when I saw Petey looking up at me through the back window.

Well, Petey sure had some good karma himself for the next day he was at the vet with Brian. After about five or six visits Petey was free of the ticks and fleas and had been given all his shots. Immediately below is a photo of Petey just two months after his adoption enjoying his newly found paradise – Brian's backyard.

By Petey's appearance alone he is a formidable watch dog but that appearance belies his sweet nature. Petey did not bother any of the adopted cats and awaits Brian's arrival home from work every day with exuberance and love. While Brian is at work Petey growls and barks warnings to any strangers that might venture onto the porch and lets them know that the premises are guarded by one of the happiest and luckiest of all the dogs on earth.

Brian and Petey have bonded to the point that they are now insepa-rable friends and living proof that there is something to all of this karma stuff after all because they are loaded with the good variety.

Walter Lamb was raised in Dearborn and graduated from St. Alphonsus High School on the city's eastside. He attended Henry Ford Community College for two years, Michigan State University for a year, and graduated with a B.A. from Madonna College (University). He has worked as a judo coach and private investigator all of his adult life. osaekomi@chartermi.net

The Deer by Dennis Underwood

It was 1969, and I was stationed in Long Binh, Vietnam. I had just finished checking out the last of the ammunition pads for the day. It had been a long, hot day. I started walking back to the break shack that was still about a half mile away. As I started up a little rise, I heard a pack of wild dogs snarling and growling. It made me stop for a moment. These dogs were not man's best friend. They were feral, never having been domesticated, and could be a serious threat to me. I was going to change direction to avoid them, when I heard the terrified cries of another, smaller animal. Coming back, I went to the top of the rise to see what was happening. As I looked over the top, I saw a pack of about eight to ten big, lean, hard-muscled dogs. They had surrounded a tiny deer and were closing in on it. The dogs took turns dashing in and snapping at the bleating, shivering deer. I was certain that any moment they would all rush in for the kill. The only weapons I had with me were a clipboard and a pen, not very much against a pack of wild dogs. Without thinking, I grabbed as many rocks as I could carry, and started running down the hill, yelling at the top of my lungs. The pack leader turned towards me. He was a massive, powerful-looking dog.

With a slow, stiff-legged, movement, he turned away from the deer to deal with me. His hackles were up, his teeth bared and he was stalking right towards me. At that moment I realized what a spot I was in. This predator and his pack could injure, or even kill me. But running downhill, I was committed to the charge, being too close now to change direction without having the whole pack after me. So I just kept yelling and throwing rocks, charging at the dog as fast as I could. My childhood snowball fights paid off. A good-sized rock made a solid hit on the shoulder of the pack leader. He yelped in pain, turned and took off. The rest of the pack saw all of this and followed him, barking and complaining all the way.

When I reached the bottom of the hill, I was shaking and out of breath, but I felt great. I had faced the pack of wild dogs and forced them to leave the deer. It was the tiniest deer I had ever seen. It was about two feet tall and must have weighed less than thirty pounds. It was lying on its side, eyes glazed with fear, panting with shock. It had a few superficial wounds, but seemed to have avoided any serious harm. As I examined the deer's wounds, I discovered that it was a doe. I knelt down and, speaking softly to her, picked her up and held her close to me. I hoped that she would not fight me or run away, and she just collapsed into me. There was still a good walk ahead of me to get to the break shack where my men and three others squads were. I had no real thought for what I would do when I got there, but I knew that was what I was supposed to do. It was a tough walk with the deer, who seemed awfully heavy after carrying her shivering, little body for a while. It was 120 degrees in the shade, but there was no shade.

She and I were both pretty done in when I got to the break shack. All the men from my squad and most men from the other three squads came out to see what was going on. Everyone wanted to do whatever they could to save this little doe. One of the guys knew that there was an American veterinarian in Saigon. Like in the movies, Army guys just know these things. Without hesitating, the Warrant Officer's jeep driver volunteered to take her. The Warrant Officer was not at the site, but we loaded up, anyway. I sat in the back, still holding her and we "borrowed" the jeep for our mercy run. I still remember holding on to her and praying that she would make it. It was a long drive and she was in pretty bad shape, but I just held her and kept hoping she would be all right. When we got to Saigon and located the veterinarian, he agreed to treat her and refused my offer to pay him. He gave her a tranquilizer, an antibiotic, and a vitamin shot. We loaded back up in the jeep and sped back to the camp.

When we got back, the men had built a stockade for her from scrap materials that were lying around from old jobs. They had even liberated stainless steel serving bowls and dug out places in the rock-hard ground to set them in. One had a salad; the other had fresh, cool water from our own supplies. All we talked about that night was the doe. Every minute or so, one of us would look over the stockade to check on her. She just sat there, curled up on her legs and shivered. We all knew that she might die from the fright she had been through, but everyone wanted her to live. She had become a symbol to all of us of something better in life than war. Instead of all of the killing, maybe we could save the life of this beautiful, fragile creature. But this is a true story, and in the morning she had died. All of us cried together and buried her in a place behind our encampment. That experience brought us closer together than anything else we had experienced together in our entire time in the war. I will always remember that little doe and how she changed us all.

Dennis Underwood is a 69-year-old Vietnam veteran. He began writing about three years ago. He is married with four adult children and two grandchildren. He and his wife live with four rescued cats and one greyhound rescued from the track in Florida. dennisu@umich.edu

Chapter 21: Skunk Tales

Two Skunks by Joseph Bongero

I saw them this morning
shortly after the sun had risen.
Was it a male and his mate
or a mother and her youngster?
They walked close together
in that funny sort of lope.
Their colors of black and white
stood out like a new pair of dice.
As they went across the yard
their bodies made a trail
in the heavy morning dew.
Where were they going?
Are they like us
going through the daily routine
of working, eating and resting?
Or, were they simply going
from point A to point B?

Joseph Bongero (1938-2011) was a United States Postal Service Letter Carrier and an English major in college. He loved being out-of-doors, observing nature and its constantly changing phenomena. He endured Parkinson's Disease the last 15 years of his life but even as the last five years meant limited mobility, he loved nothing more than being able to sit on the porches of his vacation home in Greenbush, Alcona County, Michigan, watching the ever-changing Lake Huron and landscape and searching for whatever birds, waterfowl and wildlife he could see, making records of them in his journals and often writing short stories or poems. His wife, Agnes Bongero, sent in this poem.

A Close Encounter by EmmaJean Woodyard

Full Title: A Close Encounter of the Pungent Kind

Sittin' on the swing, going back and forth, back and forth
Not a care in the world on this lovely summer evening.
Out of the corner of my eye what is it that I see
It's Peppy Le Pew inching ever closer to me.
What to do! What to do!
Sittin' on the swing, going back and forth, back and forth
Peppy eyes me; I eye Peppy Le Pew
His tail in the air, he turns and walks away
No foul reaction; no lingering "gift"
Whew! I smile to myself.
Sittin' on the swing, going back and forth, back and forth!

EmmaJean Woodyard is the executive director of the Dearborn Community Fund.

Chapter 22: Snake Tales

Triptych of a Garden with Snake by Anne Gautreau

I
A garden snake
reclined on the deck
lay so still
he was mistaken for dollar-store counterfeit.
He was more earthy than rubber though.
The right-rear appendage of the frog
lodged in his gullet
as still as garden plaster.
That immobile-frozen tableau rendered Darwin.
A pencil-thin snake
the once-agile frog
digesting and digested
married for a moment.
II
A garden snake reclined—
rear legs and lower body of the frog
bulged its mouth
in obscene tableau,
the only movement in
either a tiny
trickle of blood.
Take this and eat
Drink this and....

Nature communed
composting
fertile frenzy
of this life force dependent
upon death and digestion.

III

The clean and jerk!
Snake lifts its head one-fretful foot
sways first left then right.
Frog rides
eyes bulging
front appendages suggestive of
a victory dance.
With a look of startled triumph, frog rides
his snake-maw seat, swinging, swaying in mid-air like
some cheesy-carnival ride.
"Farewell, world. I go now to be the world,"
cries the frog, deconstructed to *fun*damentals
though none of this
alien otherness
this extraordinary naturalness
seems based
in fun nor mental.

Anne Gautreau is a retired educator and is active in the American Association of University Women, the Dearborn Library Foundation, and the Community Fund's Midwest Sculpture Initiative. Travel to over seventy countries has enriched her life.

Treasure of the Guadalupe by John Smolinski

Creekwalker and I rest a thousand meters up the mountain. Feet irritable from a weary trek through the Yucca, Agave, Creosote studded Chihuahuan desert of West Texas. The foothill trail of McKitterick Canyon calls us into the Guadalupe Mountains as the towering face of El Capitan fired by the blood orange sun, measures our progress. Three miles into the winding scorched trail guarded by cliffs of fossil formed two hundred million years ago, and two more from the trailhead of our ascent. Kangaroo Rats dart across our path and kick up red dust as if to mock. Lizards doing push-ups pause to gawk at the pilgrims interrupting their sanctuary.

Earlier, cooked by the relentless sun the rocky trail melts the glue that binds the soles of my trusty brown leather hiking boots causing first one to fall off, then the other. *Damn*. The morning sunrise is a fireball and my hiking partner and I quickly decide to backtrack to our vehicle, me looking like a *Heyuka*, hiking gingerly in sole-less boots feet baking through socks *Ooh-ing and Ahh-ing* each step of the retreat. Creekwalker drives miles to Carlsbad New Mexico's Wal-Mart, the only game in town, I buy cheap boots and hope they will last five days of hiking and camping in the rugged challenge of West Texas.

Back on the trail we take a breather, drink precious water and recline in the shade of a Ponderosa. The first cool mountain breeze of higher elevation wafts over us. I paw the dirt with a dusty boot churning up a chalky white bleached stone. Startled to see fossils of adolescent and adult rattlesnakes entombed within

I wake my partner Iris, known in medicine circles as
"Creekwalker" who is cat-napping and hand it to her.
"Rattlesnake has given you the gift of its power.
Rebirth, renewal, shedding of old skin. This confirms
the morning's visit by rattlesnake as we entered the
park. Snake is now your ally and has taken its place
on your warrior shield. Place this gift in a medicine bag."

That morning on the lone black asphalt lane into
Guadalupe Mountain State Park a young Diamond
Back lay stretched blocking our way. My companion
halted her station wagon. The rattler crawled to the
passenger side and again stretched out. Creekwalker
foreshadowed: *"Pay attention this is meant for you."*
Rattlesnake raised its head three times through the
shimmer of heat off asphalt. Each time staring at me
and flicking its tongue, then crawling out of sight.
"Watch and listen during our time here,
Rattlesnake has a message for you."

John Smolinski, an artist, poet, percussionist has had his images and poetry
published in poetry compilations such as Third Wednesday *and has*
performed musically at the Ottawa International Blues Festival as well as
other venues.

Chapter 23: Squirrel Tales

Dickey the Squirrel by Hank Czerwick

Many, many years ago, our area was inhabited by a variety of creatures. There were bears and deer. There were raccoons and opossums. There were foxes, beavers, squirrels, and skunks. There were people too. For many years they were called Indians, but we now call them Native Americans.

These people lived in the forest and relied upon the many animals to provide them food and clothing. As our area became populated with settlers from far-off lands, the native people from here moved away and the variety of animals lessened. As roads, homes, schools, and businesses were built, there was less room and food for many of the animals that were so important to each other and to the native people.

Large cities like Detroit were left with very few wild animals, while areas like Clinton Township still had some. Most of the larger animals can still be found in the northern part of Michigan, but it is the smaller ones that are still seen around our homes. Certainly there still are birds everywhere including sea gulls, ducks, and geese. But in our back yards, it is the squirrels that are most common. Oh, there is the occasional rabbit and once in a while a skunk is seen. Pee-you! Sometimes people see a raccoon and maybe a fox. But as more and more homes are built, fewer and fewer animals are left to share their habitat with us.

This then, is the story of one such creature who lived near the back yard of a little girl named Erin and her brother Vinnie.

Erin and Vinnie were typical children. They lived in a big home with their mom and dad. They played with their friends. They went to school. They went shopping, and sometimes they visited their grand-parents. Like other children, they also watched cartoons on Saturday mornings. Vinnie would lie on the floor with a pillow under his knees while Erin would be on the couch. Sometimes her knees would hang over the arm of the couch. Sometimes she would lie on her tummy. Other times she would be half on and half off the couch. The children would laugh hysterically at something funny on the TV and Erin would fall off the couch. Then, Vinnie would jump on his sister smashing her with his pillow. On one such Saturday, when both children were on the floor, they happened to look out the door-wall. There, sitting on his hind legs, and looking through the door-wall, was Dickey the squirrel. Oh, Dickey didn't know that Dickey was his name, but that is what the children called him as you will see.

Dickey looked at the children's antics with all the wonder of someone who had never seen two children romp before. Then again, Erin and Vinnie had never seen a squirrel who was so bold as to sit on their deck and watch them. Suddenly, their giggling stopped and they both slowly crawled towards the door-wall half expecting the little visitor to scamper away. But he just sat there. The children put their noses to the glass while Dickey seemed to become even more interested in the goings-on. Erin stood up and slowly opened the door. She made little "chit-chit-chit" noises which seemed to interest Dickey. He dropped to all four feet and cautiously came to the opened door. Once again he perched himself on his hind legs and sat up. His nose and whiskers twitched as he sampled the sounds and smells coming from the open door. He must have concluded that the show was over and that food, his main interest, was not forthcoming. So he nonchalantly scampered away!

Erin's mom would not have been pleased to know that Erin had opened the door. There is a risk that wild animals can bite. They are not like dogs or kitties which children can pet. Well, no harm seemed to be done and the children went back to watching TV. Next Saturday however, while the children were watching cartoons, there was a little scratching noise coming from the door-wall and when Vinnie looked to see what it was, guess what, it was Dickey again! The children pressed their noses to the glass and Dickey seemed just as interested as before.

"Vinnie," Erin said, "we should give this squirrel a name."

"Yeah," replied Vinnie, "let's call him Buzz Lightyear! No, let's call him Super-Nutty. No, let's call him Wily Squirrel. No, let's call him Wonder-tail."

"Stop it!" shouted Erin. "Let's give him a name that he might answer, just like a real pet."

As the children pondered various names, Dickey just sat there and wondered what they were doing. It almost seemed like magic, but suddenly Erin exclaimed, "He looks like he wants us to call him Dickey!" Erin again stood and slowly opened the door. "Here Dickey, here Dickey," she called. Dickey turned towards the open door and scampered to Erin. His nose twitched as before, his tail wiggled to and fro, and once again he scampered off.

"Mom, Mom," called Erin as she ran towards the bedroom where her mom was busy making the beds and straightening up. "Vinnie and I have a new friend."

"And just who is this new friend?" asked the children's mom.

"His name is Dickey, he's a squirrel, and he comes to see us every Saturday morning," said Erin as she pointed excitedly towards the family room.

"Is he on the TV?" asked Mom.

"No, Mom, he's on our deck!"

"Is he there now?"

Mom was a bit worried. If this was a squirrel that was not on the TV, she would have to investigate. She went to the family room and looked into the yard. She looked to her right and she looked to her left. Then she looked up at the large maple tree that grew in the family's back yard. There sitting on a branch, and looking right back at Mom, was Dickey. He made loud chattering sounds and furiously waved his tail about.

"Is that your little friend?" Mom asked.

The children were at her side and both said that it looked like Dickey. After all, squirrels all look pretty much the same.

"I have an idea," said Mom.

She went to the pantry and came back with some walnuts that she uses when making muffins. She gave a small handful to each child and told them to go out on the deck, to put them down, and to come right back to the safety behind the door-wall. The children stepped cautiously unto the deck.

"Here Dickey, here Dickey," called Erin.

"Chit, chit, chit," were noises that Vinnie made.

This really seemed to get Dickey's attention, although he stayed on his branch until the children were back in the house. It seemed that Dickey's mom had taught him to be just as cautious as the children's mom was being with them.

No sooner were the children in the house than Dickey ran down the tree, across the yard, and up on the deck. He immediately went to the first small pile of walnuts. First he sniffed, then he wiggled his nose, and finally he waggled his bushy tail. He picked up a nut with his two front feet and held it to his mouth just like the children do when they are eating sandwiches. Both Erin and Vinnie were delighted that Dickey was eating the food that they offered him. He fastidiously dined on Erin's offering and then moved on to Vinnie's. After finishing, he went to where the first pile was and looked around to see if he had missed anything. Then he went back to where the second pile had been and did the same thing. Being satisfied that all the nuts were gone, he scampered to the door-wall where the three observers were still standing. He stood on his hind feet and began chattering loudly as he stared at the children and their mom.

"I guess he wants more food," Mom observed. "He will have to rely on nature as I must save the rest of my nuts for baking."

"Can't we give him something else?" asked the children.

"Not for the time being," answered Mom.

Dickey seemed to again realize that no food was forthcoming and scampered away to the next yard.

At supper, the children excitedly told Dad about their new friend. He, like Mom, cautioned them about getting too close to wild creatures. But Dad was all for his children learning about and respecting God's wildlife.

"I have an idea," he said. "Tomorrow, on my way to the fire station"—the children's dad was a fireman—"I will stop at the pet store and buy a squirrel feeder, some sunflower seeds, some corn, and some peanuts. That way, you children can give your new friend a variety of proper food."

This really excited both Erin and Vinnie. They both made clean plates, helped mom with the dishes, did their school work, went to bed, said their prayers, and went to sleep just waiting for tomorrow and the big adventure that was to come.

Sure enough, the next day Dad came home with all the things that he said he would. He and the children put the feeder up on the deck, where Erin and Vinnie would soon observe Dickey coming to eat. That same day not only Dickey, but several of his squirrel friends, found their way to the sunflower seeds in the feeder. Interestingly, so did several blue jays and a mom and dad pair of red cardinals.

The feeder was a hit with all of the animals as well as Mom and Dad. This was because Erin and Vinnie were watching less TV and taking an interest in the feeder. Mom eventually bought a book on identifying birds and the children marked the book each time a different kind of bird was seen. The feeder worked well for everyone providing a source of food especially during the winter months. Dickey seemed to particularity enjoy his regular meals as he got plumper and plumper. Erin and Vinnie could tell Dickey from the other squirrels because he had a dark line of fur between his eyes and a spot on his tail that seemed to have less fur.

Dickey continued to prosper until one day in late spring he appeared at the feeder and he was a lot thinner than he had been all winter. It was Dickey all right; there was the dark spot between his eyes and his distinctive tail. Out in the yard there were two very little squirrels scampering about and eventually they came to the feeder too. Dickey seemed to take an unusual interest in these little guys, spending time with each one grooming and licking them. Then Dickey stood on his hind legs and faced the door-wall as he did when the children first noticed him. It was then that Mom noticed the row of dark nipples on Dickey's underside. It was where Dickey had been nursing the two little squirrels! Dickey wasn't a boy after all! Dickey was a girl squirrel! Were the children ever surprised when Mom explained this to them! Dickey was a Dickette!

For many years afterward, Dickette and her children were regular visitors to the back yard feeding station. Eventually, the little squirrels grew and had children of their own and they too were part of the happy family that was on the deck and the happy family that was inside the door-wall!

For Erin and Vinnie,

Mr. C., October, 2007

Hank Czerwick is a 66-year resident of the city of Dearborn and product of its schools. He retired from Ford Motor Company as an engineer and from Henry Ford Community College as an educator. His writing has been published in many magazines.

Stacie's Five Red Squirrels by Carl Goran

Stacie's ball game in a Canton park on an early spring day ended with with five tiny visitors coming home with her. While going to her car in the parking lot, she heard a squealing sound from under one of the parked cars. While investigating the source of the crying noise, she looked under a car and found five baby red squirrels bundled in nesting material that had  most likely fallen from a car's engine compartment. They were only three inches long and still had their eyes closed. Since they open their eyes at around six-weeks old, these babies were younger than that. Although the babies had some fur, they are not able to maintain their body heat at this stage and would have died had someone not rescued them. After making some phone calls to locate a wildlife rehabber, Stacie obtained my phone number. She brought them to me so that they could be kept warm and fed a special formula of nutrients from a small bottle. Within a couple of weeks, they opened their eyes and started to eat soft foods, mostly apple sauce mixed with formula and blueberry yogurt. After progressing to soft walnuts and fruits, they were moved to a larger pen that allowed them to climb on branches and learn to be squirrels. Yes, baby squirrels need to learn to climb on branches and it is a little scary for some of them. At about nine to ten weeks of age, they were placed outside in a pen with a release box to live in that would later be transferred to a tree. After they "squirreled-up" and got feisty at about twelve weeks of age, their release box, with them inside, was banded to a tree at a homeowner's seven acre wooded backyard where the homeowner supplied food and water until they left the release site about three weeks later. Sometimes newly released squirrels will leave the release site within a day or two. Other times they may stay in their release box until they feel comfortable in their new environment. If the release takes place in the late fall, it is important that a caregiver provide food for them during the winter months. Baby animals that are raised by a rehabber do not have the benefit of a mother animal to teach them how to forage for food and bury food for later in the season. They are dependent upon their caregiver for that first season until they learn to sustain themselves in their natural environment.

Carl Goran is an information technology consultant and software developer. He is an animal lover who is certified by the IWRC to rehabilitate wildlife, specializing in squirrels and chipmunks. He assists both the Dearborn Animal Shelter and animal control officers.

Sherry and the Oak Forest by Sarah Kalmoni

Once there was a family of squirrels known as the Claws, who lived in a large and beautiful forest, which was referred to as Oak Forest, because of the many oak trees. Winter season was approaching soon and the oak trees' leaves started turning into rich colors of red, gold and brown. The Claw parents were hard at work gathering everything they could find to prepare for the winter season. Acorns, pinecones and chestnuts were some of the nuts they gathered, just to name a few. Mom and Dad had two children, Sherry and Jack. Mom had just finished gathering 10 chestnuts, which were Sherry's favorite nuts. When Mom gave Sherry five of them to share, Sherry just gobbled them up and left the Claws' oak tree to explore outside. Mom was feeling sad that Sherry seemed to not appreciate how hard she looked for the chestnuts, and on top of that, gave her half of what she found. When Mom turned to Dad to let him know how she felt, Dad said not to worry and that one day Sherry would learn how to show appreciation for her family.

As Sherry was outside exploring Oak Forest, she saw two bunnies and two chicks playing by a hollow log. The first bunny looked at Sherry and asked, "What are you doing so far out here? Where is your family?" Sherry replied, "I am just exploring near my home, the Claws' oak tree. I wanted to see what's out here." The second bunny said, "There's a storm coming. You shouldn't wander too far away from home or you may get lost." Sherry said with a laugh, "Oh, I'm fine. I know where I am going. I don't need anybody." She started hopping away from the hollow log.

A few hours later, the sky started getting darker and clouds started forming. Before long, the thunder roared and lightning started striking some of the oak trees. The wind howled and the Old Owl cried hoots throughout the forest. Sherry became scared and was looking for the Claw tree. She started running around, but the rain started pouring down and it was hard for her to see where her home was. Sherry was now thinking to herself, "I wish I didn't say that I didn't need anybody. I wish I could be at home with my family." All of a sudden, she heard a snap, and a huge pinecone fell on top of Sherry's head. Everything went black.

As Sherry started to open her eyes, she was surprised to be inside of the Claws' tree. She turned her head to the right, and saw her mother carefully wiping her head with some soft leaves. Mom said, "Sherry, you took a hard bump on your head. I found this pinecone lying next to you. I was worried sick that I would never see you again." Sherry turned to her mother, and said with tears in her eyes, "Mom, I have been acting so rotten to you lately. I thought I would never find home again." Mom said, "Sherry, you are a lucky squirrel. If the bunny didn't tell me that he saw you around the hollow log, I never would have found you." Sherry thought in amazement. "You kept looking for me, even though I was so mean to you, why?" "That's what families are for, through the good and bad times. Did you know I was sad that you didn't appreciate the chestnuts I brought you? You just ran outside to play without saying thank you." "Mom, I'm really sorry. I promise to make good and that I will appreciate others with kindness." She hugged her mother tight. Mom said, "Sherry, I'm glad that you are all right and that it wasn't too late before you woke up and realized the truth." Out of the corner of Mom's eye, you could see a tear of joy.

Sarah Kalmoni is an aspiring writer. She enjoys writing short stories, poetry, essays and minibiographies about her favorite musicians in her spare time.

My Office Pet by Corey Seeman

There was no good reason to go outside on that cold January day. The negative 25 degree wind chill closed all the schools and was warning enough that it was not a day to be out if you could help it. And yet there I was, getting my coat, hat, and gloves on for a walk around the park across from work. I guess there was one reason to head out that day. The squirrels. It had been my habit every day over lunch to feed the squirrels in the park. Why should today be any different? The squirrels needed me. I believed they truly needed me.

I walked more quickly than usual as I headed through the park. While I often had company on these walks, even in winter, today, I was alone. Even the squirrels were not out and about. No doubt they were hoping to wait out this unusually cold day in their nests.

After a few minutes, I finally spotted a squirrel. He was a plump little guy looking for a nut under the snow. He looked up as I approached. It was almost as if he was surprised to see anyone out as well. He ran over to me and squeaked. He was looking right at me as if to say, "Might you have some food?" With that, I tossed a few peanuts towards his feet. I always hoped that feeding the squirrels peanuts was the highlight of their day. The work involved in eating is lifted away, much like heading out to eat at a restaurant when you cannot be bothered to make dinner yourself. For the squirrel – it was the life. No digging. No guessing.

I moved towards him as he grabbed a peanut and started to eat. I squatted near him and he did not seem to mind at all. This is what happens on miserably cold days: most are just happy to have something to eat, and they don't mind the company.

I was out only a short while, but I could feel my face growing uncomfortable in the frigid temperature. Thinking I had better move to warm up, I lunged up to start walking. Instead of moving forward, I felt myself slipping and falling backwards, feeling a sharp pain in the back of my head where it hit the frozen ground. It seemed that I was more embarrassed than hurt as I sat there.

As I started to move off the ground, I heard the squeak of a squirrel again and I looked over towards him. Strangely, he looked right at me. Then, he moved slowly towards me, in a rather deliberate fashion. I was so fascinated that I did not move from my spot on the ground, despite my desire to get off the ice. He inched closer and placed a single paw on my pants leg. In all my time walking through the park, I couldn't remember another time when a squirrel was close enough to touch me.

This was one brave squirrel. Then, without warning, this squirrel climbed my leg and sat up. I sat there in the freezing cold, in the middle of winter, on the ground of a park, with no one around, but with a squirrel on my leg. He moved towards my knee and made one last squeak.

Then in a flash, he sprinted up my leg and crawled under my coat. I had no idea what had happened and again looked around to see if anyone was watching. No one was there.

I could feel the squirrel under my coat and over my sweater nestle in. It was a strange sensation, feeling the sharp claws that enabled him to climb all the trees in the park. And yet, he did not hurt me at all. He moved gingerly from spot to spot under my coat. More settling in than anything else. I could feel his light heartbeat through his fur and my clothing as he held on. I could feel the small moves that he made as he settled in, enjoying the warmth that was so absent on these brutal winter days. It became obvious as I sat there on the ground of the park that he was not going anywhere. But it was also equally obvious to me that I should not do the same with the winds kicking up and the desire for the warmth of my office increasing with every passing minute.

But what of my new friend? Well, more like a pet now, I guessed. He held on and showed no signs of letting go. I unzipped my coat, but he moved to my back to stay warm. It seemed that like it or not, I had a companion. He chose me. I was his host.

I managed to stand up. All the while, the squirrel hung onto my sweater. I held my coat out and tried to get him to drop, but there was nothing doing. I looked around and wondered what on earth was I going to do. When you have been outside in this horrible cold temperature for only a short while, there are few good decisions to be made. I needed to figure this out and it made sense to get warm to facilitate better thinking.

With that, I headed back to my office. If I could get there, I could shake this squirrel loose and then figure out my next steps. Who knows, maybe the process of walking the few minutes back to my office would let this guy reconsider being attached to me. In my walk back to the office, he did not change his mind at all.

I entered my office with a horribly guilty look on my face. I decided the stairs might be a better option than the elevator, especially if he decided to make a run for it. I applauded my own sense of good judgment – possibly the best ever exhibited by someone smuggling a squirrel into an office. I thought we had a flexible pet policy, but I was pretty sure it did not cover this. I moved quickly, feeling the squirrel hold tightly onto my sweater as I headed to my office. What I did not see was a colleague come towards me as I headed towards my office.

"Do you have the publisher contracts?" Sarah asked.

"Nick, do you have the contracts?" she repeated after not hearing an answer.

I had been moving so quickly to my office that I did not realize that someone was trying to get my attention. In my defense, I learned that it was very difficult to consider any contract status with certain publishers when you have a live squirrel holding onto your sweater under your coat. In my goal to learn something new each day, this more than qualified.

"Uhm...I will have them later today. I just need to take care of this one...little...thing and I will get back to you," I said hoping that I could get away from her.

"I can come right in and get it – it is two emails, right?"

"Yeah, but I have this thing to do now. Let me get back to you – today. I promise."

Sarah started to ask again, but I moved past her and practically shut the door in her face. I leaned on the back of my office door with my heart racing. What the heck was I thinking? I removed my hat and my gloves, tossing them on my desk. What was I thinking? Who ever heard of a squirrel hitching a ride under a coat? More importantly, who ever heard of someone allowing a squirrel to hitch a ride under a coat? And since no one ever thought of that, the whole squirrel-in-the-office thing is completely out of the question.

I took off my coat and tossed it on an office chair. I looked down and he was not there. I did not have a mirror in my office, but I looked at my reflection in the exterior window and did not see anything. I collapsed on my seat and looked around. Nothing. I looked under my desk. Nothing. I looked on my bookshelves. Nothing.

I turned towards my computer, rubbed my hands together to get some feeling back into my fingers, and logged in. I shook my head a few times to clear the cobwebs. Gotta get those contacts for Sarah. As I was finding the contacts and adding them to the email for Sarah, I heard it. A squeak.

I paused for a moment, and slowly starting typing again. Another squeak. I turned to my left. There was the squirrel. I suppose now it was not just any squirrel...it was my squirrel. It was my pet. Here he was, in my office, enjoying the comfort and warmth of indoor heating. It was probably safe to say that he had never been indoors before. He scampered over to where I tossed my coat and started to nestle in. He seemed to be very much at ease as he found a warm comfortable spot in my coat.

What on earth have I done, I thought looking at the tail of my new pet. What was I thinking, bringing a squirrel into my office?

Then, a knock on the door. "Hey Nick, this is Sarah. Can I get the contacts so I can get on with my day?"

"Today. I will get it today. Trying to fix a little problem first," I yelled through the door. "I will get this done as soon as I can."

My mind was at a loss for what to do next. A nest...that is what we needed.

I had some extra shirts I kept in my desk for an emergency. This definitely counted. I emptied a box of books and lined it with shirts and then showed it to the squirrel. I placed a few peanuts in the new nest as an enticement to get him to use it. He looked up at me and jumped right in. He was busy fluffing the shirts and settled in. I could not believe it, a pet squirrel. My pet squirrel. And with that a smile came across my face.

It dawned on me that he would need a name. Is he a he? How can you tell? I decided it was probably not relevant.

So what about Sam? That name could work for a Samuel or Samantha – so he or she would be covered. Sam had peanuts, a nest, and a name. Maybe this is going to be a great day after all.

Seeing Sam relaxing in his nest, I reached with two fingers and gently brushed his back. For a moment, it was truly wonderful. Then reality set in. Who keeps a squirrel as a pet? What was I thinking of letting him come inside with me? I'm not that crazy...am I?

As I was thinking this, little Sam looked up at me and squeaked. I cannot tell for sure, but I was positive he nodded to me. I squinted my eyes to get a closer look, and I saw him nod again. I could not recall seeing a squirrel do that before in all my lunch hours in the park. Was Sam really agreeing with me? But how on earth could he tell what I was thinking? He squeaked again.

I leaned closer towards Sam when I heard Sarah yelling through the door. "Hey Nick, are you with me?" I started back on the email to get her off my back.

"Nick, you there? Can you hear me?"

All of a sudden, I started to feel a horrible cold in my cheeks. My fingers lost their flexibility and I could not type at all. What was happening to me?

"Nick, can you tell me where you are?" Sarah asked again.

"I'm in my office – where do you think I am?" I said, feeling colder and colder with each word that passed through my lips.

"In your office? Nick, you slipped outside and knocked your head on the ground. It is freezing, we need to get you back inside."

Sure enough, I was outside. I was freezing. I must have been out for a little bit. Sarah helped me up. But I suddenly remembered Sam...I did not want him to come into my office. I unzipped my coat and started to dance around to make sure that there was no squirrel heading in with me.

"What are you doing? It is freezing out – keep your coat on," she said.

There was no squirrel under my coat. None at all.

"Let's get you inside," she said.

As I looked towards my office, I noticed a squirrel standing there on our path. He looked up at me. It was Sam – I was sure of it. I have never been so sure of something in my life. Sarah asked me if I had a peanut to feed the squirrel. I gave her one and she bent down and gave it to him. He nodded and ran off.

"Have a good day, Sam. Have a good day," I said as he scurried off.

"Who's Sam?" Sarah asked.

"Just a friend."

"Let's get you inside. I think you need to rest."

Corey Seeman is the director of the Kresge Business Administration Library at the Ross School of Business of the University of Michigan (Ann Arbor). He enjoys his lunchtime walks with the campus pets that have graced campus for many, many years. cseeman@umich.edu

One Wild Encounter by Phyllis Tippett

winter or summer no matter which
Fairlane Woods remains
wild-animal rich
turkeys fly up the trees
no colorful tails
no foes who seize
families of deer
pause to eat hostas
as they journey through here
possums and raccoons galore
squirrels and cats
and much-much more
a few days ago I saw a new cat
a bright black and white
unusual that
often I open the door in glass wall
to take in the spring
summer and fall
then once spread-eagled I see
a squirrel on the screen
my gosh, it can't be
I moved toward the door—fresh panic my friend
the monster grew large
what things could he rend
I said, "Shoo, go away," and stretched my arm long
to slam the door
impress him he was wrong
he traversed the door top-right to off
while I sighed relief
worry finally doffed
but scratching-gnawing teeth and claws
ripped a ragged hole
to access his cause
inside the screen he raced and he sniffed

though portals were closed
which made him more miffed
he left for a spell—I thought all was done
then came his second attack
I wanted to run
fierce for sure with blood in his eye
I thought did he have a key
could the lock he pry
he muscled about—I cowered that's true
wait, it was just a squirrel
put me in such a stew
I swear—a squirrel—a tiger I saw
gruff and ferocious
with menacing guffaw
then his challenge was suddenly over
he skipped off to trees
once again happy in his fine clover

Phyllis Tippett's favorite pursuit in writing is haiku, the diminutive Japanese form that celebrates the natural world. Recently, she published a book entitled Alphabet Critters *which is available on Amazon.com.*

Chapter 24: A Turtle Tale

My Clever Pet by Saad Jawad

Today I am going to tell you about my clever pet. I have a pet turtle that is named Coach. My brothers and I named him Coach. He is not a coach for a sport. My brothers and I just thought that Coach is a nice name so that's why we named him Coach.

Coach is a very clever pet. Every day I feed Coach. Once we put Coach on the floor and he walked pretty slow—very, very slow. Coach is a medium size turtle, fits in my hand. He likes to eat his turtle food. Coach has a big tank as a habitat. He has a little rock and a log in his tank. He likes to get on the log and sit. Coach's habitat is in my basement. It is very cold in my basement, but Coach has his own heater to keep him cozy.

Once I put my finger inside Coach's tank, then he bit my finger. I started yelling and screaming. I started to shake my finger. Then Coach let go of my finger, he flipped on the table then fell on the floor. Coach's shell protected him. My brothers and I were glad Coach did not get injured. Coach also likes to swim.

I tell some of my friends that I have a turtle as a pet. My brothers and I are lucky to have Coach as our pet. We love him so much. When my brothers and I first got Coach, he came in a little bag with water in it. Now Coach is happy living in his tank with us at home. And we are happy living with him.

Saad Jawad is a third grader at the MAYA school in Dearborn, Michigan. He enjoys reading mystery books and working on his inventions.

Chapter 25: A Weasel Tale

Stoats Go Out by Christine Fischer

The Stoat High Council had given Binky ample time, but still he had not returned to the riverbank. For the fourth time that day, the stoats gathered together and drew straws. Elmer peered at the tiny twig. His turn. He reviewed the plan in his head: "1) Get the bucket of hot wings. 2) Get back." Two quick blinks of his bulbous black eyes, a mind-clearing sniff, and off he went.

Dressed in a summer-weight pinstripe suit and carrying his umbrella securely under his arm—just in case—Elmer paused to adjust his gray derby, a studious-looking topper, yet tipped slightly over one eye as to imply a hint of mischievousness, then he padded confidently out of the brush and into the street. He quickly saw what had become of Binky and the others. Greasy chicken juices and hot sauce streaked their faces and chests as the famished stoats feasted in the center of the road. As Elmer considered his options, he felt a slight shift in the air and turned just in time to see a semi-truck begin to overtake him.

He dashed back into the woods, saving his life—but losing his hat! Yet, one stoat's sacrifice, however unfortunate, ultimately led to the good of all. Elmer's tiny bowler had lodged into the truck's front brakes, and as the driver cranked the steering wheel back and forth, struggling to control the careening 18-wheeler, the rear doors burst open. The truck hurled its massive load. Seven hundred and eighty pounds of Wonder brand hamburger buns flew into the woods, sacks dropping to the riverbank, whoosh! Plop, plop! Transforming the earth into a shiny, polka-dotted wonderland.

To this day, the stoats and all the other animals of the woody area just past Fran's Tavern never have to go hungry, and the plastic bread bags make the most wonderful, cozy warm bedding. Elmer has tried storing his extra linens in the bags, but everything tends to get that musty smell after a while.

Artist, maker, sourdough-bread-baker, true-adventure-story-reader, bird-watcher-while-driving, Christine Fischer lives in Dearborn with her husband and two young daughters.

Chapter 26: A Wolf Tale

Mr. Feral de Mat by Henry Fischer

I: The Arrival

THE TRAIN CAME TO A SHRIEKING HALT in Aveyron, where Dr. B.S. Watson and I got off. A slight mist hung over the cool air.

Dr. James Weisburg, a biology professor at the University of Aveyron, saw Watson and grimaced. He stood up and waved, forcing a smile. Watson immediately seemed to notice him and quickly, yet with a tired step, came over. Both were wearing London Fog wool trench coats and gray hand-sewn top hats, holding umbrellas under their right arms, and walking like elitists in their fancy black leather dress shoes. The only differences between the two were Weisburg's blue jeans contrasting Watson's grayish dress pants, Watson's golden wire-rimmed spectacles contrasting Weisburg, who wasn't wearing glasses of any sort, and Watson's rather large suitcase. Their faces both entailed wrinkles, in relatively the same places, resembling crevices much like the moon's.

"Hello," said Watson.

They shook hands.

"Watson, good ol' Watson, how long has it been?"

"Who's counting?"

Weisburg's brow furrowed slightly, but then he smiled. "And congratulations again on your book, *Wolf in Sheep's*—"

"It's *Wolf in Man's Clothing*."

Weisburg shook his head. "I keep getting that mixed up! Clever title, anyhow. It seems your time in France has been—how shall I say it?—quite fruitful; your findings are...well...quite interesting."

Withered Watson, looking like his grandfather John, and acting like him too, squinted knowingly and laughed. "Interesting, eh? Don't give me that, Weisburg. I know why you invited me here—to discredit me, of course. And please don't humor me. I know about you biologists (especially second-rate biologists, like yourself); I know you must think my findings are nothing less than ridiculous, but"—pointing to his suitcase, tapping it, almost petting it as one would a beloved animal—"you'll soon believe me."

Just then, Weisburg noticed how ragged and worn Watson's suitcase was; there were even holes in it.

"Same ol' Watson," Weisburg laughed, trying to laugh slightly louder than Watson, "always thinking you understand everything. Well, I'll have to admit, even though your findings are interesting, they do sound a little—how shall I say it?—unscientific."

"Yes, I'll admit my book may, at times, be a little hard for the inexperienced to understand, but my presentation tomorrow will clarify any doubts."

"Yes, it may *strengthen* them."

The two men stood in the train station, trying to dominate one another intellectually, not paying any attention to the passers-by.

Soon, they exited the train station and made their way to Weisburg's Toyota, which smelled like stale cigarettes covered partly with "botanical gardens" air freshener. After Watson gently placed his suitcase in the backseat, Weisburg drove him to the Ramada. During the drive, Weisburg asked, "So, roughly, what's in the suitcase that'll make a believer out of me?"

"I suppose tomorrow will be like the good old days, eh Weisburg? But I guess those days weren't so good for you, certainly, because you could never beat me in a debate. Tomorrow it'll be your lecture versus mine. And I'll win as I always have, and you know it; and you're afraid—that's why you're trying to figure out what's in my suitcase; well, you'll see what's in here"—petting it again—"tomorrow, at the conference."

It was like they were in college again, doing anything to undermine each other. Watson had sucked Weisburg into it, but Weisburg, being an intellectual, quickly admitted (only to himself) he had been sucked into it all along.

As Watson was exiting the car, Weisburg said, "O.K., if I'm afraid, then why did I invite you here?"

Watson, it seemed, had an answer prepared: "It could be any number of reasons: perhaps a futile endeavor to get over your fear, or perhaps your elderly mind has forgotten or repressed a good number of our debates"—

"Freud's repression doesn't exist," Weisburg interrupted sarcastically, as Watson countered his interruption without countering it at all—

"Or it may simply be your envy of me: while I went to France, supported by numerous grants to further my studies, you were stuck here, condemned to waste away, almost swindled out of your precious tenure, doomed to teach nothing more than the introductory classes, which are dominated by students who rarely take any interest whatsoever in the material; or, your reason for inviting me may just be your false arrogance; perhaps it's your last feeble attempt to receive *credit* for *discrediting* my findings; or, as I said, it could be any number of reasons—mentioned or unmentioned—though the truth is, unlike you, I'm willing to admit I'm not certain. Maybe you could enlighten me."

"Let me guess," said Weisburg, "you have videos of the subject, like those who filmed 'Bigfoot.' Or maybe you have more statistics and observations—reminiscent of your book—ones that are more poetic than pragmatic; ones that replace logical reasoning with your trademarked conjecture and intuition." He went on, flooding the car with sarcasm, as Watson clenched the handle of the door: "And of course, written on the documents in your suitcase must be your greatest proof: your opinion that your subject exists and can do what you say he can; or, to be more precise, what you say *it* can. Tell me, do such meager aspects make up the body of your presentation? If so, then don't I have the right, the absolute right, to say, 'Friend, you are no scientist'? Because you've had the audacity, the presumptuousness, to write of an 'extraordinary event' while not giving even one shred of 'extraordinary evidence'! Then again, to your great credit, your 'event' may be more ludicrous than extraordinary."

"There you go again, Weisburg, playing your role as pseudo-scientist for the establishment. Ludicrous, eh? The earliest tales of apes were seen as ludicrous, and yet now it's ludicrous to deny them."

"Actually, many were monstrous exaggerations. Say, is your presentation anything like them?"

"Still trying to get an edge on me, Weisburg, eh? Still trying to figure out what's in my suitcase—so you can use it against me?"

"This is ridiculous! I'll see what's in your suitcase soon enough; then, I'll be able to, as you say, use it against you. So why not tell me now? Oh, everything you're saying is against science."

"Maybe you're against science."

"What's that supposed to mean?"

"I'll see you tomorrow, Weisburg."

II: The Conference

THE GROUP OF PROFESSORS SAT like a group of children, anxiously waiting for story time. It was already 1:30 p.m. and as more professors returned from lunch, as children do from recess—all tired out and sad that play time is over, yet eagerly awaiting the next highlight of the day—the first lecturer took the stage and gently set his suitcase down. Watson was a tall man, also quite slender, and his invigorating presence seemed to add to the anxiety. He confidently gazed upon the crowd. A nervous rush flowed through certain members of the group, mainly those who were also lecturing; it appeared especially in Weisburg, who sat close—very close—to the podium.

Watson lit up a cigarette—in recent years, an unheard of gesture during Aveyron's Research Conferences—and reached into his suit coat pocket, gracefully pulling out a shiny glass ashtray and placing it on the podium. The sweet, sting-like aroma of burning tobacco filled the room. Then, from his other suit coat pocket came a pint of Jack; he took a swig and smiled, then offered some to the frontal members of the crowd, including Weisburg. They all declined. Weisburg internally laughed, for he now knew why Watson had found what he did—there was no other explanation—Dr. B.S. Watson was mad.

The crowd, it seemed, did not know what to make of Watson's strange behavior. After taking another swig from the pint and another hit from his cigarette, he adjusted the microphone.

"This nut is finished," Weisburg laughed to himself—even though, as he stared at Watson's cigarette, he wished for a moment that he could do the same during his lecture.

"Good afternoon my esteemed colleagues and friends. What I am about to discuss here today may seem shocking, as you who have read my book know, but please bear with me, for it is my goal to show that, though my findings are shocking, they are indeed real and scientifically accurate. And though some may think my science, sociology, is not absolute in any way shape or form, I am here today to prove otherwise."

The crowd muttered with disbelief.

"During my studies of the social structure of wolves in the Champagne-Ardennes region of France, I came across a recluse, living in the wilderness, who told me that he had studied a boy who was raised by wolves. Now we've all heard the tall tales of children being raised by wolves, but there was something to this one, something in the way his eyes screamed: 'This is the truth!' The recluse told me that the boy showed no signs of being human, except in appearance. But other than that, he was an animal. He growled, pounced on and ate small animals raw; he walked on all fours and did not speak. The recluse never told me his name, and when I tried to find his story — when I tried to exhume its body from endless crypts of newspapers dating back to 1930 — I found nothing to confirm or negate it; I found similarities in a few articles, but none that I felt matched his story beyond a reasonable doubt. So all the 'evidence' I had was what many would call 'just another tall tale'; and thus, I soon realized, the only way I could get any kind of confirmation was not to research the elderly man's findings but to endeavor to reproduce them myself. I wanted to show that 'nurture' is everything and 'nature' nothing, that man is indeed merely a product of his environment; yet since I could not rightly send a human child into the wilderness (because of serious ethical, cultural, and social reasons), I decided to attempt to prove the reciprocal of the recluse's story.

"So, I extracted a cub from the wolf pack I was studying at the time, and raised it as one would a human child. This cub had large steel-blue eyes that turned yellow in the dark, and he was stronger than any wolf cub I had ever seen, which made him a good candidate for my experiment. My hypothesis was, if a human child raised by wolves acts like a wolf, then a wolf raised by humans will act like a human. So I raised Mr. Feral de Mat (the cub I extracted) to act like a human being. I socialized him with the language, beliefs, norms, values, behaviors, and material objects — which our culture deems appropriate. And just as I suspected, Mr. Feral de Mat now acts like us. Apart from his appearance, he *is* a human being. And here is my proof."

With that, he reached once again into his suit coat pocket and pulled out a medium-sized photo of the mysterious Mr. Feral de Mat. He showed it to the audience, giving it to Weisburg to pass around. As Weisburg looked at the photo, he realized that the evidence was unequivocal: the photo was of a small boy dressed in wolves' fur. Over the wolves' fur was a black suit. The "wolf" had a cigarette in his mouth. It was very clear, now. Watson was completely and utterly insane…

After passing the ridiculous fake photo to the professor sitting next to him, after deciding against the debate to tear it up right then and there, Weisburg stood up and said, "For Christ's sake, I've had enough of this. How can you do this? Watson, how can you say what you're saying and then give us that…that ridiculous photo…as your proof? What's wrong with you? That photo is merely a picture of a little boy dressed up as a wolf. Do you take us for idiots?"

Watson, hitting his cigarette calmly, broke in: "Yes, Mr. Feral de Mat is looking more and more like a human child, isn't he? Well, that's only because every day he is socialized as a human is like a layer of makeup over his fur—making him look a little bit more like a human being."

Weisburg couldn't take it anymore: "The human child that recluse found in the forest—if he actually did find a human child, and the child did what he claimed it did—was certainly retarded; for no human of average or above average intelligence could ever be raised to act like a wolf; and the same goes for turning a wolf into a human. For Christ's sake, I can't believe I'm having this conversation!"

"Isn't that why you invited me here, Weisburg? To have *this conversation*? And I'll have to say, you may have misunderstood me: I never said I turned a wolf into a human; I merely said I trained a wolf to *act* as if he were human, and the more one acts like something, the more one looks it. Your case is similar: you've acted like a professor all these years, and now you finally fit the part; but the big difference is, no matter how hard Mr. Feral de Mat tries, he will never be able to play his role as well as you play yours. So, speaking within the boundaries of science, you are right: he can never become a human being. I'll grant you that. I have, however, trained him to speak. He likes reciting passages from Shakespeare."

Taken aback by this, extremely angered by now, Weisburg said loudly, "First of all, I'm not going to debate that photograph with you any further. It's plain to see it's of a boy in a wolf's costume. Second of all, what did you mean when you said that I'm against science?"

"*First of all*, the picture is real—everyone can see that, except you. And, *second of all*, when I said you're against science, I simply meant this: as I successfully raised Mr. Feral de Mat to act as a human, so you could have just as easily been raised to act as a wolf. Perhaps you were meant to act as a wolf. Perhaps the way you are, the way all of you are, even the way *I* am, is against science. Perhaps our existence and the way we are is an accident, a mistake."

"Yes, I do believe in evolution, so I'll agree with you: it is a mistake," declared Weisburg, thinking he had Watson right where he wanted him.

"No, no, you don't understand!"

Now Weisburg was waiting for the other professors to back him up, but they remained silent. Maybe they were in shock; maybe they were too disgusted to lower themselves to Watson's level; "or maybe the only thing they're convinced of is that I'm a phony," Weisburg mused sadly.

"Weisburg, while it seems clear to everyone else here, maybe you'll never understand; though that's not my problem—my problem is that I still haven't proved to all of you, even with my photograph, that my findings are real; so, since your skeptical minds have driven me thus far, I must go the distance. Now, I present to you, Mr. Feral de Mat, himself. Mr. Feral de Mat, it's time, come out, show yourself, and answer any questions they have for you."

And with that, I jumped out of the suitcase, stretched, and answered all of their questions.

Author's note: I wrote this in my early twenties when I was reading and enjoying some of Kafka's works.

Henry Fischer grew up with many animals including dogs, cats, rabbits, turtles, crayfish, a snake, and goldfish. The next pet he would like to have is a falcon, which would be free to roam whenever it pleases. It would perch on Henry's arm when they go hunting together (as the bird did in The Beastmaster*). Henry works at Dearborn Public Library and lives in Dearborn with his wife and two young daughters.*

Author Index

www.ingramcontent.com/pod-product-compliance
Lightning Source LLC
Chambersburg PA
CBHW060234290526
45789CB00001B/43